# The Free-Lance Writer's Survival Manual

Ernest E. Mau

Contemporary Books, Inc.
Chicago

Library of Congress Cataloging in Publication Data

Mau, Ernest E.
  The free-lance writer's survival manual.

  Bibliography: p.
  Includes index.
  1. Authorship.   I. Title.
PN151.M29        808'.02        81-65180
ISBN 0-8092-5898-6              AACR2
ISBN 0-8092-5897-8 (pbk.)

To BARBARA, whose patience and tolerance have
made my free-lance career possible.

Published by Contemporary Books, Inc.
180 North Michigan Avenue, Chicago, Illinois 60601
Manufactured in the United States of America
Library of Congress Catalog Card Number: 81-65180
International Standard Book Number: 0-8092-5898-6 (cloth)
                                    0-8092-5897-8 (paper)

Published simultaneously in Canada by
Beaverbooks, Ltd.
150 Lesmill Road
Don Mills, Ontario M3B 2T5
Canada

# Contents

# List of Illustrations

# Preface

To the creative mind, there exists one word with a particularly magical allure. It conjures up images of a life-style filled with financial rewards, personal independence, and easy living. The mere mention of this word fires the imaginations of writers, editors, and others involved in one form or another of the creative arts. Often it becomes a singular goal for individuals seeking to escape the day-to-day tedium of making their livings in a fast-paced world. That one word is "free-lancing."

At one time or another, nearly every writer or editor dreams of turning his talents to the free-lance market in the search for better pay, better hours, better recognition, or greater personal satisfaction. The simple act of having selected this book from among the many publications aimed at writers and other creative types shows that you are among that group of people who find the idea of free-lancing especially attractive. Whether you are a novice just beginning your career or an established professional, I hope I will be able to provide some useful information that is not readily available from other sources.

The fictionalized media of literature and movies depict the free-lancer as somewhat of an eccentric, usually an author, painter, or composer. He is portrayed as highly successful, living in an isolated beach house, jetting around the world, leading the most unconventional life imaginable, and having few, if any, financial worries. In glamorous and romantic settings, the writer awakens around noon, often with a pounding hangover, fumbles his way through the afternoon, and parties away the night. On rare occasions, he may manage to spare a few minutes from his hectic schedule to jot down some research notes or to pound out a few lines on his typewriter. All in all, nice work if you can get it. But like the stereotyped images of detectives, secret agents, and superheroes, the glamour and romance are largely the products of some writer's overactive imagination.

Back in the real world, few people can hope to match the achievements of the fictionalized authors. The lasting literary fame of an Ernest Hemingway, the prolific sales of an Isaac Asimov, or the immense success of an Alex Haley turn out to be quite elusive and far beyond the reach of the majority of writers. Most who are willing to go out on their own must settle for more moderate and realistic goals that are more likely to be within their reach. While yearly earnings of $10,000 or more are easily within the reach of competent writers having sufficient self-discipline and good business sense, the persistent hope of at least coming close to the grand dream of fame and fortune draws increasing numbers of people into attempting free-lance careers. After all, the world of the free-lancer still is one of freedom, independent action, high pay, and numerous other benefits—or is it?

Like a modern-day Lorelei, free-lancing sounds a siren's call that lures the unwary into dangerous waters. The course to success is cluttered with obstacles—the reefs and shoals that can be nearly impassable barriers. The wise writer carefully charts his way through those obstacles rather than plunging blindly ahead, constantly rechecking and reevaluating his position as he progresses toward his goals. With a little luck and a lot of meticulous planning, he stands a fair chance of attaining a satisfactory level of success.

In developing this book, I did not intend it to be a "how-to" text on writing, preparing manuscripts, finding markets, etc. Those procedural details are thoroughly covered in other reference works already available through bookstores and libraries. I did not even set out to prepare a book on how to free-lance. Instead, I've attempted to compile a generalized guide—a chart of some of the obvious and not so obvious difficulties that you probably will stumble over at some time in your career. Like any guide or chart, the information I provide is subject to necessary alterations and adjustments that you must make to accommodate your own particular endeavor and its unique hurdles.

As a free-lancer, you are like a sailor navigating through treacherous waters toward an unfamiliar port, and you must sound out your own way in the manner that best lends itself to your individual objectives and talents. The information I've compiled is intended to aid you in identifying areas requiring particular care and in pointing up some of the problems often overlooked by the novice free-lancer in the enthusiasm of getting started.

At times, you may feel that my approaches tend to be rather negative—sometimes downright discouraging. I've taken this approach after careful consideration, since one of my objectives is to "pop the bubble" of illusion that surrounds professional free-lancing. Over the past few years, I've spent a lot of time in discussions with aspiring free-lancers, particularly those who intended to make their livings in the fields of marketing or technical communications. In nearly every case, those individuals had expectations of immediate success and high rates of pay while actually performing a minimum of work. Furthermore, most of them faced severe disadvantages in having limited experience, lacking the finances to support their intentions, or failing to develop the self-discipline necessary to function effectively as a free-lancer. Throughout my discussions with those people, and throughout this book, my intention has been and is to "lay it on the line" and "tell it like it is."

As I've scanned the existing literature directed toward writers and, more specifically, toward free-lancers, I've noted a distinct lack of attention to the basic difficulties directly associated with such careers. Very few of the writers' guides pay much attention to the organizational and operational aspects of a free-lance business, leaving the aspiring writer to stumble and flounder through those procedures on his own. At best, they limit their advice to a few specific facets such as how to find a publisher, how to present the manuscript, how to collect for a published but unpaid manuscript, and so on.

In actuality, free-lancing is not what one might imagine before starting into it; it has its pros and cons, its advantages and disadvantages, and its rewards and disappointments. I've attempted to provide a balanced view of an endeavor that is not as easy as it first seems. In so doing, I'm trying to give you at least part of the information you will need to assess the negatives as well as the positives. In the simplest terms, gaining success as a free-lancer comes down to one basic objective—*to survive*. If you can survive for a reasonable length of time, you have passed the most crucial test of all, and survival is what this book is all about.

Since I am engaged in written communications, often of a highly technical nature, this book has been slanted specifically toward writers and, by logical extension, toward editors. However, much of the material I will be covering also is pertinent to artists, designers, photographers, and the many other individuals who function in fields allied to communications and the creative arts. For those of you who are involved in such fields either directly or indirectly, it should be a simple matter to interpret the material in terms of the details of those pursuits. Again, the book is a flexible guide, not a set of rules cast in concrete. In fact, if there is one overall rule for free-lancing, it is that there are no rules. Procedures that work well for one individual under a particular set of circumstances may not work as well for someone else or under slightly different circumstances.

Many of my recommendations are designed with a full-time endeavor in mind and may seem inappropriate for the part-timer. However, some problems that are less pressing for the part-timer still exist and others may even be compounded by the fact that the enterprise is not undertaken on a full-time basis. Tax deductions are one area in which this becomes particularly evident, with the part-timer having considerable difficulty justifying deductions to which the full-timer is easily entitled.

Now I must diverge for a moment. I am quite aware that many of you are women. After all, writing is a pursuit in which women have long been able to achieve marked degrees of success. However, I also find that contrived pronoun forms such as "he/she," "him/her," and "(s)he" are unbearably cumbersome both to write and read. As a result, I have chosen to use the so-called "masculine" pronouns, but I intend them to be read in their generic sense as references to human beings without implication of gender. In so doing, I assure you that I am not attempting to ignore or slight the women who comprise a large percentage of all creative talent.

Ernest E. Mau
Denver, Colorado
December, 1980

# 1

# Free-Lancing for Profit

## WHO OR WHAT IS A FREE-LANCER?

Webster defines a free-lancer as "one who pursues a profession under no long-term contractual commitments to any one employer." It's an uninspiring definition that can be applied across a wide range of professions and pursuits. Taken literally, it makes free-lancers of doctors, lawyers, dentists, and similar professionals as well as a large portion of the skilled and unskilled, unemployed and underemployed segments of the working force. In common usage, however, the term *free-lancer* usually is reserved for individuals pursuing independent careers in the creative arts, particularly in written and graphic communications. It is this smaller, select group to which this book is directed—specifically the writers, editors, and others who spend their lives preparing materials for print or broadcast.

In general, the writer can consider the total realm of communi-

1

cations as composed of three principal divisions or fields: *editorial, marketing,* and *technical.* Each of these makes extensive use of available free-lance talents and offers many opportunities for making a living without being a "captive" employee of a company or corporation. However, it is important to understand and remember that there are essential differences between the fields, in the types of communications they utilize, in their purposes and goals, in the methods of preparing and selling materials, and in the details of the free-lancer's overall approach. At the same time the distinctions can be blurred by a certain amount of overlapping between the fields.

Although most writers function best in the field in which they are most qualified, few can limit themselves to that field to the total exclusion of the others. The technical writer may suddenly find himself working on brochures, news releases, or press kits intended to promote the product for which he has been preparing instruction manuals. The advertising or public relations copywriter may have to prepare nonpromotional articles for trade journals or corporate house organs. Similarly, the writer of nonfiction magazine articles may receive an assignment from a local company to document the use and maintenance procedures for a mechanical device or an electronic assembly. Throughout his career, the typical free-lancer can expect to make frequent crossovers from one field to another, but that's part of what keeps the job from becoming boring, broadens the writer's business base, and improves his potential for increased sales and income.

In practice, I've found that a few useful generalizations can be made about each of the three primary fields. As the economic climate of the country has changed and as local business conditions have fluctuated, I've found it necessary to shift back and forth from one area to another on an erratic and unpredictable basis. With each change of direction, it has been necessary to make major modifications in my business plan and operating procedures to accommodate the field gaining emphasis at that time. For such purposes, I view the fields of editorial, marketing, and technical writing in specific ways, and I will be making use of those views throughout the remainder of this book.

## Editorial Communications

Editorial communications include newspapers, magazines, books, television, and radio. This field is differentiated from the others by being directed to the general public without blatantly intending to sell the reader a product, service, or concept. Within editorial communications, writers can find many opportunities to sell and publish their work as authors, article writers, columnists, news stringers, photojournalists, etc. The free-lancer's efforts typically are concerned with a series of one-time creations such as single articles or books, particular news assignments, or groups of individual stories, fillers, gags, and other miscellaneous items that the writer feels have a reasonable possibility of selling. With rare exceptions, only columnists and proven news stringers seem to have a long-term working relationship with one client, while the remaining free-lancers are engaged in a constant hustle of selling new ideas to prospective buyers.

Editorial writing is the "glamour" field, especially since it includes the published authors of fictional and nonfictional books. If you describe yourself as a free-lance writer, nearly everyone immediately assumes you are working on books or magazine articles. Similarly, most aspiring writers limit their thinking to the editorial field, planning to gain their recognition through authoring a best-selling book or a series of widely read stories.

There are many reasons why this field is the first one thought of by both writers and the general public. For one, successful authors gain a high degree of public recognition through the reviews of their works, promotional tours, television appearances, autograph parties, and other direct contact with the public; just having a by-line or credit affords a degree of public recognition. Another is that the author of a best-seller can reap a financial windfall, especially if he draws royalties from motion picture, television, or serialization rights. A third reason is associated with the way writers are depicted in books and movies—the romanticism with which they are portrayed and the idyllic surroundings in which they are pictured.

Either because of or in spite of the very factors that make this field so attractive to writers and so apparent to the public, the beginning free-lancer is at a distinct disadvantage. Its strong appeal creates a highly competitive profession in which selling materials is difficult. Much of the work done in this area is speculative or "on spec," with no guarantee of financial return for the amount of time spent both in writing a manuscript and in trying to find a buyer for it. Even when a publisher is found, the rates paid for the work often are quite low and rarely compensate the writer for his full time and effort. As a result, the beginning writer or the writer who fails to establish a high demand for his work can expect to put in a lot of hours that return little or no financial reward or prestige.

As a result, I characterize the editorial field as the most difficult one in which to gain success or even to survive. Since the chances of writing a best-seller are quite slim, this field seems to lend itself best to those who enjoy a struggle for the sake of struggling, those who can afford to write for the satisfaction of writing, and those who write on a part-time basis without intending to make their livings at it. Of course, many people do achieve significant or at least satisfactory success, but it requires a lot of effort, a great deal of patience, and tremendous perseverance.

It's interesting to note that the writer who needs to earn $20,000 per year and who makes about $100 per published article would have to write and find publishers for 200 articles each year—that translates to an average of 16.6 articles per month or about 4 articles each week. On a per-word basis assuming an average rate of $0.04 per word published, that same income requires the writing and sale of a half-million words per year; 41,600 words per month; 9,600 words per week; or 1,920 words per day, five days a week. If a writer sells only half of what he produces, those numbers double; if he sells a quarter of his production, the numbers quadruple.

## Marketing Communications

Marketing communications include both advertising and public relations. In simple terms, marketing influences the general public or a defined segment of the public to behave or react in a specific way. Most commonly, the goal is to convince people to buy a product, to contract for a service, or to accept or reject an idea. Broadly, marketing communications constitute propaganda since they are always intended to sway opinions or actions in a particular direction.

The free-lancer capable of generating marketing materials can find two main outlets for his efforts: individual companies and advertising or public relations firms. Many companies organize and operate their own in-house marketing departments that prepare the brochures, media ads, news releases, editorial articles, product descriptions, and associated materials needed to promote a line of products or a specialized service. Other companies prefer to rely on the "experts" employed by advertising agencies and public relations firms to generate the same materials. Since both operations often become overloaded with work or need a fresh point of view, both are available markets for the free-lancer and can prove quite lucrative.

The free-lance copywriter generally finds that long-term associations with a company or an agency are quite possible, and that such relationships can be developed into highly profitable arrangements beneficial to both the free-lancer and his client. While the work itself usually breaks down into individual projects associated with particular products or services, the same client often has a distinct need for repeat performances to deal with each product or service being offered. Instead of working on a one-time basis with the client, it is to the free-lancer's advantage to operate under a contract of specific duration that spells out terms to remain in force for a specified period of time and that clearly defines the scope of the tasks to be performed, the rates of payment, the allowable interval for the client to make payments, and the other essential requirements of a formal business relationship.

While the editorial writer has little choice but to accept large amounts of work to be done on speculation, the marketing copywriter can avoid such situations. With a properly structured business operation, the free-lancer who works with companies and agencies has little, if any, need to do speculative work and is able to make maximum use of his time on a profitable basis. Unlike the editorial field, however, the marketing field does not provide the free-lancer with public recognition; the typical free-lancer receives no credit or by-line in a piece of promotional literature and therefore is invisible in the production procedure surrounding that material. At best, the only recognition the writer can expect in this field is that of his peers and clients who become familiar with his work through direct contact.

Writing marketing materials lacks the glamour and romance of writing novels and stories, but it does provide a steadier and more predictable income. Once away from the major advertising centers like New York, Chicago, and Los Angeles, the available opportunities decrease, but the competition for assignments also decreases. The competent marketing free-lancer in less-active and less-industrialized regions such as the Midwest can still reasonably expect to gross upward of $25,000 per year, depending largely on the effort he is willing to put out, his common business sense, and his capabilities in preparing good promotional copy.

Furthermore, while economic conditions drive magazines out of publication, force book publishers to reduce the number of manuscripts they accept, and generally erode the market for editorial writing, the same conditions cause an increase in competitive corporate marketing efforts and an expansion of outlets for the free-lancer in that area. Additionally, rising costs of doing business force many companies to trim their expensive in-house staffs and rely more and more on less-costly free-lance talent to produce their materials. A quick glance around shows that we are being bombarded by ever-increasing amounts of promotional materials, and the free-lancer should always remember that someone has to be writing that copy.

## Technical Communications

Technical communications is the most specialized field of the three, providing nonmarketing support for products and services. This in itself is a vast area, encompassing instruction manuals, engineering specifications, research and development proposals, quality control documents, manufacturing procedures—the list is nearly endless. Unlike the editorial and marketing fields, this area does not provide material for the general public but rather for a very specific audience usually having some prior knowledge of the subject.

Through the latter part of the 1970s and into the 1980s, technical communications has been the fastest growing market for the free-lance writer. Bursts of new technologies and expansions of old ones have created a continuously increasing need for additional documentation at all levels. We've seen tremendous advances in areas such as personal home computers and home video equipment, taking them from the laboratory right into our living rooms (they're predicted to become as much a part of our lives as television itself). Energy-related fields including mining, drilling, and whole new technologies for synthetic fuels and alternate energy sources have gained new priorities. Every area of technology requires writers, either to prepare sophisticated scientific and engineering documents or to reduce the information into simple terms the layman can understand. A writer's opportunities in this field alone are far greater than in the editorial and marketing fields combined.

Once having developed a working relationship with a client, the technical communications free-lancer often finds himself involved in a long-term association with that client. This is particularly true when the free-lancer demonstrates either a prior knowledge of the subject or the ability of quickly learn the essential details. Typically, free-lancers in the technical field find their tasks not as well defined as in the other fields. Rarely is the free-lancer solely a writer, a technical illustrator, a graphic designer, or any other one type. Instead, he tends to become a general consultant with strong capabilities in one or more tasks and good or at least adequate abilities in as many other tasks as possible.

Aside from the differences in subject matter and audience, free-lancers in the technical field function much like those in the marketing field. Most of the work is done under contract with a guaranteed rate of return; there is virtually no need for speculative work that consumes valuable hours without immediate profit. However, while depressed economics may actually enhance the opportunities available in the marketing field, they tend to decrease the opportunities in the technical field. As money supplies for the client companies grow tighter, technical support operations are seen as pure overhead and are among the first activities to be suspended. But this is only a temporary situation since no company that manufactures and sells a sophisticated product can continue to do so for very long without the manuals and associated documentation needed by the end user. Typically, an interruption to technical support is followed within a year by a rapid flurry of activity as the company attempts to catch up on a backlog of postponed items.

The technical field does not allow the writer to achieve much satisfaction in the way of personal recognition. Few companies allow the writer a by-line or credit in their documents, and few trade journals actually print the name of an article's author or editor. Like the marketing writer, the technical writer usually gains recognition only among others in his profession and among the people with whom he does business. Since technical writers form a much smaller group than marketing writers, even that recognition is limited. Worse yet, the most illiterate engineers suffer from the delusion that they can write technical materials as well or better than the professional technical writer, so the free-lancer quickly becomes involved in constant conflicts with those engineers.

The practicality of free-lancing in technical communications is limited by the writer himself and by the geographical location. Although a technical writer does not necessarily need a degree in engineering or the physical sciences, he does need a well-rounded background in subjects that include mathematics, physics, electronics, and so on. The writer with the greatest advantage is the one with a general knowledge of many different subjects and the ability to quickly digest and understand the basics of new subjects and new technologies; whether or not he has had any formal education in the subject usually proves immaterial.

A more serious consideration is the geographical location in which the writer wishes to establish his business. There are few opportunities for a technical writer where there are few companies dealing with suitable products or services. This limits the free-lancer to urban locations with a significant degree of industrialization. At the same time, a concentration of technological companies in an area results in large numbers of writers competing for the same assignments. So the aspiring free-lancer must make a choice between two differing approaches. On one hand is the highly industrialized location with many potential opportunities, intense competition, acquisition of a low percentage of assignments, and the necessity of charging high rates to compensate for expenses incurred during nonworking intervals. On the other hand is the less-developed location with fewer potential opportunities, significantly less competition, acquisition of a high percentage of assignments, and the ability to charge lower and more competitive rates since the work and the resulting cash flow are comparatively constant. Under either circumstance, a free-lancer who chooses his location carefully and who has the necessary abilities can gross upward of $22,500 per year.

## FREE-LANCING OR CONSULTING?

Again referring to Webster, a consultant is defined as "one who gives professional advice or services," that is, an "expert." Although many people consider free-lancing and independent consulting as being the same, there are some very distinct differences. Actually, the consultant is a free-lancer, but a free-lancer does not always qualify as a consultant. Therefore, it is more appropriate to consider consulting as a special type of free-lancing for which the primary prerequisite is some specific expertise that is in particular demand by a defined group of prospective buyers or clients.

In most cases, it is not appropriate to apply the term *consultant* to free-lancers in the editorial field. Although an individual may be an expert on a particular subject, the majority of editorial writers work with many different subjects at different times in their careers. Rarely is the editorial free-lancer called upon to give his professional advice to a publisher or broadcaster; instead, he is expected to deliver a finished manuscript or other work dealing with a particular subject. Since consulting implies direct one-to-one contact between individuals or between an individual and a group, even the expert authors of advanced textbooks cannot be considered consultants in terms of their publications.

However, consultants often are in great demand in both the marketing and technical fields. It is not unusual for an advertising agency to suddenly acquire an account from a company producing a product that is not within the expertise of the agency's in-house copywriters or account representatives. This is particularly true of the smaller advertising and public relations firms that cannot afford to be overly selective in the accounts they accept. At the same time, a new account may not be large enough to justify hiring full-time personnel to handle it. When this happens, the agency must go outside of its own staff to get the job done, usually seeking a free-lancer with some practical knowledge of the product or with the ability to learn the product and its inherent technology both quickly and efficiently. The consultant is the one who fills this need, most often at a very high rate of pay to compensate him for having his specialized knowledge or abilities.

For instance, my own full-time free-lance business involves a wide range of pursuits in many different areas. But I characterize my principal occupation as that of a "technical publications consultant." Essentially, I offer my clients a single source for all tasks needed to carry a technical document from its original conception all the way through to the camera-ready art. Additionally, I provide certain "problem solving" capabilities that utilize my experience across a broad range of technologies including computers, pollution control, medical electronics, mining, energy development, and others. During the course of preparing a document, I provide the routine tasks of graphic design, writing, editing, and preparing camera-ready art, but I also consult with my clients on subjects as diverse as planning, designing, and printing recommendations for the documents, design improvements for the client's product, engineering flaws that I detect in the device, and general recommendations that fall under the heading of "troubleshooting and product enhancement."

By functioning as such a consultant, my time and expertise become more valuable, the demands on my time increase, the qualified competition decreases, and I am able to charge premium rates for the entire service package that I offer. While this approach normally keeps me well supplied with small- and medium-sized projects and has allowed me to develop a good base of repeat clients, it also led to the single largest free-lance assignment of my career—an assignment that came from a completely unexpected source.

In the early months of 1978, I was approached by a well-known and prestigious public relations firm in my home city. We had previously worked together on a couple of small accounts, but now they had contracted to perform the public relations work for a large international mining organization. A part of their agreement with that organization included preparing an extensive state-of-the-art reference text on mining techniques. Originally intended to be a light edit of numerous encyclopedic articles contributed from mining experts all over the world, the actual job turned out to involve heavy editing, a near-total rewrite of about 80% of the contributions, and extensive reillustrating and graphic enhancement.

The technical nature and scope of the project was beyond the in-house capabilities of the PR firm, but they had no desire to lose the overall account for failure to fulfill their commitments to the reference text. In my capacity as a technical publications consultant, I was subcontracted to assume the responsibility for that text. Although their organizational structure was adjusted to make it appear that I was a member of the PR firm's staff, I remained an independent consultant working under contract at my normal consulting fee. During the following year, I edited, rewrote, and reillustrated more than 60 lengthy and complex technical manuscripts, working on a schedule of up to 20 hours a day and 7 days a week. As I said before, it was the largest single account of my career and, by far, the most lucrative.

This example serves to illustrate several important points for the free-lancer. First, there are no absolute, black-and-white boundaries between the fields of technical, marketing, and editorial communications; they are separated by varying shades of gray as they overlap each other. Second, the free-lancer who works primarily in one field may be limiting his opportunities if he fails to make contacts among the other fields; in this case, a highly technical project originated within the marketing field. Third, a free-lancer does not necessarily need a formal education in his particular area of interest; prior to this assignment, I had no experience in mining and my knowledge of the subject was limited to general reading I had done. Given the necessary reference sources and the opportunity to learn the applicable vocabulary, I had little trouble adjusting to what for me was a whole new technology.

The economic squeeze that began in the mid-1970s forced companies of all sizes to reassess the value of maintaining in-house staffs for generating their promotional and support documents. Management tends to view marketing and technical publications as pure overhead, despite the fact that their brochures, reports, manuals, proposals, and other documents are absolutely essential. Management cannot see a direct dollar return from the individuals or departments assigned to produce these publications so, when profits decline, the publications staff is among the first to be trimmed or eliminated.

To the consultant's delight, the need for the documents continues, and delays in producing them tend to create acute situations in which the projects are backlogged and customers begin to complain about the missing information. Eventually, if the companies decline to reestablish or reinstate their publications groups, they often go in search of qualified independent consultants. Normally, such companies look for an individual who can perform multiple tasks such as writing and photography, editing and design, or some other combination that can satisfy their complete needs with a minimum number of people having to be involved.

With ability or experience in the particular field and with acceptable performance on the client's behalf, the consultant can develop long-term and highly profitable working relationships with such companies.

Again drawing on personal experience, I was separated from my last full-time employer in 1975. For the previous two years I had been preparing the marketing documentation for the company's mechanical, electronic, and electro-optical products. However, the company's profits had declined sharply, and management decided to eliminate some overhead. The resulting layoff caught a technical illustrator, a technical writer in the engineering department, and me, effectively leaving the company with no in-house capability for generating new publications or revising old ones.

Within two weeks of being separated, both the technical illustrator and I were called back as consultants to prepare a trio of technical/marketing brochures for a new product line. The company had a clear and present need for the documentation, but no desire to reinstate the publications group for what they thought would be a short-term project. As it turned out, the project required several working weeks spanning a period of months and cost the company at least five times more than if they had delayed disbanding the group in the first place.

At almost the same time, an employer I had left more than two years earlier called and asked for a meeting. They planned to start a marketing communications department and were interested in rehiring me at an excellent salary to head that department. During the time I had originally worked for that company, I had been unhappy with the office politics and had a severe personality dispute with my boss, so I refused their offer. But I did offer to do their work under contract as a consultant. After ironing out the terms, we began a long association that has proved far more beneficial to both of us than it would have been had I elected to return on a captive basis. Nearly six years later, that same company has proven to be my longest, continuously active client. They account for a substantial portion of my annual earnings, and their reliability and prompt payments have earned their projects high-priority handling without premium charges for bumping other projects.

Oddly enough, I found that previous full-time employers became the hard core of my free-lance clientele. In most cases, the durations of the free-lance relationships have long exceeded the durations of my original full-time employments.

## WHY BE A FREE-LANCER?

There probably are as many reasons for free-lancing as there are free-lancers. Each of us has his own goals and expectations in life, and those are the driving forces that determine the directions our individual careers are going to take. Naturally, every free-lancer must try to recognize and work toward his own goals, and the only reasonable measure of success is the comparison the individual makes between his actual accomplishments and those he set out to achieve. A book of this scope really doesn't allow all of the possible reasons to be listed and individually evaluated, but it does help to draw some general conclusions.

The most logical reasons for undertaking a career as a free-lancer can be divided into three broad categories: *money, freedom,* and *satisfaction.* It's doubtful that a free-lancer would be able to identify any one reason for choosing to do what he does; instead he would find that he has a number of reasons that fall into any one or any combination of the three categories.

## Money

The primary consideration in any endeavor is money. We rarely like to admit it, but we all have a mercenary nature. There's an old one-liner that goes something like, "money does not buy happiness but the things it does buy sure help." Besides, we all have to meet our monthly bills and like to have something left over for our personal enjoyment. Unfortunately, inflation and a declining economy are making it difficult to afford the things we want or need, and it's no longer uncommon for both spouses in a family to need at least one job apiece just to make the budget balance at the end of the month. For all but the wealthy, the single-income family is rapidly fading into dim history.

Free-lancing offers two basic money-making options: *part-time* and *full-time.* Probably the larger number of free-lancers view it as a part-time enterprise to make a little extra pocket money, to offset the costs of some new purchases, or to improve their standards of living. A smaller number of free-lancers operate on a full-time basis with their earnings constituting their sole source of income. In either case, there is money to be made as long as there is a demand for the individual's talents and efforts. The return for a particular individual is related directly to the area of endeavor and is proportional to the extent of the individual's talent and the amount of work he is willing to do.

Traditionally, editorial writing is reputed to be the least lucrative of the three general fields. There has been little increase in the rates paid for editorial materials over the past 30 years, certainly not enough to keep pace with inflation and definitely not enough to satisfy any but the most prominent authors and writers who can sell virtually anything they can produce and for whose talents and names the publishers may actually compete.

As mentioned earlier in this chapter, the markets in the editorial field are the hardest in which to make a living or to even find a buyer. The rates paid to editorial free-lancers are on a per-word, per-page, or per-piece basis, and have little or no relationship to the difficulty of the project, the time involved, or the problems encountered. Worse yet, payment usually is not received until the materials are published or used. This means delays of weeks, months, or even years before any money is received. Worst of all, extensive effort put into work done on speculation may never find a buyer, and all of the writer's time and effort spent "on-spec" may be for nothing. Even the reputed safety of writing "on assignment" turns out to be risky since many magazines issue the same basic assignment to multiple writers and then pay only a nominal "kill fee" of 20% to 50% for terminated assignments that never make it into print.

The problems of making sales and receiving payments for this type of writing can range from merely annoying to completely disastrous, depending upon the extent to which the writer relies on editorial media for his living. For a short time in 1973, I was involved in writing short gags and filler materials that I would submit to a variety of magazines. The actual purchases within two years amounted to less than 10% of the total submissions; the other 90% were never returned, never used, and eventually forgotten. In 1980, some seven years later, a magazine with one of the largest circulations in the world and which actively solicits such contributions, finally made its first use of one of those fillers.

In 1969, I was deeply involved in photography, and many of my color transparencies were placed with "stock houses" that hold the photos on file until they have a call for a particular subject.

When a photo is sold, the stock house and the photographer each get a percentage. My first return from one of these houses was received in 1979, ten years after the photo was submitted. Even worse, one stock house disappeared from the face of the earth, along with more than 1,500 of my color transparencies, and I've never been able to take any legal action because nobody has been able to find them.

Of course, those probably are extreme cases. In 1973, I began free-lancing word puzzles to puzzle magazines in the United States and Canada. This is an area in which I have had excellent success, and I treat it as my second-line business. The puzzles provide an excellent backup to my consulting activities and can provide subsistence income when other assignments taper off. As of mid-1980, I was providing 40 types of word puzzles to 10 magazine publishers and was receiving from $900 to $1,100 per month. But even for these there is a significant delay. The time lag between submission and payment on publication for a newly acquired publisher or for a new type of puzzle sent to already established publishers ranges from a minimum of 3 months to a maximum of 36 months.

One bad experience I've had in this activity was with a publisher who suspended magazine production for a period of six months, resuming with a radically different format. When they stopped operations, they were holding 85 of my puzzle manuscripts with a market value of $10 each. When they resumed publication, those manuscripts were unusable, and their unique format for that one publisher made them impossible to sell to anyone else. The result was an outright loss of $850 and about four weeks of concentrated effort that had gone into stocking their files with that one puzzle format.

An even worse case occurred in late 1980 when another publisher folded their operation entirely. They had been requesting large quantities of material, and I had supplied some 660 manuscripts of different types and with different market values. Again, the formats were unique to this publisher, so there was no way to salvage the material for resale anywhere else. In fact, the publisher advised me that the entire contents of their files were scheduled for destruction and that the sheer bulk of material on hand would make it impossible to return the submissions even if I wanted them back. In this case, I lost about $4,330 worth of manuscripts and nearly two and a half months of intensive work.

These two examples serve to illustrate the dangers of working too far ahead of a publisher who pays on publication. They also illustrate hazards involved in trusting any company to stay in business long enough to use and pay for large volumes of materials. Of course, these kinds of things can happen to anyone at any time, and every free-lancer has to assume certain risks. In cases such as these, I have to take the risk of such failures in order to stock publisher's files with enough manuscripts to guarantee uninterrupted use and payment over periods of a year or longer. Although losses like these are serious, I operate on the assumption that enough materials will sell and that the profit margin for large-volume contributions will offset the losses.

Marketing and technical free-lancing tend to be more profitable and more reliable, especially since they permit long-term client-consultant relationships. There is little need to do speculative work; most projects are specifically assigned, are charged on an hourly basis, and are fully billable for all work up to the moment of any cancellation. When a project is assigned and terms for payment are agreed upon, the project must be paid for when completed. There should be no substantial delays in receiving payment because the consultant is functioning as a vendor to the client company and is fully entitled to be paid within 30 days, 10 days, or whatever period has been agreed upon. Furthermore, the consultant has every right to expect to be paid for his effort whether the client uses the material or not; in some cases, a company may cancel a program after the documentation work has begun, but the consultant can reasonably expect payment for all efforts up to the moment he is advised to stop work.

While most editorial free-lancers are locked into the standard rates and conditions established by their publishers, free-lancers in the marketing and technical areas are free to set their own rates within the limitations of the competitive marketplace. However, in setting his rates, the free-lancer or consultant must be able to offer his expertise at a cost lower than would be required for the client to keep a full-time individual on staff. Still the rate must be sufficient to make a good income. Typically, the free-lancer can expect to charge from $15 to $50 per hour for his time, with the higher rates being received by experienced consultants. This may sound high, but the full-time free-lancer does not receive the paid fringe benefits of holidays, vacations, sick leave, health insurance, unemployment insurance, etc., and he must cover those expenses as well as anticipated periods of time when he has no assignments or is working at less than capacity.

The free-lancer is not locked into the corporate raise structure that is designed to award an employee the minimum raise possible and yet keep him from walking out the door. Those who have been subject to corporate rulings of 3%, 5%, or 7% annual raises know the pain of watching their life-styles erode as inflation and tax increases gobble up their poor earning gains. The free-lancer in a position to adjust his rates can make appropriate compensations, raising the rates as the cost of living increases, imposing higher rates for more difficult jobs, charging premium rates of as much as 100% extra for rush jobs, building in charges for the subjective value of his experience and talent, and so on.

Most free-lancers' annual earnings are directly proportional to the amount of time and effort devoted to the job. For the captive employee, salary increases and annual earnings are fixed by management and have little or no real relationship to the complexity of the job, the employee's efforts, or proven performance. Too often, the one thing that may affect salary increases and earnings is how well the employee plays the game of office politics. Obviously, the free-lancer has the better deal—the more he works, the more he makes. And the free-lancer can make use of tax deductions and shelters that simply are not available to the captive employee, thus keeping a bigger portion of what he actually earns. Simply stated, the competent free-lancer or consultant who diligently pursues his assignments can expect to earn a higher income than can someone performing the same job on a captive basis.

## Freedom

Creative individuals know that their "creative juices" are not always flowing from 8:00 AM to 5:00 PM, five days a week. These same individuals find the highly structured and regimented work schedule of the corporate organization totally incompatible with their own lives. The situation is aggravated by a company's demands for overtime work when the individual may already be burned out. Here, the free-lancer gains a real advantage in being liberated from the routines of the workaday world. The full-time free-lancer can set his own schedule to best satisfy his own needs and creative spurts, thus maximizing his effective time and his usable output. Some find themselves at their best in the early mornings, others in the late afternoons, and still others in the wee hours after midnight. A few even find a split schedule best, working for a while, stopping, and then resuming later in the day. In any event, the free-lancer is released from the dictates of an employer whose primary interest is in having the right head count at the right time.

The free-lancer does not have to justify his actions to anyone but himself. He has no boss to whom he must explain a day's absence, no worry over trying to schedule a week's vacation in conflict with some other employee, no coat-and-tie or skirts-only dress code to be followed day in and day out. The free-lancer does not have to play the political game that pervades every business office as employees and their supervisors maneuver for the favors of upper management; to use an old bit of slang, he is freed from the necessity of brown-nosing his boss. And, the free-lancer is free to work in an environment of his own choosing—just try to write a technical instruction manual in an office with irritating background music piped right overhead, on a wobbly, wall-suspended desk surface that looked stylish to the office decorator, and with dozens of people wandering in and out of your cubicle all day long.

All of this may sound too good to be true, and, in a way, it is. The professional free-lancer must be his own management, carefully setting his own schedules, justifying his time to himself, and running his life in a way that may be more rigid than the corporate organization. The free-lancer's obligation is to his client and to the job assignment, and he often finds himself working longer than eight hours a day, more than five days a week, and without holidays and vacations. But, it's still his own schedule, subject to changes as he sees fit, and therein lies the essential freedom that writers and other free-lancers value above all else.

## Satisfaction

Personal satisfaction is the third basic reason for free-lancing. Modern methods of trying to achieve maximum efficiency require an assembly-line approach to nearly every task in a manufacturing plant or a business office, and that implies a repetitious, robot-like routine for nearly every job from production up to middle management. The writer or editor working a nine-to-five job for a company quickly finds that doing the same things over and over can become a terrible bore in a very big hurry, and boredom quickly leads to high levels of stress and extreme dissatisfaction. Typically, the captive employee faces the same problems from one day to the next. If he's an advertising copywriter, he's forever struggling to find a new approach to the same old products. If he's a technical writer, he deals with the same basic electronics or mechanics for each new member of a product line, and he fights the same engineers to pry loose each scrap of information he desperately needs to finish his project. Simple repetition is the nemesis of the creative mind, whittling away at individuality, creativity, and originality until only mechanical actions and reactions remain.

The active free-lancer gets few opportunities to become bored. When he's not actually working on a project, he's out trying to find a publisher, a new account, or a few promising contacts, or he's busily researching his next project. Very few practicing free-lancers can afford to waste a lot of time in nonproductive idling. With a little luck, the free-lancer's assignments are varied enough to pose new and different problems nearly every day. Besides, the free-lancer operates in a world of continuous learning and challenge that keeps him alert and on the go for most of his waking hours. Even the consultant, the so-called expert, finds that each job is significantly different from the last, and personal and professional growth rarely get a chance to stagnate.

For some reason, companies like to hire highly qualified employees, and then treat those employees as if they were complete morons. There is little professional respect within the corporate structure, particularly from one's superiors. It's common in many companies for upper management to deliberately block any attempts at creative contributions by the employees. I've even seen corporation presidents go so far as to direct a staff writer to sit down and shut up when he's tried to offer valid alternatives to the proposals submitted by an external advertising agency. While this is a mark of poor management, it seems that there are a lot of poor managers around, and the staff writer finds it difficult to get any respect at all. The simple act of accepting employment can relegate an otherwise skilled professional to the status of a minor flunky.

When that same writer becomes a free-lancer or consultant, the picture changes abruptly. In my own case where my early clients were prior employers, I found that I obtained immediate respect simply by being an outside consultant and charging high rates for my time. In meetings with the same managers who had been my bosses, I found that making the same suggestions I had made as an employee suddenly gained the status of expert opinions to be acted upon immediately. From a purely personal point of view, I found that to be the most satisfying aspect of my new career.

Of course, there are many other facets to achieving self-satisfaction. There are the challenges of meeting and dealing with new people (excellent therapy for the shy), of controlling and guiding business meetings, and of learning to be imaginative in developing sources of income. For some, free-lancing provides an improved outlook on life. Some people simply aren't corporate types and can't go through their lives wearing the corporate logo and devoting their existences to the company. As free-lancers, they don't have to pretend loyalty to employers; their loyalty is strictly to themselves. Throughout, there is constant personal and professional growth, with continuous gains in both knowledge and experience.

In assessing my own reasons for going free-lance, I find that elements of all three categories are applicable, but with freedom first, satisfaction second, and money third. I've long since lost my illusions of becoming rich and famous, and I've contented myself with making enough money to pay the bills with a little left over. But I enjoy the life-style. Though I get up at 5:00 AM every morning, weekends and holidays included, I prefer that to having to report to some corporate office by 8:00. Though I often find myself working 10 to 20 hours a day every day of the week, I don't look at that the same as working overtime for a company, which was something I refused to do when I was a captive employee. I enjoy working in my own home, dressed in blue jeans and grubby shirts. I enjoy the knowledge that I can take time off when I have to tend to personal errands or simply because I don't feel in the mood to work, and my only need is to reconcile that with the deadlines I may be facing.

While being a free-lancer has been far from easy, I wouldn't willingly trade the experience or present life-style for any full-time job I can imagine. Over a period of five years, I've had about 30 offers of employment, ranging up to a vice-president's title and carrying salaries of up to $45,000 a year. I've turned each and every one down without a moment's hesitation simply because I like what I'm doing now.

# 2

# The Preliminary Evaluation

## FREE-LANCING: THE IRRESISTIBLE URGE

While a few writers launch directly into their free-lance careers with little or no prior working experience, the majority begin only after some type of employment in an affiliated field. Many begin after working as editors for publishing companies, copywriters for advertising agencies, or technical writers for manufacturing corporations. Still others become free-lance writers after first having been engineers, scientists, educators, or adventurers. Since writers tend to do their best work in the areas in which they have some prior experience, their individual backgrounds often provide the subject matter and the overall approaches they will use most often in their free-lance careers.

The urge to "go free-lance" strikes about the time a person realizes that his chosen occupation is reaching a dead end. Perhaps the salary isn't good enough, he's been refused a raise, he's been passed over for a promotion, his job has become tedious and filled with make-work projects such as stuffing envelopes, or some other element of dissatisfaction and resulting restlessness has set in. Remembering all the carefree writers portrayed in books, movies, and television, the idea of free-lancing suddenly seems very attractive indeed. Once it hits, the urge is persistent and becomes an annoying itch midway down the spine where it's always bothersome and never quite within easy reach.

Once having the urge, the writer also develops an intense impatience to get started in his new life, but the decision to go free-lance is not one that should be made in haste or under stress. The sharp differences between working as a captive employee and working as a free-lancer or consultant can be sources of both personal and professional problems. A snap decision to try free-lancing can prove disastrous, and chances of success are improved by careful preparation and planning combined with a little patience.

I have twice attempted full-time free-lancing, with the interval between the attempts filled by a combination of captive employment and some part-time free-lancing. To underline the importance of proper preparation, it's useful to summarize the experiences and differences between the two attempts. My experiences were not unique by any means and are closely paralleled by those of several other free-lancers with whom I'm acquainted.

## A Tale of Failure

In 1969, I made the abrupt decision to be a free-lance photographer and writer. For the preceding four years I had been working in an engineering capacity for a large telecommunications company and had already grown disillusioned with the workaday world. So one day I was employed, and the next day I was out on my own. For about a year and a half prior to making this change, I had been experiencing some encouraging success as a photographer, winning several photo contests, obtaining a couple of local Sunday-supplement spreads and a couple of articles and photo spreads in a corporate house organ. I had also been enlisted as a part-time staff photographer for a locally published engineering journal.

It seemed I was off to a good start, and I was bristling with self-confidence. Totally positive of making it in the glamorous life of a photographer, I plunged ahead recklessly. But the dreams were short-lived, as was the enterprise itself. The whole endeavor lasted less than a year and led me right to the verge of complete financial collapse.

Later, when I was able to look back on the experience with some detachment, I realized that my failure was the direct result of four principal factors. First, I had not developed a workable business plan that would cover my day-to-day activities and provide contingency procedures for unexpected problems. Second, I had not taken the time to evaluate the available market for my services. Third, I lacked practical business experience, having gone directly from the academic idealism of the university into the restricted world of the large corporation. Fourth, I did not have the diversity of talents and abilities necessary to survive.

While it's not practical to present a chronological list of all the problems I encountered during the short life of my first business, a few generalizations are important since they affect writers and other free-lancers just as they affected photography.

My first discovery was that the local scene was overcrowded with aspiring free-lance photographers operating on a cutthroat basis just to survive. Admittedly, I was naïve, but I somehow expected to find the majority of businesses conducted on an honest level. I was completely unprepared for the world of deception, cheating, and conniving that I encountered. I found much of my competition engaged in deliberate underbidding to secure assignments, followed by overcharging when it came time to bill the account. Even the slightest hint of having secured an account with a company would result in dozens of competitors descending on that client with intentions of stealing the account by cutting rates, backstabbing, or any other technique they could use.

Unethical or downright dishonest behavior was not limited to the competition; it pervaded the clientele as well. Since my emphasis was on industrial and related commercial photography, I found my available business base somewhat limited. Most local businesses were nonindustrial, while the few large industrial corporations already were under contract to a few well-established studios. Since my overhead was lower than that of a large photo studio, I targeted my efforts to small- and medium-sized companies, but one out of every three accounts turned out to be trouble.

In Chapter 1, I mentioned the stock house that disappeared with 1,500 of my best color transparencies along with several articles. On the local front, it was not uncommon for a client to make a large assignment requiring several weeks of time and a lot of film, processing materials, and operating supplies—assignments worth several thousands of dollars. As I said, one out of three was trouble and always on the collection end. The favorite tricks were to stall payment until the work had been used and then to try returning the materials as unsatisfactory or to just refuse to pay and challenge me to take legal action. In the worst case, it took me two years of collection agencies and legal actions to finally recover only 40% of what the client owed for an electronics parts catalog that he had printed and used.

The enterprise itself required large expenditures to acquire the necessary equipment and to meet a continuous operating overhead. This left only a very small profit margin for any assignment. Eventually, I reached the point where my working capital was exhausted and my receivables were tied up in collection actions. At that point, I had no choice but to fold the business and pack my costly equipment away in the hope of using it again at some future date.

## A Tale of Success

Although the failure of my first business was both disappointing and discouraging, it was not completely without benefit. I knew what my mistakes had been, and I was able to learn from them. Knowing that eventually I would try again, I set out to do as much as possible to prevent any repetition of those errors.

From 1970 to 1975, I worked for a number of corporations as a technical or marketing writer/editor. By making certain that I never worked for any two similar corporations, I broadened my knowledge and experience across a range of modern technologies. I made it a point to become acquainted with accounting personnel and slowly gather information on corporate procedures affecting both payables and receivables. At every opportunity, I studied the work and techniques of technical illustrators and artists, learning to do camera-ready pasteup art, simple illustrations, and light graphic design along the way. When an employer had an in-house printing facility, I supervised the printing of the documents I prepared, assisting the printer with platemaking, setting up the presses, and his overall operations. In short, I studied and gathered information from as many in-house sources as possible and increased my own capabilities until I felt that I could carry most projects all the way through from their original planning stages to the final printed product.

Whenever I had the opportunity to deal with outside vendors such as photographers, printers, typographers, advertising agencies, or PR firms, I carefully developed good working relationships with the contacts I knew would be needed if I began to freelance. I studied their needs, talking to their personnel to determine where they had problems and what they really needed to best perform their own tasks. Among my interests were the procedures for specifying type that would make a typographer's job more efficient and less costly, the problems faced by a stripping artist in making negatives and plates from artwork, the procedures needed to make and reproduce color separations and halftones, and many other tasks associated with the actual production of a document.

While employed by a manufacturer of computers and associated equipment, it was part of my job to write the program reference manuals for their software packages. As part of that task, I had to learn to operate and program the computers. At the time, I didn't know how valuable that experience would be and had no expectation that I would one day acquire a high-performance business computer and word-processing system of my own.

Having already determined that my best chances would result from achieving maximum diversity, I wasn't content to increase my capabilities only within the field of technical communications. I also recognized the need for a completely different alternative as a backup, and I found it through part-time free-lancing. At first, I tried some fiction writing, but without success. In 1973, I literally stumbled over the answer to my problem; I happened to glance through a magazine featuring "word-find" puzzles. Having noticed that the published puzzles were extraordinarily easy to solve, I set out to make up a few that would be more difficult. Purely on a whim, I sent out a couple to a magazine, and the editor wrote back that they would take as many as I cared to deliver at a rate of $5 each. I quickly dispatched more samples to other magazines, and learned that I had found a large market that would pay from $5 to $15 for each of these puzzles, and they took less than two hours apiece to prepare. I've remained active in producing those puzzles from that day to this, never being far from my clipboard and a stack of puzzles in work. In 1980, a decreasing market for that puzzle type forced an expansion into other types of word games, and with the assistance of my own computer system, I began supplying 40 additional types of word games to 10 magazine publishers who accounted for 30 different magazine titles on the newsstand.

By the beginning of 1975, I was ready to try full-time free-lancing again, except for one very important point. I had developed the skills I wanted, cultivated the contacts I needed, cleared my debts, padded my bank accounts, and established a good though small backup business. I had determined that there was a clear need in my region for a technical publications consultant, both within individual companies and as a liaison between companies and their advertising agencies. I had determined that there was a minimum of competition, with no real competition for someone capable of functioning equally well across a wide range of technologies. *What I lacked was the nerve to go out and do it!*

Finally, in August of 1975, my employer disbanded the publications group and I found myself without a job, but it was the biggest favor any employer had ever done for me. The layoff forced me to implement the plans I had laid so carefully and for so many years. From that moment on, there has been no interruption to my free-lance activities. I've fallen in love with the life-style, and nothing has ever been able to tempt me back into the life of a captive employee.

## PREPARATION: ONE KEY TO SUCCESS

The whole point of the two tales I've just related is to stress the importance of thorough evaluation, preparation, and planning before plunging into the risky business of making a living as a free-lancer. The individual who skips doing such preliminary homework or who skims over it hastily and carelessly can only increase the level of risk already inherent in a high-risk business. Yet even the most meticulous planning is no guarantee of success or survival. The only guarantee the free-lancer ever gets is that he gets no guarantees.

Despite all my prior planning, the first two years in my second business were quite difficult. An economic slowdown during the second year resulted in a period of nine months with consulting assignments few and far between from both new and established clients. During that period the backup income from free-lancing word puzzles became virtually the only source of money to pay the monthly bills. However, the years spent in preparation paid off in providing me with the flexibility to wait out the dry periods and the diversity to seek out new prospective clients. After the second year, my free-lance business suddenly boomed, gaining new clients, having older clients reactivate their projects, and providing more assignments than could be handled comfortably in a normal work week. As my business grew and changed, I revised and updated my business plan to provide even more flexibility and diversity until, by the fifth year of operation, I had enough on-going activities to form an effective buffer against adverse economic changes, thus allowing me to flow with the economy instead of having to fight it continuously.

Of course, the depth of preliminary preparation is a function of the individual's pursuits. The part-time free-lancer doesn't need as thorough a preparation as the full-timer, simply because he is not relying on his efforts for his subsistence. Writers in editorial fields have little need to be familiar with printing processes or typography simply because the publishers who buy the manuscripts determine the mechanical aspects of the finished piece. Each writer has his own game plan to suit his objectives and his market, and no two writers would be expected to have the same plan.

## A PRELIMINARY INVENTORY

The first step in starting a free-lance career is to take a form of personal inventory, similar to something known in the business world as a "feasibility study." For the part-time writer not dependent upon his earnings from free-lancing, this study may amount to little more than scanning lists of writers' markets to see if there are potential buyers who might be interested in his ideas and manuscripts. A full-timer typically needs more of an in-depth study that critically examines all aspects of his planned endeavor under what engineers refer to as the "worst-case conditions." To make such a study effective and useful, the free-lancer should assume that the so-called "Murphy's Law" is in full effect; i.e., if something can go wrong, it will go wrong.

There are four basic areas of concern during this initial evaluation: *personal goals, available markets, abilities vs. markets,* and *financial capabilities.* Careful and detailed examination of each of these four areas is crucial to the writer's understanding of what he can and cannot expect to accomplish and to the development of an effective method of dealing with the problems that he is going to encounter once he begins actively free-lancing.

### Personal Goals

The prospective free-lancer should examine both his short-term and long-term goals as critically as possible. "Writing the Great American Novel" is an unattainable goal. It's nice to think about, and every writer dreams about it sooner or later. But it's come to symbolize a standing joke among writers, and it's the mark of a goal that nobody ever achieves. Even fame and fortune are beyond the reach of the vast majority of writers. Only a very small percentage of all working writers gain national or international recognition, and even fewer manage to become wealthy as a result of their efforts. Such grand dreams are not really under the writer's control and have little to do with his talent or his perseverance. Instead, sudden fame and immense profits are the result of luck and a fortunate fluke in public opinion at a particular moment in time.

It's far better for an individual's goals to be realistic and at least within the realm of reasonable possibility. While a few writers may manage to approach the stereotyped successful image of the renowned author, most of us have to be satisfied with lesser accomplishments. Hopefully, we can earn enough to enjoy a relatively comfortable life-style, meeting our bills regularly, acquiring a few luxuries, and having the pleasure of not being under the heel of some tyrannical employer.

There's an old joke that surfaces periodically and makes its rounds through the business community. "When you're up to your ass in alligators, it's difficult to remember that you set out to drain the swamp." It serves to emphasize the problem with setting goals that are too high; they tend to get lost in the daily battle for survival. The free-lance writer quickly finds that his alligators are the rejection slips, accounting problems, tax concerns, and myriad other annoyances that nip away at him each and every day.

In presenting the reasons for free-lancing in Chapter 1, I've already described many of the positive aspects of such a career, but it's important to summarize them here. First, there is the potential for increased hourly earning power. While a captive writer may earn from $6 to $10 per hour, the free-lancer can earn from $15 to $50 per hour as a consultant, depending upon the extent of and demand for his skills. Even higher rates are possible when a consultant has some unique capability not available from other sources (companies that send highly qualified specialists out on troubleshooting jobs may charge upward of $200 an

hour for those individuals). The captive employee is restricted to a
fixed system rarely allowing annual increases of more than 7%
and causing a continuous decline in real earnings. The consultant
can adjust his rates to offset inflation and rising costs, often
allowing a gain in real earnings instead of a loss. The editorial
free-lancer working with book and magazine publishers finds less
of an advantage since his earnings are limited by the payment
policies of the publisher, and his earnings may be comparatively
low. The writer working on a magazine article at $0.04 per word
and capable of composing and typing 200 words an hour (including the time for organization, contemplation, and discarded
pages) would only be earning $8 an hour, and that assumes
everything he writes is actually sold.

Second, free-lancing allows a degree of independence. It allows
the writer to set his own hours and adjust his life to best suit his
own needs. Time becomes available to tend to personal chores;
there is no other boss to whom time off and other actions must be
justified. There is a minimum of conflict between the hours the
writer finds most effective and those a corporation considers
normal business hours. There is the freedom from having to take
part in the petty office politics that are a part of every company's
operation. This list can go on and on.

Third, free-lancing provides self-satisfaction. It can permit an
escape from routine or repetitive tasks. It allows more time for
creativity as the restrictions and distractions of the corporate
office are eliminated. It affords increased respect, with the consultant gaining that respect through being a highly paid expert and
the published writer finding it through by-lines or the appearance of his name on title pages of books or the mastheads of
periodicals. Again, the list can go on and on.

Balanced against all the positives are an equal or greater
number of negatives. The most obvious is the loss of job stability
and security. Everyone is locked into certain financial obligations.
The rent or mortgage must be paid by a specific date each month.
Utility bills arrive with annoying regularity and with an annoying tendency to grow constantly larger. Credit-card charges have
a nasty habit of being billed when there is little cash to pay them

off. In addition, we have to eat, buy clothing, obtain medical aid, make repairs to damaged possessions, support our cars, and insure ourselves against unpredictable disasters. When all of these are added up, there is a substantial fixed obligation that must be met each month of each year, with only limited flexibility in shifting cash from one expenditure to another.

The monthly costs of living make job security and a regular paycheck a prime requirement for most people, so much so that the mere threat of losing a job strikes terror into the hearts of the average middle-class family. It is this dependence upon a regular and predictable income that creates the first and most difficult obstacle for the free-lancer since he can expect no regularity in the receipt of income. While individual receipts may be quite large, often there are long stretches of time between those receipts. Publishing companies and consulting clients alike seek to improve their own cash flows by delaying their accounts payable as long as possible, thus tying up the free-lancer's earnings in accounts receivable, making a shambles of his cash flow, and preventing him from predicting when money will be available to cover his fixed living costs or the overhead costs of his business.

After more than five years of continuous free-lancing, I've found that cash flow remains my single biggest problem. The cliché of "feast or famine" is the dominant feature of my operation, both in work load and cash flow. I'm constantly fluctuating between periods during which I receive several thousand dollars a month for several months and periods when my receipts drop to levels of less than a hundred dollars a month or disappear entirely. While the annual average may remain quite high, the short-term cash flow continues to be a problem under the best circumstances.

As a result, the free-lancer must learn to plan ahead, always maintaining a cash reserve sufficient to float him through all fixed and emergency expenses that may be incurred over a period of up to a year. Since creditors can be stalled only so long, the free-lancer who fails to maintain a reserve sufficient to carry him through low-paying or nonpaying intervals runs a high risk of personal disaster. If the bills aren't paid, a time comes when creditors start making repossessions, vendors stop the flow of supplies, utilities are shut down, and life gets to be quite miserable.

A less obvious problem is the loss of fringe benefits. A captive employee receives certain remunerations above and beyond his wages, including paid vacations, paid holidays, paid sick days, paid health and life insurances, paid unemployment insurance, matched-contribution investment programs, and so on. Most of these things are taken for granted by the captive employee, even though he doesn't see them as a direct part of his paycheck. There is at least one other benefit that few employees are aware of—the amounts deducted for the federal Social Security program are supplemented by the employer to satisfy the government's total required payment. This means that the captive employee only pays part of the total Social Security obligation, while the free-lancer has to pay the whole amount as a "Self-employment Tax."

Both Social Security withholding and the Self-employment Tax are determined by percentages of some maximum amount of earnings. Both apply to the same maximum amount, but different percentages are applied. In 1979, Social Security withholding was 6.03% of the first $17,700 of wages, while Self-employment Tax was 8.1% of the first $17,700 of net profit. Therefore, free-lance writers can expect to be penalized by having to pay at least 2% more of their earnings, just for being self-employed.

With no full-time employer, the free-lancer must cover his own health and life insurance needs, adding to his fixed monthly costs. If the writer also invests in photographic equipment, a video recorder, a word-processing system, or a computer system for use in his business, he will find that those items are not protected under his homeowner's insurance so he will have to obtain separate high-premium commercial insurance. Furthermore, some homeowner's insurance policies are null and void if a business is conducted on the premises or if business equipment is kept on the property, making it necessary to obtain new insurance at a higher premium. The free-lancer must handle all of his own investments, enforce his own savings plan, and provide his own retirement fund (usually an I.R.A. or Keogh plan). Vacations, holidays, sick days, and personal time to run errands or sit on jury duty are direct losses since time not spent working is time not spent earning money.

There is no unemployment insurance for the self-employed; if the business goes into a slump, the free-lancer is strictly on his own and can't go down to the local employment office to collect at least a survival-level income. In many parts of the country, it can take from 18 to 24 or more months of full-time employment to requalify for unemployment benefits once qualification has been lost through being self-employed; this means that if the business should be abandoned to return to captive employment, the individual won't be able to collect unemployment if separated from that job during the first two years.

Free-lancing also requires a willingness to sacrifice. The typical captive employee devotes about 40 hours a week to his job, with occasional paid or unpaid overtime on a Saturday or during the evenings. The free-lancer doesn't always have that luxury. Since the free-lancer's first obligation is to the commitments made to his client, it is common for him to have to work far more hours than would be necessary on a salaried job. A committed deadline must be met, even if it requires working seven days a week and around the clock for days on end.

Fully loaded with consulting jobs and tight deadlines, I've had many work weeks of up to 140 hours each, extending over periods of three months at a time. During a year from early 1978 to early 1979, the consulting assignments were so heavy and the deadlines so tight that the only day not worked was Independence Day. Even Christmas and New Year's days were considered working days, although on a reduced schedule of only eight hours. There seems to be no middle ground. "Feast or famine" is a daily rule, not an exception. Either there is too much work to be done comfortably, or there simply isn't enough to get by on.

A full-time free-lance career requires giving up a great deal of personal time. If the free-lancer or consultant is in high demand, he finds that weekends, holidays, and vacations simply do not exist. Family trips and outings often must be postponed again and again, sometimes never actually taking place. Social contacts often are reduced or cut off entirely, simply because there is neither opportunity nor time to engage in socializing without jeopardizing committed assignments. The free-lancer who turns away assignments to keep free time available, or the free-lancer who is not being offered sufficient assignments runs the risk of not being able to meet his bills, having to delay major purchases, or having to deprive himself or his family of some necessity.

If you haven't already realized it, I've just succeeded in contradicting myself. In describing the advantages of a free-lance career, I listed independence and the ability to set one's own hours. Now I've said that the free-lancer has little or no personal time. Actually, both statements are true, but not always simultaneously. The ability to arrange one's time is a direct function of the extent of the work load at a given moment. Under a light load, there is a great deal of latitude. Under a heavy load, there is little latitude, and that element of independence must be sacrificed. Since freedom exists more in the mind than in actuality, the simple knowledge that affairs could be rearranged to permit more freedom offsets the lack of actual freedom. The real difference between being captive and being free-lance is the difference between someone else determining the schedule and the individual doing it himself.

The overall assessment that every aspiring free-lancer should make involves an attempt to balance the positives and negatives. In doing so, he should prepare a written inventory with two columns—one with every positive factor and goal he can think of and the other with every negative factor. Nothing should be omitted, no matter how trivial or seemingly irrelevant. When the lists are as complete as he can make them, he should examine them objectively and decide which list outweighs the other. If the list of negatives contains even a single item that is totally unacceptable and cannot be altered to make it acceptable, the free-lancer would be well advised to delay his plans until his situation changes enough to reduce the impact of that item or to remove it from the list completely. Any remaining negatives constitute the list of things to which the free-lancer must pay particular attention in developing his plan of action, attempting to minimize their effects as much as possible.

As a further aid, Figure 1, pages 38–39, duplicates a brief

questionnaire on motivation and drive as it appears in a book published by the Small Business Administration. This is not a scientific test, but it does serve to identify some of the personal traits important to conducting a small business. Other questions may be added if they seem pertinent to an individual endeavor, and an honest evaluation should show most of the check marks on the left-hand side of the lines. Check marks toward the center or right side point up areas that may need some additional attention by a prospective free-lancer before launching into a business on a full-time basis.

## Available Markets

Once the free-lancer has identified his goals, has determined that his plans are feasible in terms of all pros and cons, and has decided to make the sacrifices, he can proceed to evaluate the available market. Again, the evaluation must be done as realistically and objectively as possible. It serves no purpose for a writer to generate manuscripts for which there are no publishers or to offer services for which there are no clients. While the writer may alter his own work to fit the market, he's not going to be able to alter the market to fit his work.

The editorial writer can find numerous listings and descriptions of publishers, broadcasters, agents, syndicates, and similar outlets for his efforts. Using these references, he can compile his own list of prospects who might be willing to purchase or at least examine his creations. From there on, it becomes an exercise in trial and error, or trial and rejection. Common jokes about the number of rejection slips a writer can expect from publishers or other buyers are not far off the mark and really aren't a joking matter to the struggling writer. No matter how many of them he's already seen, each new rejection still hurts. The average writer lacking an established name and having no proven demand for his work can expect to devote from three to ten times more time and effort in attempting to find a buyer than he spends actually preparing the manuscripts and associated materials.

Since the novice editorial writer does not have a reputation to

FIGURE 1. Rating Scale: Business Proprietor's Personal Traits

(W. O. Metcalf. *Starting and Managing a Small Business of Your Own*, 3rd ed., Small Business Administration, pp. 4–5.)

**INSTRUCTIONS:** After each question place a check mark on the line at the point closest to your answer. The check mark need not be placed directly over one of the suggested answers because your rating may lie somewhere between two answers. **Be** honest with yourself.

### ARE YOU A SELF-STARTER?

I do things my own way. Nobody needs to tell me to get going.

If someone gets me started, I keep going all right.

Easy does it. I don't put myself out until I have to.

### HOW DO YOU FEEL ABOUT OTHER PEOPLE?

I like people. I can get along with just about any- body.

I have plenty of friends. I don't need anyone else.

Most people bug me.

### CAN YOU LEAD OTHERS?

I can get most people to go along without much difficulty.

I can get people to do things if I drive them.

I let someone else get things moving.

### CAN YOU TAKE RESPONSIBILITY?

I like to take charge of and see things through.

I'll take over if I have to, but I'd rather let someone else be responsible.

There's always some eager beaver around wanting to show off. I say let him.

| | | | |
|---|---|---|---|
| **HOW GOOD AN ORGANIZER ARE YOU?** | I like to have a plan before I start. I'm usually the one to get things lined up. | I do all right unless things get too goofed up. Then I cop out. | I just take things as they come. |
| **HOW GOOD A WORKER ARE YOU?** | I can keep going as long as necessary. I don't mind working hard. | I'll work hard for a while, but when I've had enough, that's it! | I can't see that hard work gets you anywhere. |
| **CAN YOU MAKE DECISIONS?** | I can make up my mind in a hurry if necessary, and my decision is usually o.k. | I can if I have plenty of time. If I have to make up my mind fast, I usually regret it. | I don't like to be the one who decides things. I'd probably blow it. |
| **CAN PEOPLE TRUST WHAT YOU SAY?** | They sure can. I don't say things I don't mean. | I try to be on the level, but sometimes I just say what's easiest. | What's the sweat if the other fellow doesn't know the difference? |
| **CAN YOU STICK WITH IT?** | If I make up my mind to do something, I don't let anything stop me. | I usually finish what I start. | If a job doesn't go right, I turn off. Why beat your brains out? |
| **HOW GOOD IS YOUR HEALTH?** | I never run down. | I have enough energy for most things I want to do. | I run out of juice sooner than most of my friends seem to. |

back him up and cannot demonstrate a list of publication credits, he is at a severe disadvantage. Big-name writers and artists have little trouble getting their work accepted, and their submissions are brought to the immediate attention of the people in charge. The beginner, however, faces many closed doors and his materials may be returned without even being read or examined. Some publishers won't even break the seal on a mailing package arriving from someone they don't know or without a prior solicitation. The writer is left with no alternative but to try over and over again, hoping that someone will take the time to read his query or manuscript and ultimately decide to publish his work. Trial and error is the main approach to identifying and evaluating the market for editorial materials.

Marketing and technical free-lancers face an entirely different procedure in finding points of sale. In most cases, they limit their efforts to a local or regional area and must seek out suitable companies within that locale. A marketing writer naturally seeks advertising agencies and public relations firms that hold accounts closely allied to the free-lancer's own background. Alternatively, he seeks contact with the marketing departments of corporations providing products or services with which he has some familiarity. Technical writers follow much the same path, seeking advertising agencies and public relations firms that handle technical accounts and making contact with both the marketing and engineering departments of individual corporations. When a marketing or technical writer decides to become involved with books or other editorial materials, he must switch to the evaluation procedures used by the editorial free-lancers.

For marketing and technical free-lancers, there are certain research aids available. The Yellow Pages of a local telephone directory is one obvious source of categorized company names, but it provides no solid information about the size of a company, its contact personnel, or its overall activities. Most public libraries stock locally published reference books that list major corporations either alphabetically or grouped according to enterprise. Some reference books provide lists of influential contacts throughout major metropolitan areas. Other sources include professional organizations such as advertising clubs, technical communicators' clubs, public service organizations, business peoples' social organizations, and the Chamber of Commerce.

The marketing or technical free-lancer's objective is to make as many contacts as possible among people and businesses having any relationship to his chosen field. While still a captive employee, the prospective free-lancer has the further advantage of establishing contacts with the people doing business with his own employer. This can include purchasers of his employer's products, vendors to the company, advertising agencies, printers, and similar groups. Note, however, that it is both unethical and dangerous to solicit work from these groups on company time, on company premises, or from among the company's customers while still an employee. Such actions are grounds for immediate and justifiable termination of a job, and can give the individual a poor reputation among the same people he's trying to cultivate. Instead, activities should be limited to getting to know the appropriate people, learning what they do, identifying their needs, and so on. *Never get caught trying to undermine your employer's business.*

After having made a list of the possible outlets for his work, the free-lancer must examine it with a critical eye. The potential market must be of sufficient size to warrant a venture into the free-lance arena; if it is not, the demise of the venture will be quick and unmerciful. For example, a specifications writer who has spent his entire working career documenting boiler design for conventional power plants and who knows little or nothing about other technologies would find it impossible to conduct a business as a consultant in a city or region where only one or two companies are involved in the design of power plants.

What it all boils down to is that the marketing or technical free-lancer is pretty much at the mercy of his environment. He cannot expect to create a market for his talents where no market exists. The best he can ever hope for even under ideal conditions is to convince the management of new or established companies that they would achieve their needs better and more economically through the use of outside talent rather than an in-house staff. If there are no companies operating in related fields, there is no management to sway, and there is no business for the free-lancer.

## Abilities vs. Market

Assuming that the free-lancer has found sufficient evidence of an available market, the next step is to assess his own abilities in relation to the needs of that potential market. There are abilities that are marketable and those that are not.

The writer dealing with the editorial market may find an advantage in being able to do his own photography and some simple pen-and-ink-drawing. While the fiction author is concerned only with words, the nonfiction writer often needs to support his text with illustrations. Articles on subjects such as home improvements, mechanical repairs, and gardening are most salable when accompanied with color or black-and-white photos and a few line drawings. At the same time, the writer who chooses to provide his own illustrative materials should have a basic familiarity with the techniques that are used to reproduce them in printed form. For example, a drawing done in pencil or blue ink does not lend itself to the processes involved in making printing plates. Similarly, photos'that are overexposed, underexposed, or of poor contrast do not yield the best results when converted to the dot pattern of a halftone on a printed page. Conversely, the editorial writer has little need to know the procedures of setting type, pasting up camera-ready art, aligning a printing press, etc.; those tasks are handled by the publisher's production department without the contributor's direct involvement.

The marketing or technical consultant faces more complex problems. In all my discussions with aspiring free-lancers and consultants, I emphasize one factor above all others: *diversity*. Whether in talents, skills, or general knowledge, I consider diversification the single most important influence on long-term survival and success for a communications consultant. I consider it only slightly less important for the editorial free-lancer. The fewer things a free-lancer can do well, the lower his chances of success. Conversely, the more things the free-lancer can do, the larger his available market, and the greater his chances of success.

The free-lancer acting as a consultant finds that his clients expect the completion of more than just one part of the total job. The writer who works on promotional brochures rarely finds a company satisfied to let him just write the copy. Instead, they look for someone who can plan the brochure, analyze the approach, present the graphic concept, write the copy, provide the illustrations, supply the camera-ready art, and oversee the printing. In short, they seek a single individual who wears many hats. The same applies to companies contracting for their instructional manuals; few are willing to accept a handwritten or roughly typed draft and then undertake to have the artwork, camera-ready copy, and printing done on their own.

The successful free-lancer may be an expert in one field, but he also should have a range of secondary capabilities. If he's a writer, he should be able to type camera-ready copy for offset printing; he should be able to do basic graphic design work for cover art, block diagrams, and flow charts; he should be able to perform basic pasteup functions that prepare materials for print; and he should have at least a working knowledge of the mechanical requirements of the printer's art, the illustrator's art, and the photographer's art. If he doesn't have those capabilities, he had better know where to obtain them. It always is advisable for a writer to maintain close ties with qualified and reliable artists, illustrators, photographers, and printers.

The need for diversity also extends to subject matter. A technical writer who knows nothing more than computer software is hard pressed to find an adequate market for his abilities. A marketing writer who only knows how to promote large-ticket consumer goods can expect to have the same problem. Each field of endeavor in our highly specialized society comes complete with its own images, concepts, and vocabulary. The vocabulary of medicine is totally different from that of mining. The approaches used in marketing are different from those used in technical documentation. The styles employed by consumer magazines are radically different from those of trade journals.

By developing abilities and knowledge in differing fields, the free-lancer automatically improves his chances. The technical writer who can handle mining, electronics, computer software, medical instrumentation, air pollution control equipment, and other subjects has a much easier time of it than the individual who can deal only with one or two subjects. The working free-lance writer can never afford to stop educating himself. He must never stop broadening his abilities and implementing new talents.

It may sound as if I'm advocating becoming an expert in every field. Obviously, that's an impossibility for anyone. The depth of knowledge in each of many fields need not be great enough to be considered expert in that field. Instead, the knowledge need only be sufficient to allow limited performance in that field. Confusing? Not really! The writer has no intention of making his living as an artist, so he doesn't need to be a top-notch artist. But he does need to have a basic understanding of the principles of art, composition, and layout. He does need the ability to guide an artist in complex renderings and to allow for the positioning of renderings in his carefully crafted text. At the same time, he should have a feel for typography so he knows how well his copy will fit within the limited space of a brochure or a page-size advertisement.

Similarly, the writer has no intention of making his living as a photographer or printer. Still, he should know something about photography so he can assure that his copy will be accompanied by appropriate halftones in the finished product, whether he provides his own photos or they are provided by someone else. At the same time, he should be aware of the needs of the printer so any camera-ready art he furnishes doesn't have to be redone because a misplaced rule line runs into the edge of the page where the paper gripper of the press must grab the sheet.

In the diversity of subject matter, the writer need not be an expert in every possible area of knowledge, but he should have the ability to communicate with those who are experts. The best parallel can be drawn from technical writers. Contrary to popular belief, a tech writer doesn't have to be an expert in one particular field. The vast majority of technical documents really don't require a knowledge of the subject much beyond a high-school general science level. With that in mind, it's no great chore to undertake varied reading of general articles pertinent to many fields. With the basic vocabulary that can be thus obtained, the writer finds it easier to talk to specialists without stumbling around for words. When necessary, a greater in-depth knowledge can be obtained for an individual project by undertaking intensive reading on the subject as the need arises.

## Financial Capabilities

In discussions with prospective free-lancers in writing and other fields, I've found one common barrier. Nearly all of them have been financially incapable of undertaking a full-time free-lance career. Earlier in this chapter, I cited some of the financial problems faced by free-lancers, and that was not an all-encompassing list. One omission was that it is expensive to set up a business of any kind, and free-lance writing is no exception. Although writing does not have the expenses of a profession like photography with its associated costs for sophisticated equipment and supplies, writing still incurs substantial expenditures.

Of all the possible free-lance businesses such as graphic arts and photography, writing has the lowest entry cost. The basic needs are a desk, a typewriter, some paper, pens, pencils, and erasers. The usual picture of a writer shows him hovering over a broken-down 1920s vintage typewriter with sticky keys and a worn-out ribbon. They're cheap, but not always practical. While an editorial writer never producing camera-ready copy may get by with such a machine, the marketing and technical writers usually require something a bit more modern and versatile. Therein lies one of the largest expenses for a writer short of a full-blown word-processing system. The cost of renting an office-style typewriter with interchangeable type elements, carbon ribbons, and preferably selectable 10-pitch and 12-pitch character spacing will be upwards of about $45 a month. The purchase price for a reconditioned machine of this type is $850 or more, plus the cost of a service contract or the expenses of inevitable repair calls.

Writers preferring the flexibility of computerized word-processing systems can expect to invest from $6,000 to $16,000 for a suitable system. I'll be discussing word processors at greater length in Chapter 4, but here I must caution the writer against cheap systems that could be a total waste of money. The subject of word processing has caught the attention of the "personal computer" market. Many systems originally designed as hobbyist and game-playing machines now claim to be business computers and word-processing systems. Typically, these are priced somewhere below $5,500. First, the potential buyer should be aware that the word-processing capability is a function of the programming ("software"), not of the machine itself ("hardware"). The software packages can cost from $200 to $3,000, and a given package may not be at all suitable to a particular writer's needs. A lot of comparison shopping and hands-on experience is necessary in selecting the software alone. Second, lower-priced systems usually are equipped with a "dot matrix" printer that constructs letters out of individual dots. Such a printer generally is unacceptable to publishers and consulting clients alike; many publishers refuse to read manuscripts printed by a dot matrix, and the technique is completely unsuitable for camera-ready art. A good character printer, usually utilizing interchangeable "daisywheel" type fonts, will cost from $3,000 to $4,000 by itself, plus the cost of the computer, disk drives, terminals, and other interconnected equipment.

Beyond the initial startup are a wide variety of operating expenses, some obvious and some hidden. Worn equipment must be repaired or replaced, expendables must be restocked periodically, specialized tools and materials must be purchased when needed to complete an assignment. Sooner or later, every writer should purchase a reliable 35-mm camera and a few accessory lenses so that he has the capability of obtaining supporting photographs for his manuscripts. Depending on individual preference, the cost can range from about $190 for a simple store-brand camera system to more than $1,000 for a basic name-brand setup. Consultants wishing to do some industrial, product, or commercial photography may have to supplement 35-mm equipment with larger formats up to 4×5-inch film sizes and costs reaching several thousand dollars for the camera, lenses, and lighting equipment. Miniature pocket tape recorders come in handy for many writers, and they can cost from $70 to $300.

If the free-lancer decides to operate out of an office separate from his home, rent for the office space becomes a major cash outlay. Whether at home or in a rented office, the presence of a free-lance business incurs increased utility costs—more electricity for lights, typewriters, and other equipment; more gas or heating oil to maintain a higher daytime temperature in the facility; increased water consumption; and so on. Plus, there is a cost of around $500 for the essential desk, chair, desk light, table, and other furnishings of the writer's office.

Other expenses that are incurred either during startup or immediately thereafter involve stationery, brochures, résumés, advertising, and the other accoutrements of the professional business individual. This is an area often ignored by the novice free-lancer, usually to his later dismay. It is important at all times to present a professional front, and that requires a professional appearance to the business papers. While the details of these materials are discussed in Chapter 4, it should be noted here that their cost can be quite significant. For example, in 1975, I had a letterhead, a second sheet, an envelope, and a simple, two-sided, folded brochure typeset and printed in a quantity of 500 each for a total cost of about $150. In 1979, a revision involving partially reset type and reprinting in the same quantity cost $680. Advertising rates also have skyrocketed. My usual trade media ad in a local publication for the advertising and marketing community measured 4¾ inches by 2¼ inches and cost $35 a month in 1975 but $145 a month in late 1979.

There are some general guidelines that are highly recommended for beginning free-lancers, guidelines that I followed myself before undertaking my second try at a free-lance career. First, full-time employment should be continued until free-lancing becomes financially practical. The impatience of getting started may make the waiting period seem interminably long, but separating from an employer prematurely is absolute folly. As much money as possible should be stashed away in a savings account, preferably the passbook type to allow quick access when the need arises. Once the decision to free-lance has been made, other expenditures should be minimized as much as possible to help pad that bank account; those savings are going to be needed when the business is first started and throughout the first couple of years of operation. The time with the employer should be used to develop as many outside contacts as possible among the employer's vendors, business associates, etc. Incidentally, a working spouse can be a valuable asset in building the cash reserve that will be necessary for the free-lance business.

Second, the prospective free-lancer should divest himself of as many debts as possible. This means clearing charge accounts and storing those devilish plastic cards where they're not readily accessible for additional charging. However, the accounts themselves should not be cancelled, because the third point is to develop a line of credit. Once into free-lancing and lacking a full-time employer, obtaining credit becomes extremely difficult; there is no end to the problems of proving financial responsibility once self-employed, and at a minimum it requires divulging a lot of information that the free-lancer may consider confidential. A wise plan includes having credit established and available for use, without outstanding debts against that credit. It's nearly impossible to clear the debt of a house mortgage, but every effort should be made to clear special purchases such as cars, furniture, etc.

The fourth point relates to the others in that it requires the building of a substantial cash reserve. Once separated from the full-time employer, it is that cash reserve that is going to pay the monthly bills, cover the startup costs of the business, support the monthly business overhead, and provide for living expenses. Generally, it takes about two years to become established in a free-lance business and to put that business on a profitable footing. During those first two years, there are going to be extended periods with little or no income from the business but continued expenditures to keep it going. As a rule of thumb, the prospective free-lancer with a working spouse and no children would be well advised to have sufficient funds in the bank to cover all estimated startup costs, operating expenses, and household expenses for at least one full year. The presence of children in the family should increase the amount of the cash reserve by at least 25% for each child.

The amount of the cash reserve may seem inordinately high

and for many it's nearly impossible to attain. At the same time, it's impossible to predict the degree of success or failure of the business with any accuracy until it is well underway and the commitment is essentially irreversible. With luck, it won't be necessary to tap that cash reserve to any great extent, but if even half of what can go wrong does go wrong, that reserve makes the difference between survival and failure. Few free-lancers can plunge right in and make a living at it right from the first day. For the majority, there are long periods of floating along on the bank account while cultivating new projects and clients that may or may not pay off at some future date.

As an additional aid to beginning free-lancers, Figures 2 and 3 illustrate worksheets typical of those that might be used to define financial obligations. Additional items should be added to these sheets as necessary to accommodate the business enterprise being planned, but they do provide space for estimating most of the regular costs that a free-lance writer can expect to encounter.

On Worksheet 1, the column for cash needed is the selling price of the item if it is purchased outright without financing. It is the sum of the down payment and a given number of months' installments for items purchased on credit. The number of months to be allowed is an individual choice, but should be about three to six months for writers already having known points of sale and six to twelve months for writers who have not established their markets. The same applies to the monthly expenditures on Worksheet 2. The estimate of cash needed is the monthly cost multiplied by the number of months allowed, using the same intervals as allowed on Worksheet 1.

During the first two years, basic survival is the prime consideration for any free-lancer. In 1978, I received a printed piece from the Dun & Bradstreet Business Economics Department that showed the percentage of total business failures in various categories. In the service category, of which free-lancing and consulting are a part, the mailing cited a failure rate of 51.7% during the first five years, 31.8% through the sixth to tenth years, and 16.5% after ten years. With the deterioration of the economic picture since then, the failure rates undoubtedly have grown much higher.

FIGURE 2. Financial Planning Worksheet 1

## EQUIPMENT, FURNITURE, AND FIXTURES (Worksheet 1)

| Items | Cash Price | Down Payment | Installments | Cash Needed* |
|-------|-----------|--------------|--------------|--------------|
| Typewriter | $ | $ | $ | $ |
| Camera Equipment | $ | $ | $ | $ |
| Answering Machine | $ | $ | $ | $ |
| Tape Recorder | $ | $ | $ | $ |
| Word-Processing System | $ | $ | $ | $ |
| Desk | $ | $ | $ | $ |
| Office Chair | $ | $ | $ | $ |
| Filing Cabinet | $ | $ | $ | $ |
| Drafting/Layout Table | $ | $ | $ | $ |
| Lighting Fixtures | $ | $ | $ | $ |
| Initial Office Supplies | $ | $ | $ | $ |
| Miscellaneous Tools | $ | $ | $ | $ |
| Business Stationery | $ | $ | $ | $ |
| Business Brochures | $ | $ | $ | $ |
| Portfolios and Sales Aids | $ | $ | $ | $ |
| | $ | $ | $ | $ |
| | $ | $ | $ | $ |
| **Total Cash Needed (enter on Worksheet 2)** | | | | $ |

*For cash purchases, the cash needed is the total price. For financed items it is the sum of the down payment plus the number of months of installments you feel you must allocate from your initial working capital.

FIGURE 3. Financial Planning Worksheet 2

## ESTIMATED ONE-TIME STARTUP COSTS (Worksheet 2)

| Initial or One-Time Costs | Estimate of Cash Needed |
|---|---|
| Equipment, furniture, and fixtures (from Worksheet 1) | $ |
| Remodeling and/or decorating (contractor's estimate) | $ |
| Delivery and installation of equipment and furniture (suppliers) | $ |
| Deposits for utilities (from utility companies) | $ |
| Legal and professional fees (incorporation, bookkeeping, etc.) | $ |
| Licenses and permits (when required) | $ |
| Professional library | $ |
| Contingency cash (for unexpected expenses or losses, etc.) | $ |
| Special purchases | $ |
| Accounts receivable (to cover buyer's credit until paid) | $ |
| | $ |

## ESTIMATED MONTHLY EXPENSES

| Item | Estimate of Monthly Cost | Estimate of Cash Needed* |
|---|---|---|
| Owner's salary or living expenses | $ | $ |
| Merchandise and materials | $ | $ |
| Accounting costs (CPA payments, etc.) | $ | $ |
| Advertising expenses | $ | $ |
| Automobile and travel expenses | $ | $ |
| Electricity and gas payments | $ | $ |
| Entertainment costs (for clients and buyers) | $ | $ |
| Heating costs | $ | $ |
| Income taxes (prorated to monthly basis) | $ | $ |
| Interest on business indebtedness | $ | $ |
| Legal and professional fees | $ | $ |
| Office expenses (photocopying, etc.) | $ | $ |
| Postage | $ | $ |
| Reference materials (magazines, books, etc.) | $ | $ |
| Rent, lease, or mortgage payments | $ | $ |
| Rentals and leases of equipment | $ | $ |
| Repairs of equipment (include service contracts) | $ | $ |
| Retirement account (prorated to monthly basis) | $ | $ |
| Self-employment tax (sole-proprietorships) | $ | $ |
| Supplies (paper, pencils, ribbons, etc.) | $ | $ |
| Telephone (monthly bill plus long distance) | $ | $ |
| Trade and professional dues | $ | $ |
| Trash collection | $ | $ |
| Water and sewer | $ | $ |
| | $ | $ |
| TOTAL ESTIMATED CASH NEEDED TO START THE BUSINESS | | $ |

*Multiply the estimated monthly cost times the number of months you feel you need to cover to obtain the amount of cash needed to start the business.*

# 3

# Getting Started

Throughout the first two chapters, I've defined the functions of a free-lancer in three major fields, I've taken a look at the rationale for a free-lance career, and I've identified some of the positive and negative factors influencing such a career. That information was largely subjective and had little to do with procedures for starting and operating a free-lance business. The rest of this book is concerned with the nuts, bolts, and baling wire that put the business together and keep it running as smoothly as possible.

A number of writers have told me they weren't about to get involved in the concerns of a business operation. "After all," they've said, "it's only a hobby." My response is unprintable. Every free-lance writer is conducting a business. It doesn't matter whether he's working 20 hours a day on a major project or just putting in an occasional hour or two on cute fillers for a magazine. It doesn't matter whether he's planning to make a living at it or not. At some point, the objective is to sell the work, get paid for the effort, and possibly have the pay exceed the cost to become a profit. That makes it a business, loosely defined, but still a business.

Like any other business, that of the writer has certain basic requirements. While a part-timer may be able to simplify or avoid some of these things, he should include as many as possible. To provide the most information, I'm going to treat the business procedures from the point of view of a full-time activity, without qualifying them for the part-timer. I leave it to the part-timer to pick out the details that affect him directly, but I also caution him against discarding any procedure without some very careful consideration.

Getting started involves far more than just sitting down at a typewriter, tying words together into sentences, and structuring those sentences into a coherent piece of work. Even before writing the first words, a variety of things needs to be done. The essential tasks consist of structuring the business, choosing an accounting system, selecting a trade name, securing licenses, determining rates, and writing a contract.

## STRUCTURING THE BUSINESS

As a beginning free-lancer, your first decision is how to structure your business. Your choices are between setting up your own corporation or operating as a sole proprietorship. A third alternative of a legal partnership has fallen into disfavor and is used so rarely by free-lancers that I am not going to present it as a viable business structure. Figure 4 illustrates the relative advantages and disadvantages of a single (sole) proprietorship, a partnership, and a corporation. Of course, there are other business structures available, but they usually are not used by free-lance writers. Some of the other possible structures include the limited partnership, the statutory partnership association, the joint-stock company, the Massachusetts trust, and various modifications of a corporate organization.

Since I am not a lawyer, and because the legalities of incorporation differ widely from state to state, I'm not going to make any recommendations as to how you should set up your own business.

FIGURE 4. Comparative Forms of Business Organization
(W. O. Metcalf. *Starting and Managing a Small Business of Your Own*, 3rd ed., Small Business Administration, p. 24.)

## SINGLE PROPRIETORSHIP

| ADVANTAGES | DISADVANTAGES |
|---|---|
| 1. Low start-up costs | 1. Unlimited liability |
| 2. Greatest freedom from regulation | 2. Lack of continuity |
| 3. Owner in direct control | 3. Difficult to raise capital |
| 4. Minimal working capital requirements | |
| 5. Tax advantage to small owner | |
| 6. All profits to owner | |

## PARTNERSHIP

| ADVANTAGES | DISADVANTAGES |
|---|---|
| 1. Ease of formation | 1. Unlimited liability |
| 2. Low start-up costs | 2. Lack of continuity |
| 3. Additional sources of venture capital | 3. Divided authority |
| 4. Broader management base | 4. Difficulty in raising additional capital |
| 5. Possible tax advantage | 5. Hard to find suitable partners |
| 6. Limited outside regulation | |

## CORPORATION

| ADVANTAGES | DISADVANTAGES |
|---|---|
| 1. Limited liability | 1. Closely regulated |
| 2. Specialized management | 2. Most expensive form to organize |
| 3. Ownership is transferrable | 3. Charter restrictions |
| 4. Continuous existence | 4. Extensive record keeping necessary |
| 5. Legal entity | 5. Double taxation |
| 6. Possible tax advantages | |
| 7. Easier to raise capital | |

You should, however, study the available literature on the subject. If a corporate structure seems appealing, consult a competent attorney for additional and current legal advice.

One source of important information is the *Tax Guide for Small Business*, Publication 334 of the Department of the Treasury, Internal Revenue Service. The book is available free of charge from most IRS offices or can be ordered on the form provided in the back of the instruction booklet that accompanies the annual 1040 tax return form. Excerpts used in this chapter are taken from that IRS publication.

### The Corporation

The idea of forming a corporation appeals to small businesses for two reasons. First, a corporate structure appears to offer tax advantages. In many cases, there are tax shelters and loopholes accessible to a corporation and its shareholders that are not available to the individual taxpayer. When you are trying to make money in a small business, reducing your overall tax obligation is important.

Second, the articles of incorporation often allow business property to be separated from the personal property of the officers or shareholders. This means that a bankruptcy or other civil proceeding against the corporation can touch only the assets and property of the corporation itself and not those of the individual owners. For a small business on a shaky footing, this provides an element of protection for personal possessions. This can be sufficient justification in and of itself for incorporating the business endeavor.

At the same time, the corporate structure can be too complex for a free-lancer. Just a quick scan of the IRS tax guide lists complicated concerns such as deductions for dividends received, capital and retained earnings, profit computations, distributions to stockholders, liquidations and stock redemptions, an election for Subchapter S, capital gains tax, and on and on and on. The sheer number of federal and state forms and the bulk of the paperwork can quickly overwhelm you.

Furthermore, the act of incorporating incurs costs that you may find beyond your immediate ability to meet. First, it takes an attorney to wade through the legal advantages and disadvantages of the corporate structure; you're going to need his advice, and you're going to have to pay for his time. That attorney also has to prepare and file the articles of incorporation, again with a charge. When I contemplated starting a corporation in 1975, the cost of just setting it up was between $1,000 and $1,500. A second expense involves using a certified public accountant. Since few writers have the time or the inclination to study the tax laws for corporations and handle all the forms and paperwork involved, a CPA is almost always necessary, and he too charges for his time and effort.

> Once you have decided to start a business, your first considera-
> tion should be what type of business entity to use. There are both
> legal and tax considerations that will enter into your determina-
> tion. . . .

> Except in the case of a Subchapter S corporation, profits of a
> corporation are taxed both to the corporation and again to the
> individual shareholders when the profits are distributed as divi-
> dends . . . losses sustained by the corporation usually are not
> available to its shareholders. . . .

> In its computation of taxable income, a corporation generally
> can take the same deductions that apply to individuals. Corpora-
> tions also are entitled to special deductions. . . .

## The Sole Proprietorship

Your alternative is to operate a sole proprietorship, meaning that you and your business are one and the same. Under this method, your profit or loss is the difference between payments received and expenses paid out. Your personal income for tax purposes is exactly the profit shown by the business, while a business loss means zero income. This type of operation may limit accessible tax advantages when compared with a corporate structure, but it does not eliminate them. As a sole proprietorship, you still can deduct the costs of doing business, charge off bad debts, claim investment tax credits, etc. What you lack is the ability to separate personal property from business property, therefore placing everything you own at risk in the event of bankruptcy or legal claims against your business. What you gain is simplicity.

> Individuals engaging in business on their own account are sole proprietors. This is the simplest form of business organization. The business has no existence apart from the owner. Its liabilities are the personal liabilities of the proprietor, and the owner's proprietary interest terminates upon the owner's death. The proprietor undertakes the risks of business to the extent of all assets, whether used in the business or personally owned.

> **Income** from a sole proprietorship is a part of the total gross income received by the individual. . . .

My personal choice was the sole proprietorship, mainly because it was easier to handle than incorporation. Under this system, earnings and expenses are reported to the IRS on Schedule C (Form 1040). Self-employment Tax (Social Security for the self-employed) is reported on Schedule SE. The accounting procedures, computations, and forms are simple enough to handle myself without the expense of paying a CPA.

The majority of free-lancers I've talked with favor the sole proprietorship. Writers and artists seem to have no particular inclination to deal with the complexity of the corporate setup (though photographers seem to favor incorporation once they set up a studio at home or in a rented location). If you have any doubt at all about which system to use, consult an attorney—it's part of his job to remain current on legislation and changes in the tax laws that can give you an advantage or disadvantage with one system or the other.

## CHOOSING AN ACCOUNTING METHOD

Regardless of the business structure you prefer, you must

choose an appropriate accounting method before you file your first tax return. The IRS requires that you calculate and report your profits or losses in terms of a fixed accounting period and in a manner that is self-consistent from year to year. Although the IRS does not impose any specific method of accounting, it does require that your method be one that clearly reflects income in terms of receipts and deductions and that applies generally accepted accounting principles in a consistent manner each year. They also require that complete records be maintained to support receipts and expenditures.

As a free-lance writer you can choose from three basic methods of accounting: the cash method, the accrual method, or a hybrid method. Within the scope of this book, it's not practical to present all of the features and requirements of each method, but it is useful to define each method and examine its primary advantage or disadvantage to a free-lance writer.

## Cash-Method Accounting

The simplest accounting method, in terms of record keeping and calculations, is the cash receipts and disbursements method.

> The cash method requires you to include in gross income all items of income you *actively* or *constructively* receive during the year. Property and services received must be included at their fair market value. . . .

> Generally, expenses must be deducted in the tax year in which they are actually paid. However, special treatment is provided for expenditures attributable to more than one year. . . .

This method is well-suited to the free-lancer because the calculations are simple and straightforward. Receipts are recorded as they come in. Expenditures are recorded as they are paid out. Special provisions are made for depreciable items having value spread over the years of useful life and for expenses such as multiple-year insurance premiums that must be divided between the applicable years. If you submit manuscripts or do consulting work that is not paid immediately, the cash method can be a distinct advantage in not forcing you to list that work as income prior to receiving the actual payment.

## Accrual-Method Accounting

A more complex method of accounting is the accrual method and requires considerably more effort in estimating the value of work done, allocating expenditures, etc.

> Under the accrual method, all items of income are included in gross income when earned, even though payment may be received in another tax year. All events fixing the right to receive the income must have occurred and you must be able to determine the amount with reasonable accuracy. . . .

> A person engaged in a business and using the accrual method will deduct business expenses when incurred, whether or not they are paid in the same tax year. All events fixing the liability must have occurred and the amount of the expense must be determinable with reasonable accuracy. . . .

This method can prove troublesome. For example, you may deliver a draft or camera-ready brochure art to a client in mid-December, with the client delaying payment for 30 or more days. Under accrual-method accounting on a calendar-year basis, the value of that material is income in the first year even though payment is not received until the next year. The same holds true for manuscripts such as fillers that are submitted to a publisher and may not be used or paid for for several years—the values of the manuscripts are considered income in the year they are written and submitted, not the year the publisher pays for them.

A book author faces a particular problem with royalties since the ultimate value of the work cannot be fixed with any accuracy at the time of submittal. A first-time author who has been using the accrual method must then change his accounting procedure (with IRS approval) to a hybrid method. Complete conversion back to the cash method may not be possible at that point because other items of income or expense are already locked into accrual accounting.

## Hybrid-Method Accounting

The IRS does permit the taxpayer to mix and match methods of accounting to best suit the needs of the business, provided that the application is consistent and gives an accurate measure of income.

> Any combination of . . . methods of accounting will be permitted if the combination clearly reflects income and is applied consistently. Such a combination is known as a *hybrid method*. However, the treatment of certain items of income and expense must comply with the following specific requirements.
>
> If you are engaged in a business using an accrual method for computing gross profit from purchases and sales, you may use the cash method in computing all other items of income and expense. If you use the cash method in computing gross income from your business, you must use the cash method for computing business expenses. Similarly, if you use an accrual method for computing business expenses, you must use an accrual method of computing all items affecting gross income. . . .

The problem with trying to devise a suitable hybrid method is its complexity. Careful records must be kept on the treatment of various items as well as actual amounts, and you must be careful to apply your hybrid method in the same manner year after year. Actually, there doesn't seem to be any real advantage in trying to develop a hybrid accounting scheme unless absolutely necessary, and you should be able to accommodate the needs of your business under either the cash or accrual methods.

## Changing Methods

Your commitment to a particular accounting method is made as soon as you file your first tax return. While you can change your method at a later date if you find another method more to your advantage, such a change requires IRS permission, even if it involves only a single material item.

> A taxpayer filing his or her first return may choose without the consent of the Commissioner any appropriate method of accounting. The method adopted must clearly reflect income and be applied consistently.

> Thereafter, any change in your method of accounting requires the prior consent of the Commissioner. You are not forbidden to change your method but are required to obtain the consent of the Commissioner before making the change. This is necessary to put the Internal Revenue Service on notice that a change is being made and to prevent the taxpayer from gaining an unwarranted tax advantage. . . .

As a free-lancer, your tax returns may already be subject to critical IRS scrutiny. Self-employment draws IRS attention to the possibility of not reporting all income, so it is hardly advisable to deliberately attract further attention by requesting a change in accounting methods. Therefore, you should analyze your requirements carefully and select an accounting method that accommodates both present and future needs before you file your first tax return.

## SELECTING A TRADE NAME

Few free-lancers go to the trouble of selecting a trade name. However, if you incorporate your business, you will be required to do so under a corporate name so the procedure then is mandatory. If you choose a sole proprietorship, a trade name is not required but does offer some advantages. First, it provides a professional image; a trade name automatically implies a businesslike attitude that is particularly important to a consultant and only slightly less important to an editorial free-lancer. Second, a trade name lends a professional air to stationery and business cards, giving a little more clout to those items when they are received by prospective publishers or clients. There is a tendency for a reader to pay more attention to a business letter under a formal letterhead than one typed on plain white paper without a letterhead. Third, a trade name is useful when buying equipment and supplies, entering magazine subscriptions, installing a business telephone, etc. It helps identify the business expenditures and property to separate those items from personal items for record keeping and taxes.

In choosing your trade name, you must be careful not to infringe on a trademark registered to someone else. Just like patents and copyrights, infringing on a trademark can trigger a chain of events that starts with an irate letter from the registered owner, progresses through increasingly threatening letters from attorneys, and ends up in a nasty legal action. The procedure of having a trademark search performed is both time consuming and costly, and it can be done only after you have selected your trade name and defined the physical form of the name and any associated logogram (including the type font and overall graphic design contributing to their appearance on the letterhead or other printed piece). If a trademark search proves that you are not infringing on someone else, you can proceed to have your name and logograph registered.

Registering a trademark is not the same as obtaining a copyright. Copyright protection is not afforded to titles, names, or short phrases. According to Circular 34 of the Copyright Office, Library of Congress:

> Names, titles, and short phrases or expressions are not copyrightable. Thus, the Copyright Office cannot register claims to exclusive rights in the names of products, organizations or groups (including groups of performing artists), pen names, titles, catchwords, slogans, advertising phrases, mottoes, and the like. This is true even if the name, title, phrase, or expression is novel, distinctive, or lends itself to a play on words. . . .

> Some brand names, trade names, slogans, and phrases may be

entitled to protection under the general rules of law relating to unfair competition, or to registration under the provisions of the trademark laws. The Copyright Office has no jurisdiction in these matters. Questions about the trademark laws should be addressed to the Commissioner of Patents and Trademarks, Washington, D.C. 20231.

In practice, most free-lancers don't bother with the search and registration procedure because it is an extra cost. They then accept the risk of having to cease using the name at a later date if challenged by a legal owner. Others minimize the risk by using a trade name that is a variation on their personal names. Such trade names have a lower probability of having been registered than do variations on subject matter or business pursuits. As an example, for many years I used the trade name "Ernest E. Mau Associates" and accompanied it with a stylized version of my initials as a logo. My first logo design used three lower-case letters in a row but had to be abandoned immediately when I found a series of electronic parts catalogs on a library shelf that had covers and spines prominently displaying the same three letters, in the same type font and arrangement. Incidentally, the word "associates" in a trade name is as meaningless as the word "natural" on a product package. For most of the time I used it, "associates" stood for the trio of me, myself, and I.

Eventually, I decided that I needed a more meaningful trade name and began examining some ideas. I found that I had to avoid creative compounds such as "technicom" for "technical communications" because of a high probability of duplicating someone else's name. Eventually, I settled on "documentation generalist" set in a rarely used type font. Although the name itself may have been used before, my design of the physical appearance made it unlikely to infringe on an already owned trademark.

Despite what seems like a lot of trouble over a minor concern, I strongly recommend careful consideration to using a trade name. If nothing else, a good trade name provides an element of recall for your contacts. That recall ability alone has probably contributed to the acquisition of about 30% of my consulting clientele and a substantial number of my sales in the editorial market.

## SECURING LICENSES

The requirements for licensing various trades, professions, and businesses are different in every state and municipality. Before starting, you must check out the requirements of your own locale. In some cases, a professional license may be required even to conduct a business. In others, sales tax licenses for both state and municipality may have to be obtained. Since the penalties for failure to obtain a license are severe, you take a big chance if you ignore or fail to comply with local laws.

In my own case, no professional license was needed, but I did have to obtain a sales tax license. My difficulty was in getting a definition of what constituted a taxable sale since Colorado taxes merchandise but not services. Materials sold to publishers or clients out of state were no problem since they were not taxable anyway, but local sales required a decision on what constituted a product and what constituted a service. Acting on the advice of a state tax auditor who had some doubts himself, a dividing line was drawn. Work performed up to the point at which I begin preparing camera-ready art is considered a service as long as I do not actually sell or transfer title to a physical item such as a rough draft. Therefore, I do not have to charge my clients any sales tax for research, initial designs, preliminary drafts, etc., as long as all materials "loaned" to them for reading are returned to me.

Once I start work on the final camera-ready art, however, all time and other contributions to the final charge for that art are considered taxable because the artwork is a physical product. This applies to pasteup art for brochures and final-typed manuals alike. Obviously, this creates a complex invoicing and record-keeping burden since every hour and expense has to be recorded and billed in terms of being taxable or nontaxable.

The situation is further complicated by the sales taxes of different municipalities. First, their percentages vary from one suburb to another. Second, each urban and suburban area requires its own license and separate filings of collected taxes. Third, the zoning board may become involved when a request for a municipal tax license is submitted, and many zoning laws absolutely forbid any business operation within a residentially zoned neighborhood, including free-lance writing. When a consultant lives in one suburb and has clients in the core city and each of a dozen other suburbs, the situation quickly becomes unmanageable.

Of course, there are ways of beating the system. The legal address of the business can be in an unincorporated location having no sales tax; all sales and transfers of materials then are made at that location. If sales within a particular municipality are infrequent or do not total to large amounts, tax offices may allow collection and submittal on an individual basis without a formal license for that town. Another alternative is to ignore the situation entirely, but that's extremely dangerous. Penalties for failure to obtain a tax license can be as high as $1,000 a day for each day of business operation, and the taxing authority determines when the business started operation. For your best protection, legal advice should be obtained on these matters during your startup procedure.

Possessing a sales tax license can have some minor advantages. The taxing authority may allow you to keep a small percentage of the collected taxes as payment for your time and effort. In Colorado, the state allows the business owner to retain 3.3% of the total tax collected (the tax is 3.5% of the price of the product). Items subject to resale can be purchased without paying sales tax, and the definition of resale may be loosely defined. For example, film purchased for an assignment and subsequent sale of the photos can be bought without sales tax. The same provision may extend to typing paper resold in the form of a manuscript, illustration board used as the base for pasteup art, shading film, press-on lettering, etc. Often, all it takes is showing your supplier your tax license, and he will automatically delete the sales taxes from those items eligible for such treatment.

Collecting sales tax has disadvantages as well. It's a lot of paperwork and record keeping, particularly if the amounts are very small and the reporting interval is monthly. A license requires an annual application plus payment of a licensing fee. And there's no end of trouble when the Postal Service manages to lose a return and an "estimated" bill for ten times the normal amount collected arrives accompanied by a demand for immediate payment or the threat of legal action—just try convincing a tax authority that the forms were never received or that you sent the return two months ago.

## DETERMINING RATES

One of the biggest differences between the free-lancer selling to editorial outlets such as publishing companies and the free-lancer performing consulting tasks for individual clients lies in the rate structure. One is at the mercy of his buyers, while the other has complete control over his own rates.

### Editorial Rates

You can expect no control over the rates paid for your work by editorial buyers. Magazines, book publishers, newspapers, and other outlets all have fixed rates that you must accept if you want them to buy your material. Only proven writers whose work is in high demand have any real power to negotiate prices in this market.

If you check a listing of publishers, you'll find statements such as "pays $25 on publication," "pays 3 to 5 cents per word on acceptance," "pays $25 to $200" and "pays $6 plus word rate." You are left with no choice but to accept a stated rate or decline submitting or selling to that publisher. Your only latitude in adjusting your return lies in selecting the publishers with whom you wish to work.

The advances and royalties paid by book publishers also are fixed to a predetermined scale. Although previously published authors often receive more for their work than first-time authors, the rates are still under the control of the publisher. A lot of writers assume that royalties based on 10% to 15% of the list price of their book are too low, but they forget that most of the costs of a book are its production, distribution, and promotion. Those are costs that the publisher assumes and that the writer never sees. Furthermore, it is the publisher's capital that is placed at risk by accepting a manuscript. It's doubtful that the publisher's net return on his investment is much larger than the writer's earnings. In fact, if the book bombs in the stores, the publisher is the one who loses.

## Consulting Rates

As a consultant able to negotiate projects with your clients, you gain direct control over your rates. You charge what you feel your time, efforts, and talent are worth. When first starting out, you should try to determine what others are charging for similar services, decide whether you offer more or less than they do, and then charge accordingly. You also have to cover operating overhead and the anticipated complexity of the job while keeping your charges as competitive as possible.

*Flat-Rate Charges.* One way to charge for an assignment is on a flat-rate basis wherein you commit yourself to do the job for a stated number of dollars. It's a system that clients love because it tells them exactly what they are going to have to pay, and they can maneuver different consultants into a low-bid situation to minimize costs. Any request to flat-rate a job should trigger every alarm system you have. Flat-rating is the most hazardous system a free-lancer can ever use. It makes no difference whether you are just starting out or have years of experience to rely on, most assignments are completely unpredictable. Once guaranteed a fixed price, clients have no hesitation about changing the job requirements, redesigning the equipment being documented, or demanding partial or total rewrites on little more than a whim. Meanwhile, you remain tied to a fixed price for a job that requires ever-increasing time and effort.

I've made it an absolute policy to never flat-rate any job. I've seen too many product redesigns after the documentation has been started. I've seen too many projects that have been completed in accordance with a set of stated criteria, submitted for approval by the next higher level of management, and rejected, sometimes as many as eight or ten times before the client's top management finally became involved. The only compromise I ever make is to provide a "best-guess" estimate of the time and charges, but I still tie the charges to time actually spent and never make an estimate or accept a job that does not allow charging for extra work caused by client-originated changes.

*Page-Rate Charges.*   A second method of charging uses a page rate, and you quote a certain price per finished page of the document. Several writers from the Midwest have indicated that this was their policy, charging from $45 to $125 per typewritten page. In principle, it sounds better than flat-rating, but it doesn't decrease the dangers for the free-lancer. I've not been able to find any writers in my locale that use this method, and none who view it as really practical. Personally, I wouldn't use it because it makes no allowance for job complexity or the number of rewrites that a client's changes might necessitate. Like the flat-rate system, a job can grow completely out of proportion without allowing charges to be modified.

*Hourly-Rate Charges.*   The third and best rate structure is an hourly basis in which you charge a specific number of dollars per hour. The obvious advantage is that you get paid for your actual effort. Less obvious is that hourly charging discourages clients from wasting your time. When a client realizes he is going to have to pay a lot of money, he becomes cautious about making arbitrary and unnecessary changes on a draft review, releasing a project with erroneous or insufficient input for the writer, tying up the writer's time with profitless meetings and errands, or otherwise wasting valuable time and effort.

Determining an hourly charge can be a little tricky, but it's still in terms of what you think you are worth. A highly skilled writer for either marketing or technical projects should be able to command from $30 to $50 an hour. Less skilled writers may have to limit themselves to $15 to $30 an hour. Remember that it's unwise to charge much higher or much lower than the average rate your competitors offer for the same combination of talents and services. Too high a price loses clients to a competitor who can do the same job for less. Too low a price loses the respect of both clients and competitors alike. There are a lot of companies abandoning the low-bidder philosophy in favor of selecting consultants who offer a mid-range price and a proven track record. Consultants with extremely high rates are viewed as looking for a "gravy-train ride." Those with extremely low rates are considered incapable of doing the job properly.

You also have to determine how to charge different tasks that are part of an overall assignment. As separate individuals, the writer, editor, designer, illustrator, photographer, pasteup artist, and typist each have a different dollar value. If you perform more than one of these tasks, you may be tempted to use a different rate for each. I've found it more practical to charge one hourly rate for everything, with that overall rate adjusted to closely approximate the same total as itemizing the separate tasks at different rates. When I negotiate a job, I quote only the one hourly figure applied to every task and every hour involved in the project.

*Miscellaneous Charges.*   As a consultant, you also have to consider cost factors beyond the actual rate itself. First, your expenses should be billable to the client in addition to the direct charge for your work. Second, you should make the client responsible for outside suppliers such as typographers, photographers, artists, and other major vendors. Avoid incurring those costs yourself because a client who defaults on paying your bill leaves you obligated to pay those suppliers out of your own pocket. Third, make allowances for imposing rush charges of up to double your regular rates. This cuts down the number of last-minute requests and makes those you do get profitable for you and painful to the clients who fail to plan ahead.

In addition, you must never forget that competitive bidding and doing speculative work without a guaranteed return are risky operations and have many pitfalls. Since these are self-protection concerns affecting day-to-day operations, you'll find more information in Chapter 9.

## WRITING A CONTRACT

Sooner or later, every free-lance writer is bound to run headlong into the need for a written contract. Just as with rates of payment, a writer dealing with publishing houses is subject to the standard contracts prepared by his buyers, while the consulting writer is free to prepare his own contract and impose his own terms.

### The Publisher's Contract

If you restrict your writing to magazine articles, filler materials, and the like, you have little concern with publishers' contracts. Most of this work is on speculation without a written agreement. You prepare a manuscript, submit it to the publisher, and wait for either its return with a notice of rejection or its appearance in print and subsequent payment.

Written agreements do become a matter of concern when you are involved in nonfiction articles or are approached to work on a nonspeculative assignment. In either case, the agreement typically includes clauses that define the rates and conditions of pay, assignment of copyrights, a nominal "kill fee" for nonuse of the assignment, and similar points. The actual terms of the agreement are set by the publisher and are intended to protect the publisher's interests rather than the writer's. Few of these agreements allow you much chance to protect yourself since they are presented on a "take it or leave it" basis.

A more complex contractual requirement is imposed by a book publisher. Since both you and the publisher are agreeing to a large-scale and high-risk venture, the terms and conditions are defined in careful detail, but with the terms still set by the publisher. Most of these contracts are standard for a particular publisher and often are standardized between different publishing houses, with only a few deviations from one to another. Since the terms are uniform for a given publisher, the contract usually is prepared on a preprinted form, with blanks for the title, royalty rates, amount of advance, and due date for the manuscript typed onto the form. Although you may find it possible to negotiate a particularly objectionable item, you have little real choice but to either accept or reject the contract in its entirety.

Even though a book publisher's contract does not allow the writer to control the terms and conditions, a good contract defines the terms in such a way that both the publisher's and writer's interests are well protected. Examination of a publisher's contract for a book should show that they include at least the following essential points:

1. An author's grant to the publisher of specific or exclusive rights to the book, including subsequent licensing to other media such as magazines, film, syndication, and similar potential uses if these rights are not reserved to the author or his agent.

2. An author's assignment of copyrights and a notification of any prior publication in a foreign edition.

3. An author's guarantee that he alone owns the work and has the legal authority to execute the contract.

4. A publisher's agreement to publish the work *at its own expense,* complete with a statement of when the work will be put on sale by the publisher and a statement of royalty rates for both hardcover and softcover editions.

5. A complete definition of special terms affecting the author's payment as a result of discount sales or sales through special channels such as direct mail, textbooks, cheap editions, and foreign sales. This must include both the rates of payment and methods of accounting for each category.

6. A statement of the publisher's accounting method and payment schedules, including the amount of the advance, the terms of advance repayment from royalties, and the payment dates for royalties.

7. Special conditions such as holding a portion of the royalties as a reserve for returned books, withholding taxes, excusable delays, etc.

Although the contract appears complex and careful reading is required, most are straightforward and should cause you few problems. The terms and conditions have been established over a period of many years and have become fairly uniform. You should, however, be alert to clauses that specify your obligations and performance. The typical contract requires the delivery of an "acceptable" manuscript, and the publisher is the one who determines what is or is not acceptable. The contract also may contain a hidden reference to an index for the work, often glancingly mentioned under the terms for delivery of the manuscript. Indexing is a task usually performed when the book has reached the point of page proofs and the exact location of items within the book can be identified. At that point, the author may be required to provide a comprehensive index that he creates himself or pays to have a professional indexer prepare. Failure to do so promptly upon notification by the publisher can default the entire contract and result in penalties such as having to repay the advance. It also can result in the publisher having the needed items prepared *at the author's expense.*

A special note of caution—beware of any contract clause that states or implies a financial obligation on your part. The existence of so-called "subsidy publishers" or "vanity presses" can fool an unwary author. These organizations charge you to produce your work instead of paying you for the right to use it. Furthermore, they don't go beyond the printing and binding process, leaving you with no means of distributing, promoting, or selling your book. Instead, they ship you the printed books, and what you do with them is your affair.

The real danger lies in the fact that a vanity press doesn't always identify itself as such, sometimes relying on a contract's fine print to obligate the author to pay a substantial sum to cover the cost of producing the work. As a result, there are many horror stories related in writers' magazines and journals about hopeful authors who unwittingly found themselves on the hook for large bills and with no means of recovering the costs.

This doesn't mean that the vanity presses are inherently bad, only that they must be viewed in the proper perspective. Subsidy publishing is fine, as long as you accept the fact that you may have to pay a great deal just for the pleasure of seeing your name on a title page and that you probably will have a difficult time disposing of those books. Because they are essentially self-published by an unproven author, few bookstores or other retail outlets are willing to accept these works.

Unless you specifically intend to pay for publishing your own work and to absorb the resulting losses, it is best to avoid signing any contract that makes you liable for any costs whatsoever. For the most part, you should avoid publishers that advertise in newspapers and magazines under the auspices of seeking unpublished authors, incomplete manuscripts, etc. As a general rule, vanity publishers actively solicit manuscripts because their charges to authors are their source of income. The publishing houses that pay the author rarely solicit work because they are flooded with more manuscripts than they can possibly hope to produce.

## The Consultant's Contract

Acting as a consultant gives you the advantage of direct control over your own contract and your terms of doing business. It's not advisable to undertake any assignment without the exact terms spelled out in writing, even if the terms require only a letter or brief statement. Your best protection, however, is provided by using a formalized contract or agreement that defines your requirements and covers areas in which you can expect trouble.

My own philosophy is to require a general written agreement

with every client for at least the first year of our relationship. That general contract does not obligate a client to assign me any work, but it does define certain conditions for each project that is assigned. Depending upon the client's behavior during that first year, I then either revise and renew the agreement or elect to trust him on a project-to-project basis.

I've found it to my advantage to refuse to work for anyone who balks at my general terms, and I've had only two prospects in five years who have flatly refused to sign on the dotted line. In one case, the prospect actually said, "It leaves us no way out if we don't want to use it." That's the whole point! I don't allow my clients to avoid paying if they don't use the material. Too many projects are canceled in the development stages, and I'm unwilling to absorb time lost to a client who simply changes his mind.

You must consider a number of points in drawing up your own contract. To best illustrate the most important ones, I'm going to lead you through my own standard agreement, explaining my reasons for each item. The quoted excerpts are taken directly from my contract, but references to the client use a fictitious name.

*Rates and Charges.* The statement of rates and charges covers both the hourly billing and a definition of the expenses that will be passed through to the client.

The terms of this agreement are in effect until January 1, 1982, and for all assignments that have been started prior to that date.

1.  All services, including consultation, research, writing, editing, designing, proofing, preparing camera-ready art, photography, and other tasks normal and incidental to the completion of any assignment will be charged at a rate of $30 per hour, plus expenses, plus applicable sales tax. At the discretion of Ernest E. Mau, rush jobs may incur an additional 100% rush charge.

2.  Time will be charged at this rate, portal-to-portal from the office of Ernest E. Mau for all off-premises work, including trips

to the client, vendors, or any other locations. Automobile mileage will be charged at $0.18/mile in addition to time spent traveling. Public transportation will be charged at cost in addition to time spent traveling. Other expenses may include, but are not limited to, materials, special supplies, expendables, etc., with an additional 15% handling charge.

The first sentence defines the duration of the agreement, with the expiration date usually being one year from the date the contract is signed. This fixes the rates and terms for a specified period of time, and allows a revision after the first year. The expiration date is crucial to allow increases in hourly rates from year to year, but it provides the client with an assurance of a constant rate for a known period. This sentence also assures the client that any work already in progress at the expiration date will not have its charges adjusted upward; only new projects assigned after that date are subject to an increase.

Clause 1 defines the actual hourly rate and establishes that the same rate is charged for every hour spent on the project regardless of what task is being performed. As an incidental task, even typing is included under this rate. Clause 1 also informs the client that expenses and taxes are billable, and that any need to function on a client-imposed rush basis may double the hourly rate. My personal view of rush charges is that a self-imposed rush is not billable, but a client-imposed rush is. My intent is to avoid rushes by placing them at a premium to discourage unreasonable demands or unrealistic deadlines. During discussions with clients, I also emphasize that just using words such as hurry, rush, or urgent may automatically shift a project to the premium rate.

Clause 2 further defines the basis for billing in areas that have been troublesome. First, time to run back and forth for client meetings or to handle errands on a client's behalf is billable at the full hourly rate. One of my first clients had me spend four days scurrying between typographers, photographers, and printers and then expected to pay only car mileage and not time. Since time is income, making such nonsense fully billable both increases my charges and keeps a client from wasting my time on nonessentials. Additionally, Clause 2 defines the mileage rate that is billed as a direct expense over and above the time involvement, and it sets the groundwork for charging any out-of-pocket expenditures. The 15% handling charge covers the cost of paperwork involved in making purchases, paying the bills, and processing the transactions through my accounting system.

For most projects, I do not bill normal expenses such as paper, typewriter ribbons, pens, etc. I do bill back items such as illustration board for pasteup art, special press-on lettering, special paper stock to meet a unique need, unusual typewriter elements that are suitable only for the individual project, long-distance telephone calls, and any magnetic storage media that must be preserved for future revisions with a word processor.

*Conditions of Payment.*    The single largest concern in my contract deals with the conditions of payment, including default conditions, authorization of a project, and transfer of title.

3.   Billing normally will be on a biweekly basis (monthly, job segment, or other billing may be implemented at the option of Ernest E. Mau), and all bills are due and payable immediately upon presentation to ABC Electronics, Inc. All bills are considered delinquent after 10 calendar days.

A.   Delinquent bills, more than 10 days past due, will be subject to an added penalty of 0.04931% per day (18% per year), charged from the billing date to the date payment is received. Bills paid within 10 days of billing are not subject to penalty. At the option of Ernest E. Mau, bills more than 30 calendar days overdue also may be turned over for collection by other agencies, with ABC Electronics, Inc. paying all attorney's fees, court costs, and other costs of collection.

B.   Major buy-out items (commercial photography, retouching, typography, illustrative art, etc.) will be purchased and paid directly by ABC Electronics, Inc., without the financial involvement of Ernest E. Mau and without incurring the 15% handling charge.

C. All assignments, whether initiated in writing or by verbal order, are subject to all terms and conditions herein. No allowance is made for nonuse of materials, client-caused delays, or other circumstances beyond the immediate and direct control of Ernest E. Mau, nor shall any such circumstances constitute cause for nonpayment.

D. All materials furnished by Ernest E. Mau remain the sole and exclusive property of Ernest E. Mau until full payment is received. In the event of default, publication or any other use of the materials by ABC Electronics, Inc., their successors, or their assigns, is unauthorized and expressly prohibited. Title to the materials passes to ABC Electronics, Inc. only upon receipt of full payment by Ernest E. Mau.

Clause 3 establishes the billing period as my option to allow adjustment for the individual assignment. Short projects of a week or two in total duration are billed when completed. Projects such as technical manuals requiring periods for client review between drafts are billed at each stage. The delivery of each draft is accompanied by an invoice for all work done and all expenses incurred up to and including the date of delivery. Clients have been known to take several months for reviews, so this provision allows me to collect for what already has been done without having to wait for them to proceed with the next stage. Without this, the delays between successive stages of a project could make a shambles of my cash flow. Large, continuing projects that span several months of uninterrupted effort are billed at the end of each calendar month since the work and cash flow are not subject to lengthy delays.

This clause also states that bills are due immediately upon presentation, and Item A amplifies the terms of delinquency. In late 1979, I was forced to adjust the payment interval downward from 30 days to 10 days because my suppliers and vendors had already done the same. In practice, I rarely get upset if a client takes as long as 45 days because I realize that they too have cash flow problems. What I seek to avoid is a deliberate delay of 60, 90, or 120 or more days, which some companies will attempt. Unless a client can justify nonpayment within 30 to 45 days, and justify it to my satisfaction, I do not hesitate to commence collection activities.

Item A is a blatant scare tactic. In many states, including my own, there is a prohibition against imposing an interest rate unless you are a legally defined lending institution. However, I treat the penalty as a billed-through expense item since it corresponds to the interest rate my bank charges me against my personal line of credit. Since that line of credit floats me through the interval of nonpayment. the charge incurred is an expense directly attributable to any project that remains unpaid. Without exception, clients who have been delinquent have paid the penalty expense.

Obligating the client to pay the costs of collection is trickier. Commercial collection agencies are not allowed to add their charges (usually from 40% to 65% of the total bill), so using them is a last resort. I prefer to use an attorney because his fees and any court costs may be recoverable. I've probably been lucky in encountering only two real deadbeats in five years. The first eventually paid off to a collection agency, costing me 60% of the amount actually due; but they did pay the penalty charge for the entire period it took to collect the bill. The second eventually came around after a threat to file suit and contact the district attorney's office about criminal proceedings for fraud and theft of property.

Item B provides protection against incurring excessive expenses on the client's behalf and then being obligated to pay them if the client defaults. Under this provision, I refuse to contract with other suppliers for photography, typography, or printing. Instead, I act as a job coordinator but have the client issue his own purchase order to that other supplier. This prevents having to use my own capital to float the client through payment delays or nonpayment, obligating him and not me to the other suppliers.

Item C requires a written authorization for each individual

project. Verbal orders are impossible to prove, so I accept them only from clients with whom I've had extensive dealings for several years. Everyone else must issue either a formal purchase order or a letter of intent that gives me the authority to begin a job. I make no allowances for nonuse of my materials once a project has been authorized, and that condition is spelled out in this item.

Companies are fond of claiming that their purchase orders are legally binding documents, but I've heard from a number of free-lancers that they've had trouble enforcing them. The purchase order is fine as an authorization for a particular assignment if overall terms are covered in a separate general agreement such as the one I am presenting here. However, a free-lancer should not rely on a purchase order as a stand-alone document in the absence of some other agreement. Furthermore, many purchase orders have terms and conditions printed on the reverse side of one sheet. Those terms and conditions may contradict an agreement such as this and should be resolved prior to signing and returning the papers.

Item D is a definition of ownership. There remain some gray areas in the copyright laws about who owns what when work is being done for hire. This item is an attempt to skirt the problem by having the client agree that the materials remain my personal property until the bill is paid. By not paying for the work and making any use of it, the client actually commits an act of theft. I use this provision to gain leverage when I have to take action against a client, particularly after they've printed and started distributing the work. It's amazing what a threat of seizure can do to speed up a delinquent payment.

*Working Conditions.* Two clauses have been necessary to provide the flexibility necessary to the conduct of my business.

4. Whenever possible and practical, all tasks will be performed at the office of Ernest E. Mau. Should the assignment require presence at any other location, all considerations herein remain in effect at all times and at all locations.

5. The right is retained to refuse individual assignments, without prejudice to the overall agreement, under circumstances such as conflict of interest, work overloads, lack of capabilities, etc. The right also is retained to subcontract tasks as necessary to accommodate work overloads, the need for specific outside talents, or any other cause considered by Ernest E. Mau to be sufficient reason for subcontracting an assignment in part or in whole; the responsibility for the quality of subcontracted tasks remains with Ernest E. Mau at all times.

Clause 4 was included to head off a problem I encountered with a prospect who expected me to reduce my rates by working at his facility. Clause 5 simply allows me to subcontract work when necessary, and it provides an escape route when two clients conflict with each other. The latter provision became necessary when I was working with four clients who manufactured computer peripherals. There was a point where I was asked to write brochures for directly competitive equipment, and I was forced to decline the assignments because I didn't feel it was right to use what I knew about one client to the advantage or disadvantage of another. Such work would have put me in a position of having to make value judgments about the relative merits of the products and would have influenced my approach to one or all of them. Simultaneously working with two direct competitors is a situation best avoided by any free-lancer.

*Content Responsibility.* The final clause of my contract, and the most recently added, concerns the responsibility for the accuracy of the document.

6. The responsibility for accuracy and completeness of the materials rests solely and exclusively with ABC Electronics, Inc. The use of materials in whole or in part by ABC Electronics, Inc. constitutes evidence of approval. Under no circumstances shall Ernest E. Mau, his successors, or his assigns be held liable for actual or consequential damages arising out of governmental or civil actions, including but not limited to those involving misrepresentation, omission, fraud, etc.

There are circumstances in which a marketing or technical writer can be held separately and equally responsible for misrepresentation or fraud. In a civil suit or a Federal Trade Commission action against the client, the writer who may have acted under direct orders, without the knowledge of an attempt to defraud, or under deliberate misdirection by the client, can be held responsible. There have been actions taken against national advertisers that have involved the company itself, the advertising agency, the actors in a commercial, the writers, the editors, the production company—in short, everyone associated with the production of the commercial in question. Clause 6 is an attempt to minimize the hazard and place the blame where it really belongs.

*Contract Signatures.*    When obtaining a signature on your contract, remember that only an officer or legally appointed representative of the company can sign it. The agreement is worthless if signed by an unauthorized employee such as an engineer or product manager. This is the same philosophy behind contracts to purchase a car; the sales manager is the one who must sign, not the salesman who gives you the pitch.

I submit the contract for signature during the initial contact meeting with a prospect. Whenever I'm called to such a meeting, I make it a point to have two prepared copies of the contract with me. I verbally outline my terms during the discussion of the project, and present the written contract only after I have an initial indication of agreement on the terms. If the prospect has agreed verbally but hedges when it comes time to put it in writing, I interpret that as indicating a high probability of later trouble. Comments such as "the job is too small for a written agreement" or "our policy is not to sign such papers" don't get any argument from me; I simply stand up, apologize for wasting their time, and head for the door. A free-lancer has more than enough problems without encouraging someone who's going to try wriggling out of his obligations.

I also use the contract as a part of any written estimate or quotation I have to furnish. After providing the cost estimate, delivery schedule, and technical approach, I lead into a word-for-word repetition of the contract terms with the introductory line,

"The following general conditions are made a part of this quotation and further define the practices and procedures followed by this vendor on a standard basis." At the conclusion of the terms, I then add a seventh item that reads, "Conditions stipulated in any purchase order or other document shall not override the preceding terms unless they have been specifically agreed to in writing wholly separate and unique to the item in question."

# 4

# The Writer's Tools

Every writer needs certain basic tools to perform his functions, and far more is involved than just a pad of paper and a sharp pencil. You have to make numerous decisions affecting your daily operating supplies, major office equipment, and supporting business literature.

There's no way I can define your exact needs because every writer functions differently and has personal preferences. Your choices have to be based on your own functions and preferences, tempered by any specific requirements of your buyers. What I can and will do in this chapter is to identify some of the considerations that many writers may not be aware of, tend to overlook, or simply forget.

Some of the things I mention probably seem quite trivial, but each is brought up for one or both of two reasons—it either requires a significant cash outlay or it affects the salability of a writer's work. Because your survival as a free-lance writer depends on achieving maximum sales with minimum expense, the cumulative effect of even the most trivial items becomes an important part of your business operation.

## OPERATING SUPPLIES

Undoubtedly, you already know that you need a vast number of different operating supplies including paper clips, carbon paper, staples, note cards, writing pads, etc. What you may not realize is that some supplies can affect your business adversely by contributing to a high percentage of rejections or an overall dissatisfaction on the part of your buyers. It's not practical to comment on every possible item, but I should be able to convince you of the extent of their impact by picking out a few of the most important ones. In reading the following descriptions, notice my emphasis on the undesirable features, and try to evaluate each of your own choices in the same terms. Then critically examine your present supplies for any detrimental image they may produce in your buyers' minds.

### Pens, Pencils, and Erasers

Since few of your buyers see handwritten materials, you may be tempted to choose your writing instruments more for convenience than for salability. On the other hand, it may be necessary to make marginal notes on a manuscript, complete a hand-worked answer key to a word puzzle, or provide sketches or finished artwork to a publisher or client. If you stop to think about how many times you use a pen, pencil, or eraser during an average day, you'll realize they are an unavoidable part of your life.

When writers used quills and inkwells, writing was as much a graphic art as it was an art of using the language. Today, even the fountain pen has fallen into disuse, leaving ballpoint and felt-tip pens that quickly destroy penmanship. The invention of the typewriter and its general acceptance as the only means of producing salable manuscripts have virtually eliminated situations in which a writer relies on a pen for anything other than personal use. Nevertheless, situations do arise when a pen is required.

Felt-tip pens are of limited usefulness since even the fine-line varieties quickly become blunt and yield writing that is less than legible. Ballpoint pens are somewhat better for providing a fine line but still tend to blot and smudge. In either event, a publisher or a client may have difficulty reading what you have written, and the eyestrain alone can cost you a sale. Neither felt-tip nor ballpoint pens are suitable for line drawings that may be included in a manuscript. Either the line is too thick or the ink lacks sufficient density to reproduce well in printing processes. For artwork and line illustrations that accompany manuscripts, you should invest in a set of technical pens; these are available in various line widths, feature a tubular, metal point, and hold a refillable charge of reproducible drafting ink (similar to india ink).

Avoid ever using an ink color other than red or black except for a creative piece of artwork that requires particular colors. Violet and green make an especially bad impression on a potential buyer. Blue ink may look good on a written or drawn page, but it reproduces poorly in printing because the photographic plate-making process is insensitive to blue. Even red ink should be avoided unless a publisher or client requests its use for something like proofreading. This leaves black as the standard color for any type of pen you use and for most of the work you might do by hand.

No publisher or other buyer should see anything written or drawn in pencil other than preliminary sketches intended for later revision as inked artwork. Even in that limited application, the pencil used must be neither too hard nor too soft—a hard lead leaves a faint image difficult to see and a soft lead smudges easily. Pencils designated as hardness "2" or "3" generally are the most useful, and you might want to consider having one or two drawing pencils that allow interchanging leads for various purposes. A drawing pencil also requires a special sharpener or "lead pointer" that allows an extended section of lead to be inserted and rotated until the desired point is obtained. Again, the emphasis is on clarity and ease of reading; even personal notes have to be read at some time, and smudges or faint images only make the job more difficult.

Erasers also contribute to readability problems or sketching difficulties when they smudge or fail to remove a line completely. The erasers on the ends of pencils are the least desirable and cause the most smudging. One good choice is a "gum" eraser. Another is a draftsman's "kneaded" eraser that can be worked by hand to a desired shape and flexibility; this type is useful for cleaning light pencil lines from artwork and printed copy without destroying the image itself.

You should consider having a few "nonphoto blue" pencils, either as complete pencils or as leads for your drawing pencil. These are nonreproducing and are a light blue color. Their advantage is that they are invisible to the printer's platemaking process (though not to some copying machines) and can be used for marking guidelines and instructions on camera-ready art. They also are handy for marking manuscript pages where the use of pens or black pencils may be undesirable, hence the term "blue-pencil" for marking edits, deletions, and revisions.

### Adhesive Tape

You probably take your transparent mending tape for granted and use whatever you can find. For many writers it rarely becomes a matter of great concern except that its use should be avoided as much possible. However, if you prepare camera-ready art for manuals or similar documents, you use a lot of this stuff to splice materials together, and the wrong type can lead to a real disaster.

"Cellophane" and "transparent" tapes often have an adhesive that deteriorates with age, becoming either gummy or dry and taking on a brown color. When camera-ready pages for a document are filed and later retrieved for revision or reprinting, you may find that one tape has become stiff and crumbly while another has oozed a sticky adhesive and glued pages together. Even worse, the adhesive may have reacted with residual chemicals in the paper to leave a dark brown stain that makes printing difficult or impossible without a complete rework.

Without naming brands, there is at least one tape that doesn't have these problems. On the roll, it is a translucent milky color. Pressed onto a page it becomes transparent without the shiny surface of a cellophane tape (which also can be a problem in printing). Over a period of several years, this tape remains flexible, does not leak adhesive, and does not take on a brown color or seriously stain the paper. Writers preparing camera-ready pages should never use any other tape, and it's highly recommended even when the application does not involve long-term storage.

To diverge for a moment, the subject of aging brings up another consideration not properly a part of office supplies. That subject is photocopying. When you want to have a draft or document copied for your client's files or your own, you will find two types of copiers available. An electrostatic copier uses a special paper with a treated surface characterized by a silvery or metallic appearance. Over a period of time, this paper breaks down and becomes brittle, often with the copied surface peeling or flaking off and destroying the image. Bond copiers use plain paper that lasts longer in files, though the paper does eventually age and discolor. However, some bond copiers use a heat-set image that sticks to surfaces like plastic notebook covers, so some care in storing them still is required. To provide the longest possible storage life for your copies, use a bond copier and store the pages where they are not in contact with plastic, metal, or glass surfaces.

## Paper Stock

Your choice of typing paper is critical. Publishers reject manuscripts submitted on unacceptable types of paper such as erasable bond and onionskin, usually without reading them and without comment. Camera-ready pages prepared on the wrong paper may prove unprintable or may yield a low-quality image in the final printed product. In either case, you create a major problem for yourself by picking the wrong paper stock or trying to be overly economical.

The same basic requirements for paper apply whether you are typing a manuscript for a publisher or pages for direct reproduction in a printing process. The paper must be white. It must be a standard 8½×11 inches. It must be heavy (dense and thick) enough to prevent reading the typed copy from the reverse side. It must have a matte surface that is neither glossy nor highly textured.

Reserve the use of textured or colored papers for stationery items, and then use fancy papers as conservatively as you can. For manuscripts or camera-ready pages, use only standard white bond paper designated 20-pound basis weight or heavier. Some papers such as 20-pound white "offset" also are acceptable, but you need not spend the extra money for a "text" paper grade. Avoid using an "enamel" paper that has a shiny surface and will resist efforts to type on it.

The so-called "erasable bond" paper is specially treated to prevent typewriter ink from setting immediately and is never satisfactory. Any you might have on hand should be packed away or destroyed to avoid the temptation to use it. Similarly, onionskin is never acceptable and should be used only for personal letters being airmailed to foreign countries where the light weight is an advantage in lowering postage costs.

Your best prices on suitable paper are obtained when you buy it by the ream or carton. Pads or small packages of typing paper are a false economy and eventually cost you more than buying paper in bulk. One source of paper is an office supply store having a bond copier for public use. These stores often sell reams of inexpensive paper they stock for the copier, and they may sell it at a lower price than a ream of regular typing paper. Another good source is a printer's paper supplier, some of whom warehouse precut 8½×11 paper and will sell reams or cartons to individuals. A third source is a print shop. For two years, I had a printer who set his waste aside for me. Paper used in aligning a printing press often is discarded even though it may not have a printed image; if precut to the right size and meeting the other requirements, those discards can be a cheap or even free source.

You should also note that many papers have a right and a wrong side. These papers have a different finish or "tooth" on either side of the sheet, and the two sides take printer's ink and typewriter ink quite differently. Some reams are labeled to show the printing or image side (usually the smooth side) of the paper stack contained within, and it is that side that should be used for typing. I make it a practice to leave the paper in the wrapper, peeling the wrapper halfway back on the printing side only. Then I can remove a sheet only with its image side up, and I always get the correct side into the typewriter. If you notice that a heavily inked typewriter ribbon leaves an image that bleeds around the edges of the letters, try using the reverse side of the paper and the problem may correct itself. The extra expense of a paper stock finished on both sides is unnecessary since you only type on one side.

## Typewriter Ribbons

Your selection of an appropriate typewriter ribbon is as critical as your selection of typing paper. For manuscripts submitted to publishers or used in any way other than as printing masters, inked-fabric ribbons offer the best economy and usually are acceptable as long as they are well-inked and provide a clear, dense impression.

Fabric ribbons are not acceptable for camera-ready pages. These require the use of carbon-film ribbon for quality reproduction and subsequent readability of the printed product. Even though a special typewriter is necessary, carbon-film ribbons also give an improved, professional image to typed manuscripts intended for any use, and they give the writer a slight edge in impressing a publisher or other client.

Regardless of the type of ribbon used, it should be black. Some corporations have taken to using colored ribbons for typing on their stationery because it lends itself to the overall color scheme of the letterhead itself. In typing manuscripts or printing masters, you should never get involved with colored ribbons, and even a two-color red and black ribbon is a waste of money. If your typewriter is built for a red and black ribbon, try substituting an all-black ribbon of equal width to extend its useful life and reduce your costs.

If you use a fabric ribbon, it's good practice to run a worn and poorly inked ribbon only for your own review drafts. As soon as you start work on pages intended to leave your personal possession, switch to a fresh, well-inked ribbon. It's been to my advantage to keep a number of ribbons on hand, rotating them through stages of use as they wear. New ribbons are stored in sealed containers until needed. An old and worn ribbon is used for rough drafts and is replaced by another newer one for final typing. When that second ribbon begins to show too much wear the drafting one is discarded, the final-typing one is downgraded to a drafting ribbon, and a fresh one is removed from storage to serve as the new final-typing ribbon. This provides maximum ribbon utilization and assures that a good one is always on hand when needed. Incidentally, the storage life of unused fabric ribbons can be extended by sealing them tightly in foil and then refrigerating them.

Carbon ribbons are good for only a single pass through the typewriter, so they are not subject to rotation. However, if you have a machine capable of accepting either type of ribbon, it costs less to use fabric ribbons for drafts and personal copies, installing a carbon ribbon only when you are ready to begin the final typing pass. You should be cautious of bargain ribbons because they often yield poor print quality. Furthermore, some carbon ribbons have a specified shelf life after which they transfer less carbon to the paper so the image decreases in clarity and overall quality as the ribbons age.

## Correction Media

It's impossible to avoid correcting typewritten pages, but the method should provide the neatest, least obvious correction possible. Physical erasure should be avoided at all costs. At its worst, an erasure leaves an unsightly thin spot or hole in the paper. At its best, it makes the surface rough so that a letter typed over the correction bleeds into the paper fibers and becomes more of a blot than a letter.

Thin strips of white correction tape also should be avoided.

These strips stick to the page and cover the error. The correction then is typed on the tape. It's a crude method that gives an ugly appearance, makes the page uncomfortable to handle, and demonstrates a careless, unprofessional attitude to a prospective buyer. Eventually, the tape peels off the page, takes the correction with it, and sometimes leaves a discolored smear. On camera-ready pages, the tape edges cast shadows that are picked up in the plate-making process and become printed black lines in the finished product.

Overtyping media such as the white strip on a self-correcting ribbon or loose sheets coated with a similar material are somewhat better. To correct an error, the typewriter is backspaced, the correction sheet or ribbon is positioned over the error, and the original error is retyped to fill the letters with white powder. Then the typewriter is backspaced, and the corrected entry is typed. This works fairly well with a carbon ribbon, but not with a fabric ribbon where the correction powder absorbs and spreads the ink. If the page is subject to a lot of handling or even vibration and friction in a mailing envelope, the powder works loose and literally uncorrects the error. Again, this is not suitable for final typing pages intended as camera-ready printing masters.

Correction fluids offer a more permanent fix. These are formulated to be partially absorbed into the paper fibers and to cover the error completely. The correction is typed right over the dried coating. Carefully done, the technique lends itself well to carbon ribbons, provided the fluid is completely dry before the correction is typed. However, the inks used on fabric ribbons tend to be absorbed by and dispersed through the fluid, forming a grayish blot when trying to cover an error. The method is not good for camera-ready typing because there is a distinct contrast and density difference between the correction and the rest of the page—a difference that shows clearly in the printed product and may even look like a different type font. Careful handling is required; excessive flexing of the paper can chip or flake the correction, effectively uncorrecting the error.

The one other method of correction involves a mechanical procedure rather than the use of some supply, but it is a handy method. Known as "cut-and-splice," this is the only practical way of changing a typewritten page so that the change is invisible to the printing process (though it may be visible to a photocopier). Within limits, it can be used for manuscripts and other documents, but only with discretion. If you don't know how to use it, I'll describe it in the following steps. With a little practice, you can learn to change words, sentences, and whole pages if necessary.

1. Using the same ribbon and paper stock as the base page with the error, type the desired correction on a new sheet. Be sure to surround it with plenty of white space.

2. Carefully position the correction sheet over the original, aligning the letters both horizontally and vertically. A light table or a window can provide backlighting for better visibility. Letters can be added or deleted by running the correction across several words and adjusting the spacing between the end words. Some large corrections are more easily handled if the correction sheet is on the bottom.

3. Without disturbing the positioning, place the two sheets face up on a suitable cutting surface.

4. With a sharp instrument, carefully cut around the correction and through both sheets at the same time. Make certain not to cut into any material to remain on the original page (you only have a fraction of an inch to work with between words). Most people prefer to use an X-acto® knife equipped with a sharp-pointed #11 blade.

5. For best results, cut only with the tip of the blade and with the handle angled outward away from the correction. If the correction sheet is on the bottom, angle inward instead. Two vertical and two horizontal cuts give good results.

6. If properly done, you can remove a small piece containing the error from the original sheet and a piece of the same shape containing the correction from the overlay. Proper angling of the knife makes the hole in the original a hair smaller than the piece with the correction.

7. Observing the earlier recommendations in this chapter, place a piece of mending tape on the back of the page so the adhesive faces through the hole.

8. Carefully position the correction in the hole, guiding it with the knife until it fits exactly. Then press it against the tape.

9. Turn the sheet face down on a clean surface and burnish the tape with a flat tool. This presses the edges of the page and the correction together for a near perfect match.

When the page is examined, the correction should be nearly invisible and in perfect alignment. The fine cut line does not show in the printing process as long as there is no actual gap between the pieces. Unless the correction is near the edge of the page, few readers realize it's there because they don't feel the tape on the reverse side. Though cut-and-splice sounds tedious and time consuming, practice makes it faster than most other techniques when the corrections are all made at once on a finished document.

## OFFICE EQUIPMENT

As a writer, your basic office equipment consists of a desk, a chair, a lamp, a filing cabinet, and a typewriter. Those are the necessities. Then there are the luxuries like a camera, an answering machine, a tape recorder, or even a complete word-processing system. Although you can operate with a bare minimum of equipment, you can also develop a dependence on or a desire for some very sophisticated aids.

There's little that can be said about desks, chairs, lamps, and cabinets. The desk and chair must be comfortable enough to spend a lot of time there. Reclining executive chairs are nice, but they're costly. The desk should afford plenty of working area and sufficient storage for all the pens, papers, clips, and miscellaneous items you need to have at hand. It should have a typing extension or an auxiliary stand that is several inches lower than the main surface; typing with the keyboard elevated too high is extremely fatiguing. The lamp must provide adequate illumination of your working area to prevent eyestrain from trying to peer through shadows. The filing cabinet should provide sufficient storage for manuscripts, invoices, and business records; a two-drawer cabinet may suffice. These items are strictly a matter of personal taste and budget allowance, but be sure to obtain items you can live with for a long time and won't outgrow quickly.

## A Typewriter

The selection of a typewriter is an entirely different matter. A good, reliable machine is essential to any writer and has to be chosen on the basis of business needs, not according to personal preference or even according to budget. Acquiring a bargain typewriter is no bargain at all if it's incapable of turning out the kind of work you need. Few publishers or clients are going to bend their requirements just so you can get by with a cheap machine. If you can't type, you had better learn how. You can't always depend on someone else doing your typing for you.

The least expensive typewriter is a manual portable. It's nice as a backup machine or for taking on a trip, but it's not altogether practical as a primary machine. If you deal only with the editorial market, you can get along fairly well with one of these for the majority of your work. Book and magazine publishers will accept manuscripts as long as they are neat, easy to read, and meet any specified requirements. If the typed manuscript does not meet a publisher's requirements, however, it will be rejected immediately.

The disadvantage of a manual portable is that it provides no flexibility. It accepts one kind of ribbon and one variety of type.

The minute you get a request for a special piece requiring the use of a carbon ribbon or a different type style, you have a problem and either have to purchase or rent another machine. Incidentally, most publishers express a preference for pica type while a lot of consulting work requires elite type. If you can't remember which is which, pica (or 10-pitch) is the large type, and elite (or 12-pitch) is the small type.

The electric portable is the next step up, but its only advantage is a little less work to push the keys. A few models are on the market with interchangeable ribbon cartridges, but the rest have the same limitations as the manual portables plus the fact they don't work when the power goes off. Those that have interchangeable ribbon cartridges may provide a carbon-ribbon capability but still have only one fixed type style. Again, the machine is fairly well suited to the majority of editorial work but is too limited for camera-ready pages required in consulting work.

The third step is the nonportable, office typewriter, but unless it offers interchangeable type fonts, it has no advantage over the electric portable—it's essentially the same machine, only bigger.

The final step, short of a computerized word processor, is the office typewriter with selectable type elements. Over the past few years, more and more of these machines have appeared, largely due to the expiration of patent protection on the rotating-ball type element. These machines can combine quick changeover from one type style to another, alternation between 10-pitch (pica) and 12-pitch (elite) type sizes and spacings, self-correcting carbon ribbons, and other desirable features. Most, however, force the purchaser to select carbon-only or fabric-only ribbons.

For the starting free-lancer, such a machine may seem a real luxury, but it can be well worth the investment. By choosing carbon-ribbon operation, the multiple type fonts and selectable type spacing open the door to doing camera-ready documentation. The versatility of this machine makes it suitable for virtually every writing project in the editorial, marketing, or technical fields. A writer providing camera-ready work quickly finds that this is the only configuration that lends itself to the preparation of those materials. Although the purchase price can be high, most manufacturers' representatives have leasing plans available for the current models. Older and less sophisticated models often are available for rent on a week-to-week or month-to-month basis from local office-machine stores.

In purchasing a typewriter, or any other major piece of equipment, you should remember that the whole cost is not deductible as a business expense in the year of purchase. Items with extended lives have to be depreciated over the expected life of the item according to one of the accepted methods specified by the IRS. If the item has an expected life of five years, a portion of the cost is deducted in each of the five years. When rented or leased, however, the actual costs of the rental are fully deductible when incurred.

Conversely, purchases may be eligible for an investment tax credit in which a percentage of the price is charged off as though it was income tax paid directly to the government. Rentals are not subject to investment tax credit, and leased items may or may not be according to whether or not the lessor has retained the credit rights.

Furthermore, rentals include the costs of repair service, so a breakdown is fixed without additional out-of-pocket expense. Leased items may or may not have the repair costs included, according to the contract terms. Purchased items are repaired at your cost once the warranty has expired. Since sophisticated equipment can be expensive to repair, it is advisable to obtain a service contract on any major purchase. Typically, the monthly cost of a service contract is between 0.5% and 1.0% of the purchase price. While such a contract can get to be a burden, costs of routine repair can far exceed the cumulative contract cost for some kinds of equipment.

## A Camera

Eventually, you will want to have a reliable camera, regardless of the type of writing you are doing. Sooner or later, it's to your advantage to be able to provide photographic documentation of some project. In the editorial field, your need might be to illustrate the steps of a how-to book or article. In the marketing field it might be to cover the opening of a new manufacturing plant or an awards ceremony. In the technical field it might be to show the step-by-step procedure of disassembling and reassembling a device. For some projects, photographic coverage is absolutely essential and failure to provide it hurts or blocks the ultimate sale of the work. At the same time, it's not practical to hire a professional photographer for every project that might be enhanced by such support.

The paramount consideration in acquiring a camera is how well the photographs lend themselves to final reproduction in the publication process. In general, larger film sizes provide better reproductions. With black-and-white film, enlargements made from small negatives show the coarseness of the film grain and emphasize defects such as dust on the negatives. With color film, transparencies (not prints) are required for publication, and small transparencies are difficult to use in the engraving or color separation processes involved in their publication.

Cameras providing instant prints are useless for publication work; the overall lack of image quality and the sizes of the prints make them unsuitable for printing processes. Pocket cameras using 110 film and the split-frame 35-mm cameras are poor choices because the small image sizes on the film provide insufficient detail for prints and halftones (black and white) or color separations. The minimum size normally acceptable is a full-frame 35-mm camera, with even larger cameras preferred for commercial product photography, calendar illustrations, and other work requiring high detail in the finished work.

Some markets have very distinct requirements. Calendars and many high-quality art books require film sizes from 4 × 5 inches to 8 × 10 inches and, consequently, very large and cumbersome cameras. Architectural and product photography require correction for distortions in perspective and necessitate large-format cameras that allow correction of the perspective.

Of the many types and sizes of cameras to choose from, a writer's best choice for initial investment is the full-frame 35-mm single-lens reflex (SLR). Although the film size may be too small for some markets, it is accepted widely enough to be practical for most applications you are likely to encounter. The biggest advantage is portability since the 35-mm is easy to carry around and can be used in situations prohibiting the complicated setup of a larger camera.

Assuming that you are in the market, remember that you usually get what you pay for. Cheap cameras and lenses often give poor images that cannot be reproduced properly in print, and your investment turns out to be wasted because the photos are unusable. Still, you have to compromise because the entry cost into photography can run to several thousands of dollars as a function of brand names and the number of gadgets a salesman can talk you into buying.

Unless you have some specialized need, your first investment should be in a medium-priced camera costing from $250 to $350 when equipped with a standard 50-mm or 55-mm lens. It's advisable to pay an extra $50 or so to substitute a "faster" lens of the same focal length but with a larger maximum aperture for low-light photography. Normally, this substitution is on an either-or basis at the time of purchase; the dealer keeps the original lens and you pay a small price difference to acquire the replacement.

The most practical cameras have through-the-lens light metering that measures the light actually seen by the camera. The type of metering and subsequent exposure control is a matter of personal preference, and there are numerous choices available with fancy names such as match-needle metering, LED indication, center-weighted metering, aperture priority, shutter priority, etc. These things may affect the purchase decisions of experienced professionals, but they are of little concern to a writer seeking a camera for only occasional use. Your interest is in having a camera that provides a good image under the majority of conditions, not a camera capable of functioning under every possible adverse condition. Your emphasis should be on seeing the whole image in the viewfinder, without having to move your eye around, and having the viewfinder show whether or not the exposure is set properly.

Before making any purchase, it's wise to study a few back issues of a photographic magazine, paying particular attention to any product evaluations the magazine makes. Learn what is available, what the various features really entail, and what you really need to accomplish your own task. Make your decision as realistically as possible, taking care to avoid the trap of excess gadgetry that a camera salesman is going to pitch.

Having selected a camera, there are a few essential accessories that you should consider. A good initial system needs only three lenses of different focal lengths to achieve most purposes. The 50-mm or 55-mm lens that comes with the camera is your "normal" lens and is used for general-purpose shooting. An accessory 28-mm or 35-mm "wide angle" is useful when you have to cover a large area in a single shot; the 35-mm is usually sufficient and gives less distortion than a 28-mm lens. An accessory 135-mm "telephoto" lens is useful for making objects appear closer and doesn't distort the image as much as a longer telephoto lens. You may be tempted to buy a "zoom" lens or a "macro" (close-focusing) lens, but you should reserve that purchase for a later date. Zoom lenses are convenient, but few offer the image quality obtainable with a fixed-length lens. Macro lenses are useful for specialized work requiring extreme magnification of the subject, but rarely are used in day-to-day shooting.

A device known as a "doubler" or "extender" may be useful in that it makes your 50-mm lens behave like a 100-mm telephoto and your 135-mm lens behave like a 270-mm. These devices have their uses and double your availability of lens choices, but they also degrade the image quality, regardless of how well they may be designed. Still, the relatively low cost makes a doubler a tolerable expense.

Additionally, every lens you purchase should be equipped with a "skylight" or "ultraviolet" filter that stays on the lens at all times. The purpose is not so much to improve the picture as to protect the front lens element from rain, dust, and fingerprints. Water spots and dust on a lens can quickly destroy its sharpness, and cleaning should be minimized to avoid scratches from abrasive dust particles. Fingerprints can actually etch into lens surfaces, quickly ruining an otherwise good lens. It's always to your advantage to replace a $15 filter rather than a $250 lens.

Your final accessory should be an electronic flash unit. Small units can be obtained for less than $100 and are adequate for most situations requiring flash. Of course, you can get as sophisticated as you desire, but you should reserve any high-cost purchases until you are thoroughly familiar with the capabilities of your standard equipment and have resolved your exact needs.

The most important thing is not the kind of equipment you use or the number of gadgets you buy. Instead, it's how well you use what you have. You must study the instructions that accompany each item of equipment, and you should spend some time studying how-to photography books and magazines to learn the basic principles. Then, you have to practice. The more you practice, the better you become. Remember that you are a writer, not a professional photographer. You're not setting out to compete with the photo professionals but only to supplement your own capabilities and to meet your normal needs. Avoid becoming a gadgeteer; if you can't use what you have and use it well, some fancy new gadget isn't going to help.

When you shoot for an assignment, remember that film is a lot cheaper than time. Don't rely on a single shot to capture the event you are trying to portray. Instead, bracket the normal exposure with varying degrees of under and overexposure, shoot from different angles, try shots with and without flash. Using several rolls of film to capture a single event is better than having to go back and do it over again or missing it altogether.

## An Answering Machine

It's nice to have an answering machine for your telephone. In addition to simply taking messages when you're away, it allows you to screen incoming calls while you are working. A good machine can be set to answer on from one to four rings, so you can wait for the caller to identify himself before deciding to interrupt your work.

Cheap, battery-powered units available in hobby stores should be avoided. They don't last very long, offer few features, and provide a scratchy announcement to the caller. In a price range from about $150 to $350, practical units offer the selection of the number of rings allowed, the selection of more than one prerecorded message, indexed recording and quick access to individual incoming messages, remote dial-in to retrieve messages when you are away from the office, and a vast number of practical and not so practical enhancements.

My own choice was a $200 machine that I leave activated 24 hours a day. It's set to answer on the fourth ring, after which it informs the caller that I'm either unavailable or couldn't reach the phone before the intercept. When I'm busy working, I often let the machine take all calls. Since it also announces the caller's message audibly while recording, I can identify the caller without actually answering the phone, deciding at that point whether the call is important enough to interrupt work in progress and intercept the caller before he hangs up.

One point of extreme importance; the telephone company requires that it be notified of any device connected to the telephone lines. They insist on making certain that the purchased unit is compatible with their lines, and they usually charge for a service call to install a wall jack or to verify that the unit is suitable. They cannot prohibit your use of a purchased extension phone, automatic dialer, or answering machine, but they can make it difficult to connect the device. There are penalties for failure to notify the telphone company of the connection of an extra device: they can discontinue service, they can bill retroactively for an extension and assume you had the extension from the first day of telephone service, or they can take legal action.

Don't go on the assumption that the phone company will never know about your added device. Most telephone company central offices are equipped with sophisticated and automated electronics that scan individual telephone lines at random. Most devices you can connect to the lines can be detected by those scanners, so they can find your device without ever entering your home or office. Naturally, there are ways to defeat attempts at detecting extra equipment, but the methods are illegal and can lead to criminal actions for fraud and theft of services if discovered.

## A Tape Recorder

A portable tape recorder is one of the handiest accessories. You can use a recorder for taking research notes or for keeping a complete record of business meetings, telephone calls, and other daily activities that you might otherwise have to note in writing. In selecting a suitable recorder, you need not be concerned with high fidelity sound reproduction. Your interests are in simplicity of operation and adequate recording of conversations.

In selecting from the many types of units available, your principal requirements should be that the unit is small and lightweight, battery powered (rechargeable if possible), and unobtrusive. Lugging around a large unit, even a standard cassette model, can be a nuisance. Most of your use will be in situations where it's impossible or inconvenient to connect a cord to a wall outlet for power. Furthermore, you don't always want the recorder to be the center of attention; in a business meeting, it's best to position the recorder where it's not in a direct line of view so everyone is more at ease.

In recent years, some very small and very practical units have appeared on the market. The smallest use a "microcassette" that measures only $1\frac{1}{2} \times 2\frac{1}{4}$ inches and can provide two hours of recording time. The recorder itself can fit into a shirt pocket or purse and is only slightly larger than a pack of cigarettes. Some of these provide two-speed operation and have a capstan drive for improved sound. Even with the built-in condenser microphone, such a unit is adequate for recording everything said in a conference room, yet still can be used in a library environment where a soft voice is required.

The real advantage of a miniature recorder is that it can be set on a table and soon forgotten by people involved in a meeting. It's so small that it doesn't intimidate people as much as a larger recorder would. It's so easy to carry around that you can replace your normal pen and notepad, relying on the recorder for keeping virtually every scrap of information you need.

Some caution is necessary, however. There are people who do not want their conversations recorded, and you must obey their wishes. You are legally required to notify a telephone caller that you wish to record a conversation, and you must do so prior to starting the recording. When requested to terminate recording, you must do so immediately. You must also cease recording if a speaker indicates that his next remarks are "off the record." Never record someone without their prior knowledge and consent; to do so is an invasion of privacy and at the very least may cost you a prospective client or interview. Additionally, never record an artistic performance in a theater; performances are protected under copyright laws and statutory law, making unauthorized recording a criminal act. Photographing a performance also is prohibited under the same laws.

Along similar lines, the expanding field of home video recording has opened a new field for consultants and has added a new tool for writers. With a little experience and careful selection of equipment, a marketing or technical writer can offer clients the availability of videotaped training programs for office and manufacturing personnel. Some companies can use videotapes as a means of introducing new employees to the company, training field service personnel, augmenting educational seminars, and providing overall documentation of products and procedures. By planning, scripting, and executing such video projects, the writer finds a whole new world opening up.

Additionally, a writer may be able to justify a video cassette recorder as a research tool. A fiction writer may use it to study and review movie scripts and story presentations. A marketing writer can compile and study commercials and promotional techniques. A technical writer can develop a library of educational programs as a review of different technologies. The possibilities are nearly endless and may allow a writer to qualify at least part of the cost as a business expense and deductible to the extent of business use.

## A Word-Processing System

A computerized word-processing system is the ultimate writer's aid. Regretfully, costs ranging to $16,000 or higher put them beyond the reach of beginning free-lancers and most established writers. But prices are dropping and equipment is improving, so it won't be long before a large number of free-lance writers are able to afford these machines.

In Chapter 1, I've already mentioned some cautions concerning word processors. The most notable is the need to avoid the dot-matrix printer. To repeat, publishers and consulting clients quickly reject written materials prepared on such a printer. To find out why, all you have to do is try to read 100 pages printed with that technique. It won't be long before you literally have spots in front of your eyes. Ballistic line printers that print an entire line of letters at one time are no better. The individual letters are unevenly spaced, float above and below the line at random, and have varying ink densities.

The only suitable printer is one that prints a single character at a time and uses some form of spinning or rotating type element. The most common printer of that style is known as a "daisy-wheel" printer and uses a type element that looks very much like a flattened flower; each character is positioned at the end of a long spoke, and the entire wheel spins to position the character under a hammer that drives a spoke forward to strike the ribbon and paper. Figure 5 illustrates the differences between the printed images obtainable with various printers, using an enlarged letter to show the loss of readability that may be suffered when the wrong printer is selected.

FIGURE 5. Comparative Printer Styles

*(Courtesy Qume Corporation, Hayward, CA)*

**Ballistic**          **Dot–Matrix**          **Ink–Jet**          **Daisy–Wheel**
**Line Printer**       **Printer**             **Printer**          **Printer**

It's also necessary to be wary of the personal computers that supposedly have been converted to business systems and word processors. The programming or software controls the available functions, and some word-processing packages contain features that are designed to make a visual impression on the software buyer without enhancing usability. For example, you'll find few occasions to type within a perfect circle or fancy outline, no matter how pretty it looks in the showroom. Another problem is that many systems are designed for short items like business letters, reports, and other documents only a few pages long. If you work with large manuscripts, brochures, technical manuals, and similar lengthy documents, a particular word processor may cause more problems than it solves.

I also must point out that there is a difference between a dedicated word processor and a computer configured for word processing. The first is a unit dedicated to one function and one function only—word processing. It's an expensive unit priced anywhere from $8,000 to $16,000 or more and offers little or no general computing capability for bookkeeping, depreciation schedules, inventories, etc. The second type is a general-purpose computer suitable for all computing tasks and performing word processing under the direction of one of many possible programs. Obviously, the latter type offers greater flexibility to a small business since it can be turned to other tasks when not needed for actual work on written text.

This leads to a consideration of machine utilization. Once a machine is acquired, its overall cost in terms of purchase price, maintenance expenses, supplies, interest on financing, and electrical power can be broken down into a cost per hour of actual use. The more hours a machine is in use, the lower its hourly cost. For example, assume you buy a unit for $15,000 cash (no financing interest), obtain a service contract for $110 a month, and use the machine for five years. For simplicity, ignore the cost of supplies and electrical power. If you actually use the machine an average of 30 hours a week (7,800 hours total), your cost is $2.76 per hour. If you use it 50 hours a week (13,000 hours total), your cost declines to $1.66 per hour. If you could find a way to keep it busy 24 hours a day and 7 days a week (43,680 hours total), your cost would be only $0.49 per hour.

The objective is to keep the machine busy enough to justify its cost. If you purchase a general-purpose computer and can devise useful programs that run while you sleep or are away from the unit, you can optimize your costs. It may be difficult, but I know it's not impossible because that is exactly what I did.

I purchased a $15,000 system in late 1978 and proceeded to develop programs that would run on the machine without my attention. During the day, the system is a word processor that handles every word I write from personal letters to complete manuscripts and the camera-ready pages for technical manuals. It also handles all of my accounting, maintains an inventory of all business and personal property, does my billing, and manages a large mailing list for addressing letters and brochures. When I'm finished using it in those applications or have to leave the office, I switch the machine to another program such as one for producing word puzzles. Under a normal schedule, I never shut the machine down except for maintenance. Overall, I calculate my cost of using the machine as about $0.89 per hour with all costs included. Its rate of return to me averages $8.00 an hour.

Once you reach a point where a word processor becomes a good investment, you find yourself in a whole new world. The convenience and capabilities soon make you totally dependent on the machine, and a good system is designed to make life much easier. Although it's not practical to list all of the possible features, a few are worth mentioning to whet your appetite. The format of the printed document can be controlled. Changing from 10-pitch to 12-pitch type or back again, altering margins, and switching from single to double spacing only require changing an appropriate entry in the printing instructions. With a typewriter-quality character printer running at 45 characters per second, a new copy of a manuscript can be typed at a rate of about a page a minute with single spacing or two pages a minute with double spacing.

Editing is quick and easy, and an entire document can be searched for occurrences of specified words or letter combinations. Common typing errors can be located and corrected throughout the entire document in a matter of minutes by specifying that the system replace all words spelled one way with words spelled another way. Paragraphs can be moved from one part of the text to another in only a few seconds. A word processor also can provide a flush right margin whenever necessary, automatically center lines on a page without counting characters, and insert boldface and underlined words wherever you need them.

Best of all, repetitive copies of letters, résumés, outlines, client lists, and similar materials each look like an original typed just for the recipient. Quite simply, word processing is a marvelous tool for a writer.

Despite all of its many attractions, I must warn you one last time to proceed with caution. A word processor or computer is a major investment and every aspect of both the machine hardware and the programming software should be investigated as thoroughly as possible. Study the available literature on the subject, talk to owners of similar systems, and never trust a salesman's word. Insist on a complete demonstration of any system under consideration, and then insist on some time alone with it at the showroom to test it for yourself. Request (buy if necessary) the instruction manuals for the systems you like, take them home, and study them carefully. Above all, don't be too hasty. The whole computer field changes so rapidly that if you can't find the perfect system, you'll probably find it six months from now. Don't be threatened by a salesman who says, "prices are going up next month." The costs of computer components and systems are declining rapidly as production increases, and they should continue to decline in comparison to available features for many years.

## BUSINESS LITERATURE

The last major category of a writer's tools is that of business literature. Once again, it's a consideration often overlooked or ignored, but it constitutes the principal means of contact between the writer and the outside world. On the premise that you are conducting a business, you need certain pieces of paper as business tools to present a professional image. As an editorial writer you can get by with the standard stationery items of a letterhead, second sheet, and envelope. You might also need a business card. As a consultant, you need all of those items plus a personal résumé, a client list, and possibly a brochure. No matter what your field is, you also need a professional portfolio.

Since a consultant is under more stringent requirements than an editorial free-lancer, I'll describe the individual items from his viewpoint. Before discarding any particular idea as irrelevant, consider it in terms of presenting a businesslike front to the people with whom you deal. The more professional the image you present, the more sales you should be able to achieve. Nobody likes a novice except another novice, so it is to your advantage to put forth a little extra effort in making a good impression. If you don't feel you can do a good job of designing your own material, then it is worthwhile to have an artist or graphic designer do the work.

## The Stationery

The letterhead, second sheet, envelope, and business card are the four items that compose your business stationery. As such, they should be of similar appearance and coordinated design.

The letterhead usually contains your business trade name, address, and phone number. If you have a logo design, it should appear as well. It does no harm to add a line or two immediately below these items that defines your business and the services you offer. The second sheet can be a blank sheet of the same paper as the letterhead, or it can have the logo in the same position as on the letterhead. I prefer the second approach because it provides continuity between the two sheets and serves for rapid identification of a second sheet when it becomes separated from the main letterhead. In my case, I use a two-inch letterhead with the lines defining my functions positioned to mark the bottom of that space and running across the width of the page. The upper right corner has the name, address, and phone information. The upper left corner has a stylized logo. My second sheet has only the logo in the upper left corner.

The business card and envelope are reorganizations of the basic letterhead. For the card, it's best to omit the lines defining the business and limit yourself to the logo, name, address, and phone number. If you feel that you need a definition of your business, it can be printed on the back of the card. The envelope should show only the logo, name, and address.

FIGURE 6. Basic Set of Business Stationery

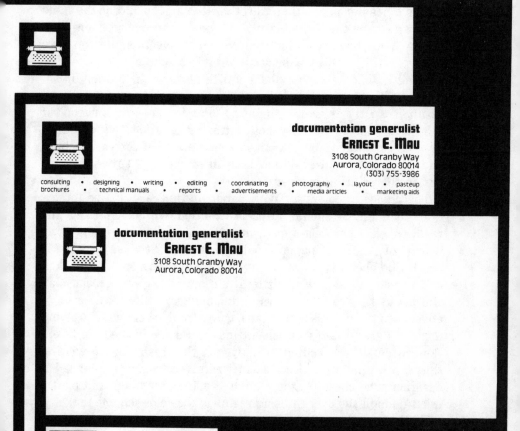

Figure 6 illustrates the stationery package that I created in accordance with these guidelines. Notice that the appearance of each piece is coordinated with the others to provide a uniform visual impression.

To present a professional appearance, the four items should be matched as closely as possible. Although the business card requires a heavier paper than the other items, it should be the same color and have the same texture. Business stationery is one area in which you have room for creative paper selection, but you have to be careful to select paper that enhances your image instead of eroding it. The paper may have a nice texture like a linen finish, but some coarse finishes don't take the printer's ink very well and result in spotty or uneven printing. Particular care is needed if the design includes heavy bold lettering or a logo with a large area to be covered by ink; these are what printers call "solids" and require special attention both in selecting a suitable paper and in the printing process itself.

The choice of colors for both paper and ink are just as important. The pieces should attract attention without hurting the reader's eyes. The best appearance is achieved with conservative, warm colors. White paper should be avoided because it looks too much like cheap typewriter paper. Cream colors are overworked and overused, attracting little attention. Blues and greens may work, but they're cold colors and some recipients may be quite adverse to them. This leaves tans, grays, pinks, yellows, etc. Avoid using a paper that is garish—it may get some immediate attention in that it gets routed directly into the trash. As I'm writing this, I'm looking at a piece recently received from a free-lance PR designer who chose bright orange as a base for black and brown inks. Though the overall design is nice, the color scheme makes it difficult to read and actually makes me want to throw it away.

It's also wise to avoid nonstandard approaches. Most of the material you send out or leave with clients does not get an immediate response. Instead, it is placed in a file for future reference. Undersize letters drop down inside file folders or in stacks of similar literature, becoming lost almost immediately. Oversize papers rarely make it to the files at all; they're easier to discard than to fold or trim. Folded materials or those placed inside folded covers suffer a similar fate. Your best bet is to use standard 8½ × 11 inch paper and standard #10 business envelopes.

Business cards are subject to similar restrictions. The standard business card measures 2 × 3½ inches, and a deviation by more than ¹⁄₁₆ inch can be a disaster. Most business people keep the business cards they receive in either a special wallet or a special file box made for cards of a standard size. For a while, there was a trend to use an oversize card of about 2¼ × 3½ inches on the assumption that it would stick up above the others in the file. Wrong! Most went on a nonstop trip to the trash can! The same was true of the trend toward double business cards folded in the middle. They didn't fit the system so they wound up in the incinerator.

Cards smaller than standard have the same problem as small stationery; they slip down too far in the file and are overlooked at a later date. If you flip through a card file, you'll find that you control the motion with the top edges of the cards; when a card is shorter than the others, it moves forward in the stack right along with the card immediately preceding it. Similarly, the layout of the card should be horizontal rather than vertical. Vertical cards aren't easily read in a file box or card wallet.

One final point. Embossed papers and cards, though expensive, can make a good impression if they are well designed. Embossing (raising) the paper for a logo is quite popular, but raising it without printing on it does not make it legible. On the other hand, avoid the "raised lettering" technique like you would a social disease. This technique uses heat to melt a powder and fix the resulting fluid substance onto the paper surface so that the dark letters stand up above the paper. In the first place, this technique is in general disfavor and does not give a modern professional image. Second, the raised type eventually sticks to any plastic, metal, or glass surfaces it contacts. A business card of this type placed into a plastic folder becomes impossible to separate from that folder within a very short time.

## The Résumé

Every public library is stocked with books that tell you how to prepare a résumé, all of them assuming that you will be using it to look for a full-time job. As a free-lance writer, your use of a résumé is somewhat different, so the résumé itself is different. Obviously, you're not looking for full-time work, so you're not as concerned with someone reading it quickly. Instead, the résumé is used as supporting information when a publisher or prospective client requests additional background. For the most part, people who ask for a résumé have an interest in reading it, so you are not faced with the problem of having to summarize your life within one or two pages. Your essential requirements are to explain your employment history, list your major publication credits, list awards you've received, identify your professional memberships, cite your special skills, detail your personal data (including education and military experience), and possibly list some good references.

Under employment history, you proceed chronologically backward from most recent to earliest. Be sure to list your free-lance occupation complete with trade name as your most recent employer. Although most recommendations call for a single-line explanation of what you did for an employer, you'll probably do better with a full paragraph of 8 to 12 lines. Be sure to blow your own horn a little, particularly under the entry for your free-lance business. The descriptions of each job should be complete enough to provide all pertinent facts. While you should list inclusive dates of employment, your title, and the company name, address, and phone for each job, there is no reason to list the cause for leaving an employer.

Under major publications, try to list as many as possible, even if you didn't get a by-line or credit. Each publication should be listed by title, publisher or magazine name, date, and other information necessary for its location and identification. Standard bibliographic listings are probably the best. Remember that books printed and distributed by an employer other than a publishing company can be included, but routine technical manuals or brochures usually are omitted. Similarly, reports prepared for government agencies and produced by the Government Printing Office can be listed. If you have fillers or games published regularly in magazines or newspapers, list the publishers or the magazine names and specify that you are a regular contributor. In this section, every entry counts, so include as much as you can possibly think of, even if it seems unimportant.

A section on awards should include every professional recognition you've received, including competitive awards in writing, photography, or other creative arts. Don't omit honorable mentions or items seemingly unrelated to actual writing. You are trying to show accomplishments in as many areas as possible. If, however, you have been out of school for a couple of years, you should not list academic awards (hold them for the section on education).

A section on professional memberships is valuable, particularly if you are or have been a member of an organization affiliated with your free-lance pursuits. Specify whether you are a current member or a former member. Include all offices held.

In a section on skills, mention those you feel might be appropriate. If you can type, state the approximate rate. If you know computer programming, name the languages you can use even if you're not an expert. If you know several conversational languages, list them. If you are familiar with or own a word processing system, list it. Even seemingly unimportant skills like developing film, printing photos, copyrighting documents, and various other skills can help make a favorable impression.

Under personal data, describe your educational background, complete with any awards, scholarships, or academic honors. State your military experience and include any pertinent special training. Finally, if you wish, you may list such data as marital status, birth date, etc., though employers are now legally restrained from seeking this information to relate to potential employment.

At the conclusion you can list references. Most résumé experts recommend against this practice because an individual will only list good references so it's a meaningless exercise. But you need a place to list some contacts, by personal name and not just company name, and this is as good a place as any. It won't hurt, and it can help.

When you have all of the information together, consider how to present it best. Design a document that is easy to read, clearly separates each major area, and is attractive to the eye. For your purposes, forget all you've heard about never exceeding two pages. If you need four pages, use four pages. Since your use of the résumé assumes prior interest on the part of the reader, you're not going to lose him partway through. If each category is clearly set off from the others, the reader can pick and choose what he wants. The most important thing is to have all of the necessary information at the reader's fingertips.

If you have a second sheet of stationery with a logo printed on it, overprinting your résumé onto that sheet gives you another coordinated piece and helps convey the impression of professionalism you are trying to achieve. It's not always good practice to use a complete letterhead as the base for a résumé because it's too easy for a reader to confuse the résumé and a cover letter.

### The Client List

As a separate document, the client list is most applicable to a consultant. A résumé is designed to list jobs and personal history, but the client list is used to fill in the information missing from the description of the free-lancer's business. The objective is to answer two questions asked by new contacts: "Whom have you done work for?" "What did you do for them?"

Usually provided under a complete letterhead, the list contains a brief two- to five-line description of each major free-lance assignment, including the client's name, city, and state. Although you don't have to include the mailing address, phone number, or personal contact, you should define the type of product or service involved, the tasks you performed, and the intent of the documentation. A typical entry might read something like:

XYZ Electronics, Inc., Denver, Colorado. Research, write, edit, illustrate, and prepare camera-ready art for technical and marketing documentation, including instruction manuals, data sheets, fliers, brochures, etc. The documentation involves numerous product lines and services associated with data processing equipment, computer peripherals, magnetic tape products, and software development programs.

For the free-lancer just starting out, a list of clients isn't available. As the business grows and new clients are added, the list lengthens until it becomes sufficiently impressive to be a major sales tool. If you have only a few clients, list even the most trivial ones. They can be removed and replaced with important ones at a later date. It is preferable to place the most important clients at the top of the list, without regard to alphabetical or chronological order. Eventually, the list should look as though it is a purely random selection.

You don't have to remove a listing just because a client is not currently active. If you head the list with, "Partial List of Clients," you don't commit yourself to meaning that all of them are current clients or that any of them have been particularly large accounts. You should, however, delete any from whom you've had trouble collecting your money; it's amazing how bitter a deadbeat gets when someone goes after him for what he owes, and he will accuse you of being the bad guy anytime he's asked for a reference. It's better to leave him off the list rather than to let him take out his misplaced vengeance on your reputation.

## The Brochure

A simple advertising brochure can be your most effective sales tool. It need not be overly complex, but it should be compatible with the rest of your business literature. You will find it looks best when printed with the same ink and on the same paper as your business card. Just remember that this is a formal brochure and as such it must have a highly professional appearance.

There's no harm in judicious use of halftones (photos) to punch up a brochure, and the text itself should be prepared by a professional typographer using either foundry type or phototype. The physical appearance should immediately associate with your overall image, using the same type fonts for the trade name and text as you use on your letterhead. Your logo also should appear prominently on at least the front of the brochure. You have a great deal of creative latitude, but you still want to avoid harsh or overbearing appearances that might discourage your reader.

One of the most useful formats is a six-part brochure arranged to fit both sides of a single 8½ × 11 inch sheet. Proper arrangement and double folding give you a front cover, a back cover that can be designed for self mailing, and four usable "panels" for a description of your business, your background and qualifications, your areas of expertise, etc. When folded, a brochure like this fits nicely into a #10 business envelope.

Figure 7 illustrates one side of the unfolded sheet that I use as my brochure. When folded into thirds, the bottom panel becomes the front cover and the center panel becomes the back panel. In a previous design, the center panel was blank except for a return address, making that brochure a self-mailing piece that could be used without an envelope by simply sticking on an address label and a stamp. In this design, the reverse side also contains three panels printed upside down in relation to the front side (head to foot printing) so that the brochure reads properly when unfolded.

If you haven't had experience at preparing camera-ready art for printing, the job will be a lot easier if you work with an experienced graphic artist. The layout has to be arranged so the folds provide the borders for the six panels, with the folded borders evenly spaced as though they were margins on a page. The job is complicated by having to trim the sheet slightly shorter than 11 inches; since one section folds into the center, it is slightly smaller than the other two and forces balancing the entire brochure against that size difference. A small mistake in positioning any element can ruin your entire printing when you go to fold it. You're better off to pay for an artist's time rather than risk having to pay for a useless press run and wasted paper.

A couple of other points might save you some unpleasant and costly surprises. Be careful in selecting a paper texture, particularly if you are using large areas of solid ink or halftones. Some papers just don't give good results for that kind of printing and

**FIGURE 7. Simple Brochure for a Consultant**

# miscellaneous services

Documentation services may be contracted as a complete program, including consulting, planning, researching, writing, editing, designing, finalizing, and coordinating single documents or entire communication projects. The services are also available individually, such as writing and editing only, for clients preferring to have direct control over one or more facets of the project or those wishing to use their own in-house capabilities for particular tasks.

Other services may include photography, scripting, media coordination, ad placement, and similar tasks on a limited basis. The documentation services are available to companies, advertising agencies, and public relations firms. Liaison services are also available between industrial and technical companies and their advertising agencies.

# experience

Diverse experience includes more than a dozen years of documentation for technical, industrial, scientific, and commercial communication projects. Brochures, advertisements, manuals, reports, audiovisuals, technical papers, promotional campaigns, etc., have been done for:

- Instrumentation
- Data Processing
- Software Development
- Air/Water Pollution Control
- Residential Products
- Telecommunications
- Digital Tape Products
- Industrial Process Control
- Electro-optical Equipment

- Electronics
- Minicomputers/Microcomputers
- Environmental Consulting
- Civil Engineering
- Medical Equipment
- Cryogenic Fluid Handling
- Photographic Processes
- Air Purification Systems
- Various other endeavors

# documentation generalist

# ERNEST E. MAU

3108 South Granby Way
Aurora, Colorado 80014
(303) 755-3986

you could be stuck for the cost of an expensive but useless paper stock. "Felt," "leather," and "laid" finishes are particularly difficult to print and should be avoided for halftones and solids.

Most papers are cut to run "grain long" through a printing press to minimize curling. Since the folds cross the grain line, you can break the paper and end up with a ragged, unsightly edge. With some papers this can be avoided by machine scoring the fold lines to press them into the surface, but other papers may have to be cut and printed "grain short."

Considerations of paper texture and grain are best discussed with a qualified printer, preferably one who does only high-quality printing. Try not to use a neighborhood quick printer for this item; what you may gain in convenience, speed, and price will cost you dearly in the loss of quality. In fact, you should use a quality printer for your stationery as well and reserve the use of instant printers for mundane items.

If your design is closer than ⅜ inch to any edge of the paper, be sure to advise the printer that he may have to order oversize paper and then trim off the excess. If you fail to do so and the printer doesn't have a gripper edge to feed the paper through the press, you may have to redesign the art or pay for the unusable paper.

## The Sample Portfolio

No writer should be without a portfolio. Try to keep as many copies as possible of everything you do; extra copies are important in case you have to leave some samples with a prospective buyer. Your portfolio is your most important sales tool because it shows what you have accomplished. It should, therefore, represent the entire range of projects and subjects you have handled, and it should cover as much of your working history as is practical.

You start building your portfolio with the very first project you do for an employer. Just because you are a captive employee doesn't mean you can't show off your work. Writers who fail to collect samples of all their work inevitably end up regretting it, and a fast way to lose a prospective client is to reply to his request for a sample by saying, "Well, I worked for five years in that field, but I didn't get any copies."

I really can't emphasize this point strongly enough—getting samples of printed work is a top priority for any writer. I've been in the position of interviewing potential employees for companies and as potential subcontractors to my own business. If someone can't show me any samples, indicates that he's never bothered to collect any, or makes excuses for not bringing any along with him, all discussion ends there and then.

When I'm coordinating a printing job for a client, I obtain my samples directly from the printer. Once I've completed a job, it's common to have no further contact with the client for an extended interval which makes it difficult to obtain samples from him. Each printer I normally recommend knows that I want samples and that my continued recommendation may depend on whether or not I get them. Since printers routinely overrun a job to assure that the usable number of copies is at least as large as the ordered number, I simply have them set part of the overrun aside. It doesn't cost the client, but it satisfies my needs.

In organizing the portfolio, you can use notebooks, folders, or any other practical and attractive method of displaying the work. The method of presentation is not as important as having a good variety of samples organized in some logical order. My own approach is to have a notebook for each major employer or client, grouping the samples within each notebook according to the type of document (brochures, news releases, manuals, etc.). I also maintain a separate and larger notebook with a scattering of widely varied documents organized by subject matter. The first group of books allows me to select the one most closely allied to the interests of a new prospect and show him the depth of my work in that field. The miscellaneous notebook is used to show maximum diversity when meeting with a new prospect involved in a field in which I have no prior experience. Either approach works equally well, depending on the circumstances.

A final note on the subject. If you only have one copy of a sample, never leave it with or mail it to anybody. No matter how much someone promises to return your sample, they never quite get around to it. If someone asks for samples to examine more carefully, give them only ones of which you have more copies. As soon as you get back, make certain you replace those samples with the reserve copies so you don't accidentally forget them when you go out to a later meeting.

## Using the Literature

There are many ways to use your basic assortment of business literature. What may be effective for one individual in one locale may not work for someone else or in a different locale. In soliciting my clients, I've had fair luck with one approach, but it's not necessarily the best one for you.

I use my brochure as my primary sales piece for general mailings and to leave at meetings. Given a list of low-probability prospects gathered from many sources, I shotgun them all with the brochure. A smaller list showing higher probabilities might be gathered from one specific reference and would receive both the brochure and the client list. High-probabilities such as companies known to use writers in my field or those with a known need receive the brochure, client list, and résumé along with a cover letter.

If someone expresses interest after any stage, I then supply any items that have not been sent already. If samples are requested and I have them available, I may or may not send them along; the decision is based on the degree of interest expressed by the contact. With today's high printing costs, it's not practical to send every available piece to every possible contact, so some sort of preselection is necessary to achieve an element of economy.

## The Business Letter

There are a few points to be made about business letters, whether they are used on an individual basis or as cover letters for general mailings.

It's unwise to deviate from the accepted forms of a business letter. They should be clear, concise, and in accordance with formats that may be found in any standard reference book. The preferred form is a block format in which paragraphs are separated by a blank line but are not indented from the margin. The best readability is achieved when every line of the letter (including the date) is flush to the left margin.

It's tempting to use a preprinted cover letter for mass mailings, particularly if you can have names, addresses, and a personalized salutation typed onto the printed form. The problem is that the letter looks like a preprinted form with typed information. Most secretaries are trained to intercept unimportant mail, and such letters rarely get past their desks. I've seen a somewhat higher percentage of penetration to the executive's desk without the cover letter; the secretaries sometimes can't decide whether the brochure or other insert is important, so they pass it through. Regardless, I prefer to omit a cover letter rather than use a preprinted one.

With the availability of right-margin justification on word processing systems, there's a tendency to think that a letter looks better with a flush margin on the right to match the one on the left. Again, the problem is the trained secretary who immediately recognizes that format as machine printed and therefore unimportant. If you happen to have the capability, do not right justify your business letters—leave that margin ragged to make it look more like an individually typed letter.

# 5

# The Writer as a Salesman

Being a free-lance writer means being a good salesman. Referring to the dictionary, a writer is defined as, "one who practices writing as an occupation." In order to consider any pursuit an occupation, you have to get paid. To get paid as a free-lance writer, you have to sell your work. To sell your work, you have to play the same marketing games as any other business, small or large. If you can't or won't get out there in the real world and peddle yourself and your work, you cannot call yourself a writer no matter how many manuscripts are collecting dust in your files.

When you begin free-lancing after having been a captive employee, you have to make a major transition. As an employee, your only real opportunities to play salesman probably involved finding a new job from time to time. With any luck, you faced the chore of selling yourself and your abilities only once or twice every few years. As a free-lancer, selling yourself and your work suddenly becomes a part of your daily life and is necessary for every manuscript you write, every publisher you contact, and every client you solicit.

I'll go so far as to say that being a good salesman is more important than being a good writer. Even work of poor quality can be sold to someone if the presentation is convincing enough, but the best work may go nowhere at all if not backed by an aggressive sales approach. For novice free-lancers, at least, one thing is certain—it takes more time and effort to make a sale than it takes to do the actual writing. As with virtually every other facet of a free-lance career, there are distinct differences between writers selling to the editorial markets and those functioning as consultants to individual businesses, and it's necessary to consider them separately even though any one writer may cross back and forth between them.

## EDITORIAL MARKETS

Visit any bookstore or library and you'll find volumes of information on how to write, prepare, and sell your work. Subscribe to any of several writers' magazines, and you'll be inundated with articles and opinions on the same subjects. As soon as you try to obtain a comprehensive overview, you realize that there's no end to the number of printed words intended to help get your words into print. To further complicate your life, some of the information is good, some of it is not so good, and much of it is contradictory. Just scanning two years' back issues of a single writers' journal reveals dozens of different and often opposing opinions on how to approach a publisher, whether or not to use a literary agent, where to get ideas, when to pay to have a manuscript edited professionally, and so on.

All of that information leads to one conclusion: there is no single right way to do things, but there are a lot of wrong ways. Simply following the steps to success outlined by one author doesn't mean you, too, are going to be successful, but failing to heed the warnings can lead you straight to failure.

When I started the research for this chapter, I fully intended to present a set of recommendations that summarized the valid procedures for selling a manuscript. Much to my disappointment, and probably yours as well, I found the task impossible. No matter what approach I settled on, it was useful only for a small segment of the available market and then only under a particular set of circumstances. Rather than mislead you by trying to tell you what should be done, I can only tell you what should not be done. You have to decide for yourself whether a literary agent would be to your advantage or disadvantage, whether you benefit or not from eye-to-eye contact with a publisher, whether or not you want to risk assignments that may pay only a 20% kill fee for nonuse, etc.

As a free-lance writer, you are unique. You will not be using the same methods and approaches as any other writer but will, instead, be developing your own techniques. In so doing, you have to play a game of percentages, picking out the procedures that seem most appropriate, trying them for a while, and discarding those that don't work. I do recommend, however, that you spend some time reading through as much material on the subject as possible to identify methods that may be applicable to your particular pursuits. Don't let all the tales of woe discourage you too quickly. There is money to be made in this market and with a salable idea, a professional approach, a lot of perseverance, and some luck you should be able to put some of that money into your own pocket. In Chapter 11, I am including a list of additional reading; the list is not all-inclusive, but it should help you get started.

## Identifying Markets

One of the first things you need is a comprehensive listing of available markets, one that is categorized by type of publication and subject matter and that gives the names and addresses of the publishers as well as contact personnel, rates paid, special requirements, etc. The most valuable and easily obtained reference of this type is a book called *Writer's Market*, updated and published annually by Writer's Digest. The book is available from any bookstore and can be ordered if they don't have it in stock.

The current edition is available in the reference section of most public libraries.

A quick scan of the major sections reveals markets in consumer magazines, sponsored publications, farm publications, professional journals, book publishers, and subsidy book publishers. A section on miscellaneous markets lists authors' agents, syndicates, and similar points of sale. Under the heading of consumer magazines alone, there are more than 40 major subject classifications, each containing a number of individual publishers or magazine titles.

You also can develop some useful lists of your own by gathering information from the mastheads of magazines on a local newsstand and from title sheets of books at local bookstores. I've found many magazines on newsstands and in business-office waiting rooms that are not listed in the *Writer's Market,* some of which have proven to be valuable points of sale. Similarly, local or regional book publishers and some trade journals are not included in the reference listings but are valid prospects for a writer's work. Some imaginative searching for sources of names and addresses is to your distinct advantage since the prospects obtained in that manner may not be flooded with as many contributions as the ones listed in a standard directory.

## Are Free-Lancers Needed?

There are markets and individual publishers within a specific market that do not use free-lance contributions. These publishers rely entirely on their own in-house staffs for all their work, but they don't constitute a particularly large portion of the overall editorial market. You are most likely to encounter a publisher like this among specialized professional journals or in low-budget operations such as word-puzzle magazines.

As a general observation, few outlets are available for fiction or poetry, and those that are available are difficult to break into. Fiction is the primary glamour field and is the one most writers like to pursue. As a result, the competition is fierce and the acceptances are few in comparison with the number of submissions. Poetry is a low-demand item, but a lot of aspiring writers like to think of themselves as poets. The limited market for poems is always overcrowded, and the chance of success is limited.

On the other hand, nearly all nonfiction publishers use free-lance contributions, and there remains a large and untapped outlet among trade publishers and specialized magazines that have difficulty attracting competent free-lancers in their specific fields. Many of these publishers find the use of free-lancers particularly attractive because it costs them far less than keeping writers on staff. The free-lancers give them an element of flexibility, allowing them to pick and choose submissions that best suit the publication's needs and that offer fresh views and ideas. In some cases, the use of an individual or unusal style and point of view is highly desirable, and the need to pay only after a piece has proven usable helps the publisher reduce his overhead costs by not having a salaried writer wasting time on an idea that may prove fruitless. A free-lancer with a degree of expertise in a scientific or technical field may have the further advantage of finding a publisher who simply cannot afford to keep such a specialist on the full-time staff.

At the same time, many publishers take a very conservative stand when contacted by a free-lancer with whom they are not already familiar. They are understandably leery of giving assignments to someone whose work they don't know. Unless the final piece comes from a regular contributor, they have no way of knowing in advance whether or not it will be usable. Some free-lancers promise to deliver an item, and the publisher finds himself coming up short because the story is never delivered; at best, the publisher loses the element of control over the final piece. While most free-lancers act in a reputable and professional manner, there are those few who don't. Once burned, a publisher becomes wary of all free-lancers just for his own self-protection, and the majority of writers suffers for the sins of a few.

It is this concern with professionalism and broken promises that forces most publishers into having free-lancers work on speculation until they have proven themselves. By not committing the publication to something that won't be delivered or that won't be usable even after delivered, the publisher is using the only means of self-protection he has available.

Since the primary concern is to get the magazine out on time, many publishers won't even rely on a single assignment for one possible piece. Instead, they issue the same assignment to several potential contributors in the hope that at least one usable piece will be received. When more than one piece is submitted, they can pick the best one and pay the other writers nominal kill fees.

I remember a time, not long ago, when working on assignment was the free-lancer's ultimate goal. After all, it proved that the writer had been accepted as a regular contributor and pretty much guaranteed the appearance of his work in print. Today, that's no longer true! A writer can receive assignment after assignment for years, never seeing his work in print and never receiving anything more than the kill fee. Again, we have the few unprofessional and unethical free-lancers to thank; their failure to deliver what they promised has hurt us all.

## Professionalism as a Sales Aid

No matter what approach you may adopt for selling your work, professionalism is necessary. It's a two-pronged consideration in that you must make the prospect believe you are a professional and then actually perform accordingly. Earlier, I indicated I could only advise you of what not to do in selling your work, and this is the area of primary concern.

Although a few rejections of a piece you consider outstanding might make you think otherwise, it's helpful to realize that editors and publishers are human beings. Like the rest of us, they have their bad days and their individual preferences. Like the rest of us, they are not always successful in keeping their personal attitudes completely separated from their jobs, and subjective opinions occasionally get in the way of truly objective criticisms. You may not always be able to avoid such situations completely, but you can avoid aggravating them.

Imagine for a moment that you are an editor at a publishing house. From the hundreds of unsolicited queries and manuscripts you receive, you have to select only a dozen or so that can actually be put into print. Your primary concern is to select those that give your publisher the highest probability of selling the finished work, whether it be a book or a magazine. If the publisher consistently loses money because your selections don't sell, you soon join the ranks of the unemployed; so simple self-preservation dictates that you eliminate all but the best.

Your first criterion is subject matter. It's relatively easy to cull out the submissions that are totally unrelated to your publisher's interests, but that still leaves quite a stack of materials that may or may not be usable. As you eliminate more and more submissions, the decisions get harder and harder. Sooner or later you begin to look for the contributions that have the most professional appearance.

Somewhere down deep inside, you know that a writer who shows a truly professional approach in presenting his manuscripts probably takes his work seriously. Such a writer is likely to deliver a finished piece and deliver it on time to help keep production on schedule. He is apt to put more effort into his manuscript and any rewrites, thus minimizing the costs incurred in putting the work into print. Choosing the work of a writer who looks like a professional just makes more sense than settling on one who might never carry through on the project.

While I still have you in that editor's chair, imagine that you have to read through a dozen or so "finished" manuscripts that you didn't ask for in the first place. Just for the fun of it, you happen to have a slight but annoying headache that puts you just a little on edge. You reach for the next submission, and your fingers immediately tell you that this writer used erasable bond paper. Right then, you know you're going to have trouble reading it! As you scan the first sheet, you see that the typewriter ribbon was too worn to leave a clear image and that the letters are more a muddy gray than a dark black. To give you a little more fun, the author single spaced the type to conserve paper, crossed out a few lines and wrote their replacements with a soft pencil, and then managed to spill a cup of coffee that stained the upper right corner of every page. I leave it to you; would you bother to read it or would you reach for a rejection slip?

If you think this example is extreme, you're wrong. Every editor can tell you that he sees just those kinds of things every day, and some submissions are even worse. As a writer, you want the editor to read your manuscript. Everything you can do to improve your chances of having him do so enhances your chances of getting an acceptance. Common sense alone should tell you that professionalism in your work and your presentation is of paramount importance, and the first impression you make on the editor will be a lasting one. The following list contains a few of the things you can do to make that first impression a good one:

1. Use a formal letterhead for your query and cover letters; it costs a little more but makes a better impression on the reader.

2. Make your query and cover letters as brief and to the point as possible. If it's a query, accompany it with an outline detailed enough to show exactly what you intend to do and how you intend to do it.

3. Use only quality paper with good, black typewriter ribbons. The more readable the work, the more likely it is to be read. Never use onionskin or erasable bond paper and never type with a colored ribbon.

4. Make any corrections as unapparent as possible. Holes in the paper, strikeovers, globs of correction fluid, and other unsightly messes are the mark of an amateur. If you can't type without a lot of errors, hire someone to do the final typing for you.

5. Don't submit pages that are smeared, stained, or dog-eared; retype them or have them retyped. Keep your manuscripts away from food and drink and out of the reach of children, pets, and other hazards.

6. Use standard business letter formats for your correspondence and a standard manuscript format for your work. If

you don't know what the current formats are, obtain a reference book on the subject. Don't try to get creative with your formats to attract attention; it's likely you'll get the wrong kind of attention.

7. To make it easier for the editor to read your manuscripts, use double spacing throughout and use pica (10-pitch) type whenever possible.

8. Picture yourself as the editor. If you would rather not have to read something, an editor wouldn't want to read it either. Remember that the editor is a busy individual and try to do everything you can to make his job easier.

Just presenting a professional image isn't much good if you don't perform accordingly. You have to deliver the goods as promised. Once you agree to provide a manuscript, you must provide it and provide it on time. If you are asked for a rewrite, do it. If you are asked for illustrations, do them or have them done. If you are obligated to provide an index, do so within the time interval specified. Maintain the highest possible standards for your work at all times, and do everything you can to accommodate the needs of your publisher. In short, prove you really are a professional.

Sometimes, putting forth a little extra effort can yield tremendous rewards. As an example, while I was involved in working with various types of word games for different publishers, I started computerizing various types that I would find in my publishers' magazines, usually modifying the approach to provide better versions than what they were already using.

One day, an editor of a publication suggested that I send some samples to another publisher to expand my business base. The recommended publisher, who shall remain nameless, had never been a successful market for me in the past, but I sent off some new samples anyway. Two weeks later, I received a threatening letter informing me that the publisher would be taking action against me for copyright infringement. That publisher claimed total copyright protection for the basic concept of some half dozen different puzzles. The claim was not for a specific puzzle as published but for the appearance, style, and overall method of preparing those puzzles even though they were regular features of other magazines.

After my inital surge of panic began to die down, I checked my file of copyright information, finding the appropriate government documents that disallowed copyright protection for three areas: (1) ideas, plans, methods, or systems; (2) blank forms and similar works; and (3) titles, names, and short phrases. These were Copyright Office Circulars 31, 32, and 34 respectively. With those documents as ammunition, I responded to the threat in terms of having created the computerized methods myself, having done so under the instructions and guidelines of other publishers, and having operated under the umbrella provided in the three Copyright Office circulars. I included copies of the circulars with the applicable areas underlined.

At the same time, I wrote to every other publisher using word puzzles, advising them of the threat I had received, explaining my stand on the issue, and enclosing copies of the same three circulars. I also advised them that they would have to make their own decisions concerning the use of the materials in question, but that I was not withdrawing my submissions from the market until such time as the troublesome publisher would provide adequate written proof that they had circumvented the normal provisions of the copyright law. Had they been able to do so, I would have had to withdraw my materials immediately, but they were unable to provide that proof.

Of course, I lost any opportunity to ever sell to the publisher in question, but they never pursued the matter further. I don't think they expected to run into someone who deals with copyrights and keeps the pertinent information on hand at all times. It's reasonable to assume that the publisher was merely trying to scare off some possible competition.

The value of the exercise became apparent only when I started receiving responses from the other publishers. They too had been bothered with the same threats, so my identification of the applicable legal provisions had been helpful. Furthermore, I impressed them adequately enough to earn a higher priority on considering and using my own submissions. The net result was the loss of one low-probability prospect and nearly doubling my sales among almost a dozen other publishers. That little extra effort in contacting the publishers and offering them the opportunity to avoid using questionable materials gave my professional image a real boost and translated directly into more dollars in my pocket.

## The Percentage Game

Selling your editorial work is a hit or miss proposition. Even with the most professional approach, all of your good ideas and manuscripts are not going to be salable to every publisher or to any one publisher in particular. In fact, a substantial portion of your work may never find a publisher. To survive, you have to play a little game of percentages. Simply stated, the rules of this game are to generate as many different works as possible, offer each work to as many publishers as possible, and rely on the laws of chance to sell a sufficient number of ideas and manuscripts.

Your ideas, outlines, and manuscripts are your stock in trade. The more of them you have, the better your chances of having some salable ones. Therefore, you never can stop generating new materials, and you must think and write continuously. Ideas can come from many sources including personal experiences, general reading, and even watching television, but you have to learn to examine everything you encounter in terms of story or article possibilities. If you can find a different twist, a way to amplify an experience, or just a way to play the devil's advocate, you may find an idea that will sell. But all the ideas you may have do no good if they're not down in black and white, so you also have to write them. Even if something seems irrelevant or of no interest, don't discard the idea until you have examined all of the alternatives and all of the possible uses or points of sale.

Once you have something written, you can't sell it unless you send it to a publisher. Hiding a piece of work away in a file cabinet just because you think it might be rejected doesn't help at all. It may hurt to get a rejection slip for a piece, but at least you've given it a chance. Paraphrasing an old cliché, "it's better to have tried and been rejected than never to have tried at all."

It's in the process of actually submitting a piece of work that the percentage game works best. I remember a time when the standard advice was to offer an idea or manuscript to only one publisher at a time, waiting for his response before submitting the same item to another publisher. That was the ethical and professional way of doing things. The disadvantage was that an average time of about a month and a half to receive the material back allowed only eight tries a year. Since it takes a lot of luck to find one publisher out of eight willing to accept a particular piece, the method was time consuming and discouraged many writers.

More recently, it's become acceptable to offer the same piece to several publishers at the same time, resolving any conflicts between multiple acceptances when and if they occur. From the publishers' view, this method may be less than desirable because they may accept an idea only to have the author elect to go with another publisher. However, it does provide them with more material to select from and a higher probability of finding something they can use. From a writer's view, this is the only practical approach, and the fact that many other writers are using multiple submissions literally forces a new writer to do the same.

The simple logic is that single submissions allow only about eight tries a year, but eight tries of a dozen publishers each allow 96 total chances for the same piece in the same period. Although this means more writers and more manuscripts are looking for a publisher at any one time, the odds of finding one publisher out of nearly a hundred are about twelve times better than one out of eight. In playing the percentage game, it's numbers that count, and the higher your numbers, the better your chances of succeeding.

## CONSULTING MARKETS

Defining the sales procedure for a consulting writer is considerably more straightforward than for an editorial writer. Many of the elements of chance and hit-or-miss operations can be eliminated, reducing the task to a logical business procedure. Instead of trying to peddle an idea or a manuscript, the consultant sells himself and the services he offers. Instead of offering the same material over and over again to unseen publishers, he works on a head-to-head basis with individual clients having specific and easily identified needs. Instead of randomly selecting prospective buyers who may or may not want what he has to sell, he seeks to attract desirable clients and have them solicit his services. Given a good marketing plan and the willingness to do some basic groundwork, the consulting writer can expect to have a far easier time of it than the editorial writer.

## The Marketing Plan

No consultant can develop a good client base without having some type of marketing plan for his services. Regardless of what individual techniques you decide to use within your plan, the ones you do adopt must penetrate the market segment you are going after. If you are writing advertising copy for consumer goods, it doesn't do any good to promote your services through an engineering journal. If you are interested in writing technical manuals, there's little advantage in advertising your services in a suburban community newspaper.

In devising and implementing a marketing plan, you have six basic approaches to consider: purchased advertising space, "free" publicity coverage, direct mail, telephone solicitation, personal sales calls, and word-of-mouth referrals. The advantages and disadvantages of each approach have to be weighed in terms of overall costs, expected results, and penetration of the desired market.

In Chapter 2, the need for preliminary evaluation of personal goals, market availability, and applicability of talents to the market was described at some length. The information gathered during that evaluation process is invaluable in structuring a marketing plan. You should already know whether your business has the potential for working in your locale, and you should have a pretty good idea of just which companies and contacts are important. Now the task is to find a systematic way of reaching the key personnel of those prospects and to let them know you are available to solve their problems.

*Purchased Advertising Space.*  It seems logical to assume that advertising your business in local papers and professional journals would be a good place to start. It's also a costly way of achieving what amounts to only nominal market penetration. The costs alone may be prohibitive, involving both the materials to prepare the advertisement and the purchase of space in the publication.

Classified-style advertising can be dismissed immediately because you are seeking executives and purchasing authorities in other businesses, few of whom read classified ads. General-circulation newspapers for cities, suburbs, and neighborhoods are designed to reach the public and not the specific individuals you are after so they can be eliminated as well. That leaves "display" advertising in specialized publications as your only useful medium, and both the preparation of and space for such display ads tend to be expensive.

You may not find a suitable publication in which to place your ad. Most major cities have a large organization of professional advertising and marketing people, often operating under the auspices of the American Advertising Federation or in some way affiliated with that organization. In many cases, they publish a local magazine for their members, and that magazine or others like it can be a useful vehicle for a marketing writer. Similarly, most metropolitan areas have some type of business newspaper that can be useful to a marketing writer.

A technical writer has fewer possibilities because he has to reach engineers and scientists who normally don't receive or read business newspapers or advertising journals. Other than national trade magazines which are very expensive, the technical writer often has no direct advertising media in which to convey his message.

There are some additional possibilities in highly specialized and one-of-a-kind publications that spring up occasionally. Some professional organizations publish directories of businesses operating in certain fields or in particular locales. The local Chamber of Commerce and "blue book" publishers may also get involved in such projects. I've even seen a private enterprise that produced a giant wall poster for business offices, displaying the ads of other businesses in the area that could provide necessary services. As a last resort, there is the Yellow Pages section of the local telephone directory. The biggest problem with all but the telephone directory is the circulation of the item in question.

At one time or another, I've tried all of the professional directories and posters available, and they've all had the same problem—a relatively high cost for the space and virtually no circulation among the local businesses. In one case, I bought space on a graphic arts wall poster that was supposed to be distributed to 5,000 local businesses; I even provided the producer with my own list of companies who could make use of the poster. In actual fact, none were distributed directly. Instead, the producer printed a notice in a local magazine that they were available at his office or at a local art supply store for pickup by anyone interested in having a copy. Since few people bothered to make the trip to obtain the posters, few copies made it into circulation and the net result was a total waste of my money.

Advertising in the Yellow Pages has its own problems. First, you must have a business telephone, in itself an expensive proposition for a small business that does not rely on the telephone. Second, the cost of even a single column inch of advertising space may run $75 or more a month for the entire twelve-month life of the directory. Third, appearing in the directory attracts more people trying to sell you something than people interested in buying your services.

One other point is worth mentioning. Most people misunderstand the actual purpose of advertising and assume that merely placing an ad is going to sell their product or service. If you can get an advertising professional to stop justifying his job for a few minutes, you might hear him admit that advertising in and of itself never sells anything. In pitching a consumer product, all ads are supported by numerous other techniques including the positioning of an item on a shelf so it strikes the customer's eye before its competition, couponing and discounting techniques, high-powered salesmen to wear down resistance, and an unbelieveable number of other sneaky tricks. For nonconsumer products, the advertisement merely paves the way for the actual sales pitch. With luck, it might serve to create a positive product image or at least make the prospect aware of its existence, but the sale itself relies on the face-to-face confrontation between seller and buyer.

The same principle holds true in advertising a consulting business. You can make the market aware of your existence, particularly if you have a trade name or logo that sticks in a reader's mind. You may be able to rely on an ad to give you a slight edge when you walk into a meeting because the person you talk to remembers "seeing that name somewhere before." However, you can't rely on it to generate actual sales.

For three years, I placed periodic ads in a weekly business newspaper, a monthly magazine targeted to advertising and marketing professionals, and every annual professional directory I could find. As a result, I found myself on several hundred uninteresting mailing lists and received up to 15 telephone calls a day from people trying to sell me something or get me to invest in something. In three years, I received exactly four calls (attributable to the ads) concerning the possible use of my consulting services, and only one of those turned into an actual assignment. What I did achieve was a certain recognition or "name" that made it easier to reach a prospect by phone, by mail, or in person. Although many contacts couldn't remember where, they all remembered having heard of me or having seen my name or logo. Just that alone made the costs of advertising worthwhile to me, but it might not be as worthwhile for you.

*"Free" Publicity.* An often neglected marketing possibility is that of no-cost publicity. While advertising costs money to keep your name out in front of your prospects, there are ways to

accomplish much the same thing with only the costs of paper, envelopes, and a few postage stamps.

Most local newspapers have a business section or column devoted to activities on the local scene. Even the newsletters and other periodicals of professional organizations provide no-charge coverage of newsworthy events of interest to their members. From the moment I set my business into motion on a full-time basis, I've made it a point to send out news releases for each new development. I've sent releases for starting up the business, each new client signed, and each major project completed. I've kept the local media advised of my activities as much as possible, and retained close ties with local organizations of advertising people and technical communicators alike. Approximately 80% of my news releases have made it into print, with the principal metropolitan newspaper accepting and printing nearly 50% of them.

Again, just the appearance of my name in print kept it alive in the minds of the people I needed to reach, and the editorial coverage I obtained served to reinforce the image I built with purchased advertising.

Other useful techniques have included being listed at no charge in directories of influential contacts, speaking at occasional professional meetings, helping companies and advertising agencies locate personnel for staff positions, assisting other writers in finding full-time employment, etc. These items may seem unimportant at first, and helping companies find staffers or helping people find jobs seems contradictory for a consultant who relies on companies not being staffed to meet their needs. But the overall purpose is to enhance my image. An executive who's had my cooperation in locating someone to handle work I'm unwilling to take on, or to fill a full-time slot, tends to remember me when he has work I can handle. Someone who has had my assistance in locating a job owes me a big favor, making him a valuable future contact. If I refused to do such things, I might see a short-term advantage, but I would only hurt myself in the long run.

The objective is to maintain a high profile. The more obvious you are in the business community, the more opportunities you are offered. It doesn't pay to be shy or humble when you're trying to promote your business; if you are, people just ignore you.

*Direct Mail.* By mailing your business literature to executives and key contact personnel, you can direct your efforts more precisely than with advertising and publicity coverage. Throughout your daily activities, gather all the names and addresses you can from business directories, newspaper help-wanted ads, the business sections of the newspapers, and any other sources you can identify. Some local business papers publish lists of new companies, new business telephones, and new sales tax licenses. When you have a sufficient number of names, spend some time addressing envelopes and send off your business literature.

The biggest disadvantage of direct mail is a relatively high cost for a low return. A small consulting business can't afford to print literature in large quantities of 10,000 or more copies at a time just to get the quantity discounts a printer offers for large jobs. Instead, a press run of 500 to 1,000 copies of each piece is more likely to be within the budget allowances. Considering the costs of preparing the camera-ready art, buying the paper stock, and having the actual printing done, it's reasonable to expect per-piece costs of $0.05 for envelopes, $0.20 for two-sheet résumés, $0.10 for client lists, $0.50 for brochures, and $0.10 for cover letters. This totals to $0.95 per literature package, without including time spent, typewriter ribbons, address labels, and other miscellaneous expenses. Adding $0.18 per piece for postage, the cost becomes $1.13 for every complete set of business literature sent out.

Simple multiplication shows that the cost of conducting a mass mailing to 500 prospects is $565. Although that cost may be spread out by having individual pieces printed at different times, it remains a cumulative cost that must be considered a part of the promotional expense.

The results from direct mailings often are disappointing. Many of the packages never reach their intended targets, getting lost in the mail or being intercepted by an efficient secretary whose job is to shield the boss from unimportant matters. Even those that do get through to the intended reader have to hit when there is a distinct need for the services being offered. Those that don't hit at the right time end up in a file and are likely to be forgotten.

Again, it comes down to a game of percentages. A response

from 3% of the recipients of a mass mailing can be considered outstanding. A response rate of 1% can be considered good and is within reasonable expectations for a small consulting business. A response rate of 0.5% or less is not uncommon. This means that you can expect to average one inquiry per hundred mailings. If you can succeed in converting 20% of the inquiries into actual assignments, you can expect to obtain two clients per thousand mailings. If the assignments secured as a direct result of 1,000-piece mailing do not have a total value that exceeds $1,130, you suffer a net loss just in terms of the total costs to send out your literature.

There are a number of ways to lower the cost of direct mail solicitation, including using a lower class of postage, printing literature in larger quantities to lower the per-piece cost, using self-mailing brochures that do not require envelopes, and reducing the number of pieces actually used in a mailing. The latter consideration requires some method of preselecting and qualifying prospects to determine who receives what.

My own preference is to categorize according to low-, medium-, and high-probability contacts. The low-probability group includes names and addresses gathered from general lists such as the phone directory and local business directories, companies for which I do not have the name of an individual executive, and other prospects not known to use staff or consulting help in preparing materials. That group is the largest of the three, and receives only the brochure in an envelope at a cost of $0.70 each.

The medium-probability group includes names gathered from specialized sources such as lists of manufacturing companies that would probably require technical manuals. That group receives a brochure and client list in an envelope at a cost of $0.80 each.

The high probability group includes the names gathered from sources such as want ads, personal contacts, and other sources that reveal a direct and specific need for my services at some point in time. That group receives the full package of brochure, client list, résumé, cover letter, and envelope. The addition of the two-sheet résumé pushes the mailing into a new postage classification and raises the cost from $1.13 to $1.28 per package.

Direct mail does not necessarily draw an immediate response. Mailing out 500 items on Monday doesn't mean that you can expect a call by the following Monday. Whether or not a prospect responds to your literature is a direct function of his needs at that moment. If he expects to have a future need, your literature goes into the files, hopefully to be retrieved weeks, months, or even years later. Once in a while, I get calls from companies that haven't received any literature for as long as five years. The materials were stuffed into a file, and they happened to stumble across it at a time when they had a need to produce a particular type of document.

Direct mailing does, however, enhance the image you try to create through advertising and publicity. An overall design that provides strong visual identification between media ads and mailing literature allows one to reinforce the other. Used as part of a multi-directional approach, direct mailing helps establish a small business as a part of the total business community.

*Telephone Solicitation.* Using a telephone to solicit business is a tedious, time-consuming, and often unprofitable pursuit. While it is useful to follow up on high-probability mailings and even some medium-probability mailings, simply calling companies at random rarely has any value.

The presence of an efficient secretary or receptionist in the prospect's office makes itself quite evident. Unless you can direct your call to a specific individual and convince the secretary that you have a valid reason for calling, you probably cannot get through to your target. Just dialing a number and asking to speak to "whomever is in charge of marketing communications" is like trying to knock down a concrete wall with a spitball. Talking to anyone in a personnel department is just as useless, and that's where most of your calls are routed.

I reserve telephone solicitation for cases where I know the prospect has a specific need and I know the name of the individual I want to reach. If I have a referral from someone else, that usually helps me get past the barricades. For instance, a line such as, "Mr. Brown requested that I speak to Mr. Smith as soon as possible," works wonders for getting past that devoted secretary. Of course, it is necessary to have a valid reference, preferably a name the secretary knows from past contact.

On the occasions when telephone solicitation is necessary, it helps to know something of what the prospect is doing. One big disadvantage in making calls down a classification of the telephone directory is that you have no idea what the individual prospect really does. If you are seeking manufacturing companies for whom you can provide technical literature, it's hard to differentiate a directory listing for a sales representative from one for a manufacturer. Before you can even a place a call, you have to know something about the company, what it does, who's in charge, and the extent to which they use written communications. You have to be able to justify taking a busy executive's time by having a specific direction for your conversation. You do yourself more harm than good with lines such as, "I was wondering if there would be any way I could help you with some project?" It's much better to be able to say something like, "I've heard about your atmospheric modeling project, and I'd like to discuss some thoughts I have that might be helpful."

*Personal Sales Calls.*  If telephone solicitation can be profitless, blind office-to-office sales calls or "pavement pounding" are worse. All of the problems of getting past closed doors on the phone are multiplied when you show up in person. Any good receptionist or secretary knows that once you get in you're going to take up a lot of someone's valuable time. As a result, you get steered to either personnel or purchasing, neither of which puts you in contact with the decision-making authority you are seeking.

I've tried this approach often enough in the past to have abandoned it in total disgust. The only time I use it now is when I happen to be meeting with a client located in an industrial or business park with a high concentration of other prospects in the immediate area. Even then, I use it only if I have a few hours to kill in getting no farther than leaving some literature with receptionists. At that, I rate the chances of making a sale as next to zero.

There are two notable exceptions. The first is a result of meeting with a regular client who informs me that he gave my name to someone who had indicated a need for a consultant. My regular client then can give me all the information I need, including the name of the person to talk to, the nature of the prospect's business, and an idea of what that prospect may be needing. With that ammunition and with the regular client as a reference, I have what it takes to talk myself past the receptionist and secretary and into the presence of my target. Failing that, I at least get an appointment with the individual. There even have been times when a regular client has gone so far as to call the prospect and make the arrangements for a meeting.

The other exception is the result of spotting an interesting help-wanted ad in the newspaper. Past discussions with corporate accountants have given me a fairly good feeling for the total costs of hiring a full-time employee, including not only direct salary but all of the fringe benefits. For example, hiring a full-time technical writer at a moderately high salary of $20,000 a year can cost a company upwards of $30,000 a year with training, vacations, paid holidays, unemployment insurance, Social Security contributions, investment matching, retirement funds, etc. For some companies, the figure may even approach $40,000 a year.

Analyzing my past billings, average time needed to complete certain types of jobs, and similar factors has provided me with documented proof that I can handle the needs of many companies at a total cost far below that of a full-time employee. By eliminating a client's need to pay fringe benefits and wasted time such as sick days, even my highest consulting rates can compare favorably with the costs of a full-time employee.

Armed with all that information and more, I strike directly at the prospect's vulnerable point—his finances. I appear at the company's door without an appointment and without any warning, expressing extreme concern over the want ad that just happens to be dangling from my fingertips. The strategy is to convince the receptionist that I want to save them an unnecessary waste of money in hiring someone they may not need. It's not a lie because I can do just that while still lining my own pockets.

Receptionists are not decision makers; they have to check with someone and can be convinced to call on a vice president or departmental manager instead of the personnel department. As a result, I get in to see an executive while the waiting room is full of applicants trying to get to the personnel manager.

Once past the receptionist, it's easy to make a sale. The matter of money is a company's most sensitive point, their soft under-belly. By aggressively detailing the ways I can save them money, describing the ways I've done it in the past, and outlining some impressive sounding but relatively routine approaches to their problems, I usually leave with a signed contract and the smug knowledge that I've just eliminated a job opportunity for a lot of applicants. That last statement sounds cruel, and it is! But it's also necessary for my own survival!

*Word-of-Mouth Referrals.*    All the marketing approaches you adopt won't do you as much good as referrals from satisfied clients. If you do a good job for a client and behave in a totally professional manner, word gets around. It does take time to develop a good base of referrals, but when that base reaches a sufficient size, your business can become nearly self-sustaining.

It's reasonable to expect the development of a good client base to take about two years. During those first two years, finding assignments can be difficult, and you have to devote a lot of time to just hustling new clients. But once you have the base developed, those satisfied clients become your own sales force, dropping your name at meetings and among their own associates. Suddenly, you may find that calls start coming in from people you've never contacted. Unsolicited comments such as, "Mr. Smith mentioned you and I'd like to meet over lunch to discuss some possibilities," can become almost commonplace. That's the position every con-sultant wants to achieve. When that starts to happen regularly, you know you've made it—you've beaten the odds and survived in your own business. While you still have to face a lot of problems and probably will see long dry spells as the economy fluctuates, the worst part is behind you.

The importance of clients who make frequent referrals is so

great that you must guard your relations with them as carefully as possible. You can't afford to let professionalism slip even the smallest bit. Meeting deadlines, keeping promises, and providing the best materials possible are all parts of your image. If you make just one mistake, do just one thing in an unprofessional manner, you negate all of the hard work put into building your business. Bad news travels fast, and if a client feels he's been cheated or misled, that word gets around too—usually faster than all the good recommendations combined.

If you forget everything else in this book, remember just one point! *Satisfied customers are your best salesmen!*

## Sources of Leads

I've already mentioned many sources of valid leads such as telephone directories, blue books of local corporations, help-wanted ads, the Chamber of Commerce, and professional organizations. There are some other sources that are not as immediately apparent.

There are companies that specialize in providing mailing lists and mailing services. In many cases, you can purchase lists of preselected names from these companies at a cost of approximately $0.10 to $0.25 a name. Some local magazines and trade publications also allow their mailing lists to be purchased. The important thing is to specify the parameters you want used for the selection process. If you want only engineering titles within a certain geographical region, you must specify the titles and the postal zip codes that are of interest. If you want only managers and higher, you have to specify that. If you don't establish your requirements carefully, you can end up paying a lot of money for names you don't want and can't use.

Local vendors are another good source of leads. Printers, typographers, graphic artists, ad agencies, and many other companies can help you locate potential clients. For example, a printer who receives poorly prepared camera-ready art can advise you of a company's obvious need for professional help. Similarly, a vendor in any field may be approached by someone looking for help in putting together a document; if that vendor is aware of your existence, he can make a direct referral and literally put the prospective client right on your doorstep. Graphic artists and designers often get requests for help with the written text they are illustrating, so they too are important sources of referrals. What I'm saying is don't ignore the allied communications arts, even if they seem totally irrelevant to your own pursuits. The objective is to get referrals, and you get more of them when more people know of your presence and capabilities.

Membership in professional organizations is valuable. By meeting with the people working in your own lines of pursuit, you find out which companies use staff writers and may be understaffed from time to time. You get to know what's going on in various companies, giving you the background you need to negotiate with them when and if you should have an opportunity. However, don't rely too much on personal contacts or acquaintances. Most people in marketing and technical communications jealously guard their jobs. Any consultant who can replace them is a real threat. Advertising people, in particular, are clannish and very cautious about talking to anyone outside of their own groups. In advertising and marketing, pirating clients is a part of daily activities involving both attempts to steal someone else's client and protecting ones already under contract. As a result, many of these companies try to avoid giving a free-lancer any information that might allow him to steal a client.

As just one example of the potential benefit of membership in a club, I've been approached by a department manager of a large local corporation that has always utilized an extensive in-house staff for their communications. Both that manager and I are members of the same professional organization, and he called to advise me that the company is reorganizing the support operations (probable translation: a lot of people may be laid off or fired). The intent is to start using an outside consultant to handle much of the work formerly kept for the staff. By being members of the same group, that manager knew me and knew that I handle exactly those types of assignments, therefore he knew where to ask for help. At the same time, I got advance warning of a developing situation that could prove quite profitable.

Still another source of leads comes through information sharing. Depending on the level of competition you face, it's not always the best policy to keep secrets from other free-lancers. Not every potential assignment can be satisfied by every individual, and simply referring a prospective client to another free-lancer or advising the other free-lancer of the situation can actually increase your own business. What you create is "goodwill." The prospect who gets a list of other consultants when you turn him down is going to remember your effort to help and probably will call on you again for something you could handle for him. The free-lancer who receives a referral is apt to remember it later and return the favor, even if you have to prod his memory occasionally. Regretfully, too many professional communicators fail to communicate among themselves and limit their own opportunities.

Of course, some caution is necessary. You don't want to give away valuable projects that you could handle, and you shouldn't do so just for public relations. The projects I pass along to someone else are those that involve something I don't care to do such as promoting a product I consider of no value or those for which I have no time available. If I can handle the project myself within my own time frame, I won't pass it on to someone else.

Consulting writers have to be alert to local happenings at all times. New opportunities pop up almost out of nowhere, and the writer has to keep a close watch on the newspapers, local business announcements, and similar media. New corporations moving into an area offer numerous opportunities for both marketing and technical support work. New retail stores and public facilities often require promotional aids such as brochures, news releases, and advertising. Events such as fires, traffic accidents, land developments, solar energy installations, and many others offer a wide range of possibilities for journalistic writers, particularly if they can be supported with photographic coverage.

Some specialized businesses offer even greater possibilities for writers highly skilled in certain subjects. For example, the rapidly expanding field of personal home computers has resulted in numerous computer shops opening in shopping centers and local business parks. In many cases, these shops have part-time programmers preparing their software, usually without adequate documentation for the user. A writer who is moderately knowledgeable in the computer field can find almost unlimited work in preparing the manuals needed for those software packages. This is particularly nice because some of those shops may be willing to exchange equipment and software for the documentation, so it can be a good way to obtain the basics for a word-processing system or to enhance a system already owned.

The important thing is to be as creative as possible in searching for new assignments. If you can find sources of information not already overworked by other free-lancers, you can develop an almost competition-free market for your services. The absence of competition, in turn, allows you to develop a larger business base, achieve a better income, and improve your chances of survival.

# 6

# Confronting a Client

As an editorial writer, you can expect few occasions to meet with your editors and publishers on a face-to-face basis. Instead, you probably conduct your business either by mail or through a literary agent. Even telephone conversations are limited, and most publishers express a distinct preference for conducting business by mail.

As a consultant, however, you have direct client confrontations quite regularly and conduct most of your business either in person or by telephone. Since most consulting projects are up against rather tight deadlines, few clients are willing to put up with the delays that can occur when materials are sent through the mails. As a result, meetings are conducted when you first negotiate your contract, when your client releases an assignment, when a draft is reviewed, and when materials are delivered.

Of all of the possible meetings, the most important is the initial contact—the sales meeting at which you attempt to convert a prospect into an active client.

## INITIAL CLIENT MEETING

The first time you set foot in your client's office is the most critical time in your entire working relationship with that client. In fact, it determines whether or not you will have a working relationship. Of course, there is no way to guarantee a successful first meeting, but there are some considerations that can prove helpful.

### Gaining an Advantage

Nearly every initial meeting turns into a kind of minor conflict in which a lot of maneuvering is done on both sides to gain some advantage over the other. The client naturally seeks the advantage because it gives him leverage in negotiating terms and lower rates. You seek the advantage for much the same reason except that you want your own terms and higher rates.

The initial meeting is not unlike an interview with a potential, full-time employer. When you are unemployed and desperate for a job, the prospective employer can sense your urgent need, knowing immediately that he has you at a disadvantage. The more desperate you are, the more likely you are to accept whatever he may throw your way. On the other hand, if you already have a job or aren't worried about securing immediate employment, you can approach the interviewer with a casual attitude that tells him you're not going to grab at any crumbs. In the first case, the interviewer has the negotiating advantage, but you have the advantage in the second case. If the employer's needs are great enough and your attitude is casual enough, you can negotiate the salary, fringe benefits, and working conditions across a wide range simply because you're not pressed to accept anything at all.

As a consultant, the situation is very much the same. If you show a desperate need to obtain an assignment, or any hesitancy at all in discussing your terms, the client can seize the advantage and manipulate you into settling for something less than you are seeking. But if you don't show a need for the client's assignments, you can turn the situation around and manipulate him, especially if he has a clear need for your services.

One advantage is achieved before you ever meet with the client, determined by who solicits whom. Your best position is established when it is the client who solicits your services rather than you approaching him. When he is the one who initiates the contact, you know immediately that he has a definite need and that he must satisfy that need. If you have contacted him, he knows that you are the one with the need. This is one reason for stressing the importance of word-of-mouth referrals; the contacts made in this manner are automatically to your advantage simply because you are not the one doing the calling.

A certain amount of aggressiveness also is necessary. If you impress the client as something of a weakling, he feels he can force you to back down on rates or conditions you might wish to impose. From the moment of the first handshake, its absolutely necessary to impress the client that you are 100% professional, that you know exactly what you are doing, and that your will is not going to be broken.

The simple act of shaking hands conveys a great deal of information in both directions. Every businessman will tell you that he hates a dead-fish handshake and is impressed by a firm shake combined with good eye contact. A limp wrist, diverted eyes, or a shake broken too quickly all indicate an element of weakness. Whether a man or a woman, your handshake should be firm and positive, and your eyes should be on those of the other person. At the same time, don't play the little game of seeing who's going to break the handshake or the eye contact first. Trying to stare down a prospective client is just as bad as appearing weak.

The ability to maintain good eye contact without staring remains important throughout the business meeting. People who avoid meeting someone's eyes, as we all tend to do from time to time, are characterized as shifty-eyed and somewhat weak. You gain a very definite advantage by being able to maintain good eye contact throughout your talks with the client.

The biggest consideration in developing an aggressive attitude is overcoming shyness. The problem often is compounded for writers who have spent years working for companies where their self-confidence has been eroded by constant treatment as a subordinate. As a consultant, it's helpful to remember that you are no longer subordinate to anyone and are the equal of even the highest levels of corporate management. You own and operate your own business! You are the chairman of the board, the president, and all of the vice presidents rolled into one! There is no reason to feel inferior to anyone with whom you might be meeting, and any indication that you do feel inferior again opens the way to the client gaining an advantage. Nor can you go into a meeting with a superior attitude because that alienates the prospect almost immediately. The best approach is to behave as an equal, regardless of what level of corporate management you encounter. The feeling of equality breeds self-confidence, and that in turn is conveyed at a meeting as a subjective impression. The greater your self-confidence, the greater the client's confidence in your abilities and professionalism, and the greater your advantage in carrying on the discussions.

A related point has to do with the level of corporate management at which you conduct your business. The contracting of consultants requires a management level high enough to be able to implement those decisions. Therefore, it is good policy to restrict business discussions to those in a position to make the necessary decisions affecting purchases and costs. Rarely does the average product manager, engineer, or personnel manager have the authority to make business decisions on a company's behalf. As a result, you probably will find yourself talking more to vice presidents and presidents than to their subordinate workers. Your discussions with individuals lower in the corporate hierarchy probably will be limited to specifics on a particular project such as the design details of a device, the marketing strategies for a product, and so on. This is another reason for learning to feel comfortable with upper-management individuals since they are more likely to be the ones whom you are going to have to impress.

Conducting a business meeting requires practice. As you meet with more and more executives, you find that you grow increasingly comfortable in their presence. As your self-confidence increases, you can gain control of the meetings with growing frequency, directing the meetings in the manner you feel is best. You also find that you develop a sensitivity to the prospective client, learning to size him up quickly and find the points that are to your best advantage. You also can develop the ability to identify potential problems such as a company operating on a shoestring budget and possibly unable to pay your bills, an executive who is elusive and unlikely to honor his commitments, or a rampant disorder that might indicate trouble in getting the information you need to complete an assignment. All of these things are important to your survival as a free-lance consultant since you can't afford a client who reneges on a deal, doesn't pay his bills, doesn't provide adequate information, or attempts to cheat you on your rates.

## Preparation

One method of gaining an advantage in a business meeting is to arrive fully prepared. First, it demonstrates a professional attitude. Second, it shows an interest in the client and his possible assignments. Third, it is simple self-protection.

An obvious consideration is your physical appearance and grooming. You may prefer to work in ragged jeans and a sweatshirt, but that's hardly appropriate for a business meeting, at least not for the first few meetings. Since you are out to make a good impression, you must look like a business person. That means dressing for the occasion just as if you were a high-powered executive. It also means being conservative in what you wear; upper management levels tend to frown on extreme styles, even though they may be in vogue for social events and evening wear. A man's or woman's business suit should be of conservative cut and a color not too flashy; the closer you can come to matching the style of dress expected of the client's personnel, the better off you will be.

Rules of common sense also apply to hairstyles, beards, manicures, and all other items of personal grooming. Although full-time employees have been given a lot of latitude in recent years, you are faced with making an impression on an executive who may have a personal dislike for "natural" hairdos, scraggly beards, or dirty fingernails. Doing your own thing is fine, but not if it costs you the respect of a prospective client and, ultimately, a good-paying assignment.

Once you have worked with a client for a period of time, it may be permissible to relax your standards somewhat. For example, it's not always necessary to wear a business suit just to drop off a completed manuscript. Simple errand running like that can be accomplished in everyday dress without seriously affecting the client's feelings toward you. Nevertheless, when you are scheduled into a formal meeting for a draft review or project evaluation, it is advisable to switch back to business dress regardless of how long you have worked with the client.

It's advisable to do a little preliminary homework before going into your first meeting with a new client. First, you should have some idea of what the business entails. There's little use in trying to develop a client that you can't handle. For example, if you write only materials for the electronics industry, it may not be to your advantage to set up a meeting with a client manufacturing underground drilling machines for the mining industry. Second, you should check out the financial standing of the company. Larger companies are listed in indexes and other references that can tell you their financial status, number of employees, etc.

A fast check with the Better Business Bureau, local credit firms, and the Chamber of Commerce can provide general information about the prospect's financial standing. Few free-lancers can afford to get involved with a client who has a reputation of defaulting on bills, postponing payments for excessive periods, or abusing customers. It's also good practice to request that the prospective client have copies of the latest annual report and financial statement ready for your examination at the first meeting. Although these measures are not an absolute guarantee against being burned by a client, they can help shift the odds in your favor.

By finding out what the prospective client actually does, you can select the appropriate samples to take with you to the meeting. If you've done a lot of work in the particular field, you can take samples that show the extent of your abilities in that area. If you've done little or no similar work, you can select diversified samples that illustrate a wide range of capabilities. At the same time, you should put together a package of information to leave with the prospect. Depending upon the type of business literature you are using, you should leave one copy of everything pertinent. That means a copy of any brochure you use, your client list, and your personal résumé. If you feel the prospect is serious enough to warrant it, you also might want to include a few samples that can be left for later examination (samples probably won't be returned, so don't include anything you don't want to lose).

You also should have a prepared contract to present to the prospect. It should be addressed directly to the company and should have your rates and terms fully defined. Agreeing to something at a meeting and then sending a contract for signature later is unadvisable. Some of the agreed upon items may have been forgotten or the client may have had too much time to reflect on your terms. It's better to be able to present the contract and obtain the necessary signature before the end of the first meeting.

Two copies of the contract should be prepared, both under your business letterhead and each identical to the other. You should keep the original copy for your files and allow the client to keep the second copy for his. Don't let the client retain the signed original since it's the one you need to prove any later claims. If, during the course of the meeting, you decide to change something in the contract, it can be written in and initialed by both parties without having to prepare a whole new agreement.

It's only natural that good preparation will enhance any meeting. It allows you to feel comfortable and enables you to show off your skills and abilities to their best advantage. If you have to stumble around for the answer to a question or apologize for not bringing the right samples, you interrupt the flow of the discussion and may lose the prospect's interest. It keeps coming back to one major consideration—being totally professional and businesslike.

## Presentation

Whether you like it or not, your actual presentation is a sales pitch. You're not trying to hustle used cars, but you are trying to sell a particular service. It's best to avoid an attempt to con your client and to rely on a thorough but low-key presentation that spells out what you can do for him and what you expect in return.

The logical place to start is with a description of the services you can provide, whether they be limited to the writing or expanded to include all aspects of a project from initial design through to the printed product. Your samples are your ammunition! As you page through the sample book with the client, explain a few of the more appropriate projects you've done, describing how you approached them, the problems you faced, and the things you did to turn out work of the highest possible quality. Don't be ashamed to show a few things that didn't turn out as well as they should have, but be prepared to discuss the reasons.

I keep a few samples of documents that proved miserable failures, and I use them to illustrate what can happen when someone who is not a professional writer decides to exercise authority in overruling the advice that a company is paying premium rates to receive. Be careful, however, to avoid disparaging remarks about a previous employer or another client. Such remarks do not make a good impression and leave a prospect feeling that you might say the same things about him.

In describing sales calls in Chapter 5, I mentioned the use of financial advantages as a way to get past some closed doors. The only time I've found it advisable to discuss financial considerations before actual capabilities is when I've had to use them as leverage. Normally I reserve any mention of finances until after I've completed my presentation of capabilities and services, and I never mention my rates until I'm ready to start actual negotiations.

Once you've convinced a prospect of your ability to handle his projects, you have to present the financial considerations. Talking money is the most difficult part of any meeting, and you have to put your charges into perspective for the client. Most executives are used to thinking in terms of employee salaries ranging somewhere around $8 to $10 an hour, so simply stating a consulting rate of $30 to $50 an hour can be a real shock.

It's usually better to prime the prospect by first telling him what he doesn't have to pay. For example, he doesn't have to pay vacation days, holidays, unemployment insurance, Social Security, sick leave, pension contributions, investment plans, or any of the other fringe benefits enjoyed by captive employees and paid by the companies. He also doesn't have to pay a salary for nonproductive working hours. I'm always careful to point out that my full-time employment averaged nearly four hours a day wasted on talking to fellow employees, stuffing envelopes, running errands, and just waiting for the day to end. I've also observed that many other employees run about the same average or slightly higher for their wasted time. Using a ratio of two-to-one for hours paid to hours effectively worked, I point out that the actual salary to support a captive employee can be twice the hourly rate quoted; i.e., $16 to $20 per hour without fringe benefits.

By the time all of the fringe benefits, training costs, and miscellaneous costs are included, that full-time employee may be costing the company as much as $25 or more for every hour of actual productive time.

From that point, it's easy to demonstrate that a $30 an hour consulting rate paid only for time actually spent on a project is economical from the client's point of view. To clinch the argument, other advantages include a fresh outsider's view of the project to closely accommodate the end user's needs, new approaches to old problems, the availability of diverse experience, the avoidance of lay-off or termination problems when the project is completed, and so on. If the financial aspects are presented properly with emphasis on benefits to the client, few prospects will even flinch at the hourly consulting rate.

It's also effective to point out any cost-cutting measures used as a routine part of a project. This is even better when you can pull out a few examples and explain where money was wasted. One good area to demonstrate your concern with the client's costs is full-color printing. I've had clients who have insisted they wanted color printing when there was no color in the product. Since I believe in using color only when absolutely necessary, I proceed to offer alternatives such as limited two-color printing. When I outline the comparative prices, most clients immediately opt for the simpler printing method, and I have proved my interest in their budget by gaining them a cost reduction that can amount to half of the original estimate.

Once having sold the prospect on abilities and economies, the discussion of terms can commence. Since the prospect already should recognize your concern with keeping his costs as low as possible, you should have little trouble getting his agreement to your specified payment intervals, penalty clauses, and other contractual terms. Once he has verbally agreed to the major terms, you can present the written contract for signature. As soon as the prospect sees that written agreement, he may start to back off a bit and maybe hedge on what he's already agreed to. To soften the impact, you can stress that the written agreement is standard for all clients, that it defines and locks down your rates for a specific period of time to protect him from an upcoming increase, and that it only obligates him to pay for projects assigned. If the agreement does not obligate the client to assign any projects, it allows him an escape route by not giving you any work. Your interest is to make certain that you are paid for any work you do get.

The one major stumbling block in a contract such as the one I've outlined in Chapter 3 is that it doesn't allow the client to avoid paying for work he doesn't use. That is the one consideration that usually draws a question, and it's necessary to state that you do not intend to give him that right. Your justification is that your time is your income and that many projects may never be used because clients cancel their programs. You can explain that you cannot afford to let that happen, but that you will do everything possible to make a project acceptable within the limitations of the information you are provided. I state that I will correct any problems that are my fault at no additional charge, but any attributable to a client's misinformation or changes will be billed at the full rate.

If a client continues to balk at the written agreement, it's best to avoid doing business with him. If your terms are reasonable and are acceptable to most other clients, the one who is reluctant to sign most likely is the one who hopes to get the work done and then avoid paying for it. On the two occasions when that has happened to me, I've simply walked out the door and ended all discussion there and then. I'd rather not acquire a client of that type than to spend a lot of time on a project and then not get paid.

## CONTINUING RELATIONSHIPS

The duration and profitability of a consultant-client relationship is largely a function of how well you live up to your initial image. This means that once you have established a professional and businesslike appearance, you must act accordingly throughout all future dealings with the client.

Your integrity and reputation must be spotless. When you promise to do a job, you have to get it done. When you commit to a deadline, you must meet the date specified. If you give an estimate, try to make it an honest estimate that you won't have to overrun later; it's better to lose an assignment or two by overestimating than to consistently bill charges higher than your estimate and perhaps lose clients entirely.

It's important to refuse assignments that you can't handle. If a project appears to be beyond your capabilities, tell the client. You can offer to try, but you don't want the client waiting indefinitely for something you know you may not be able to deliver. The same holds true for a project that constitutes a conflict of interest between two clients. One or the other (or both) should be refused to prevent future problems. If you undertake two conflicting assignments, say the advertising brochures for competing companies, you open the door to accusations of unethical behavior and may be accused of pirating proprietary information.

In either case, it should be the client's option to use your services if you don't withdraw them completely, and he should be advised of any circumstances that might inhibit your performance on his behalf.

If you do have to refuse or withdraw from an assignment, make an effort to locate someone else who can take on the project. There may be a possibility of subcontracting a particular job, or you can at least lead the client to an individual who can take care of the immediate needs. A lot of free-lancers hesitate to make such references for fear of losing a client permanently. But I've found that it serves to keep people happy and to eventually generate even more work. A client referred to somebody else is far more likely to call back at a future date than one who is just left hanging with the task of finding help on his own. I also keep a file of information on currently active free-lancers in my area, using it to provide referrals for companies calling about projects in which I have no interest. Again, it's good public relations, and the companies remember my assistance at a later time when their requirements are more closely aligned with my own interests and abilities.

Many people needing the help of a free-lance consultant have little idea of what the job might actually require. As a result, there may be many possible alternatives, some of which are more expensive than others. Of course, the consultant can choose the most expensive route and probably put a little more money in his pocket for the one assignment. On the other hand, sacrificing a few dollars to adopt the least expensive method can improve repeat business. Still other methods can shift the expenses from one pocket to another.

For example, recommending a large piece be typed on over-sized pages for reduction to standard size in printing is a way to cut printing costs by using less paper and fewer press runs. However, it also increases the amount of work necessary to prepare the camera-ready art. If you are the one preparing the camera-ready art, proposing this to a client could divert more money into your business and can be made quite attractive if it still saves the client some money on the total costs. At the same time you're increasing your own profits, you're impressing the client with a concern for his budget and almost guaranteeing that he's going to come back to you for the next assignment.

Throughout all your dealings with buyers and clients, maintaining a truly professional attitude is one of the best ways to assure continued survival. Your reputation should be as untarnished as possible.

# 7

# The Writer vs. the Tax Man

Free-lancers draw an inordinate amount of attention from the Internal Revenue Service, largely due to the possibility of not declaring all money received as income. Filing Schedule C (Form 1040) to declare a profit or loss from a sole proprietorship automatically raises IRS suspicions. Operating a free-lance business increases those suspicions dramatically. To compound the problem, Schedule C contains the question, "Did you deduct expenses for an office in your home?" A "yes" answer to that question makes the tax return even more suspect because the IRS has specific restrictions on qualifying a home office as a business expense.

Although it's not practical to summarize all of the IRS requirements and restrictions in this book, there are certain considerations that are of particular concern to a free-lance writer. Specifically, these are the requirements for bookkeeping, declaring all income, available deductions, an office at home, equipment depreciation, investment credits, estimating taxes in advance, self-

161

employment tax, and manuscript losses. For simplicity, I am assuming a sole proprietorship organization for the business. Unless otherwise noted, excerpts are taken from the IRS *Tax Guide for Small Business*. Since I am neither a tax lawyer nor an accountant, I can only point out problem areas and report some of the comments I've read or heard over the years. I cannot give legal advice, nor do I intend to do so.

Advice received directly from the IRS is not necessarily binding or enforceable in a court of law. Advice received by calling one of the IRS information numbers is particularly dangerous because the IRS is under no obligation to honor their statements at a later date. Even the information contained in the IRS tax guides and instruction sheets is no protection against an auditor's decisions that can be based on completely different provisions of the tax law.

In short, you can assume that there is no right way to complete an IRS form. No matter how closely you follow the instructions, an auditor can, if he wishes, counter the procedure you follow with a contrary set of rules neatly tucked away in some forgotten volume of tax law. The best you can do is to complete the forms as honestly as you can, recognizing the major restrictions and regulations. It's also necessary to remember that the burden of proof is on you, not on the IRS. The civil-law concept of "innocent until proven guilty" does not always apply in dealing with the IRS.

## BOOKKEEPING REQUIREMENTS

Major accounting systems have been described in Chapter 3. Accurate and complete records are essential to proving your tax liability and the accuracy of your statements to the IRS.

> You must keep records to determine your correct tax liability. Regardless of your bookkeeping system, your records must be permanent, accurate, complete, and must clearly establish income, deductions, credits, employee information, etc. The law does not require any particular kind of records. . . .

> You are required to keep the books and records of your business

available at all times for inspection by Internal Revenue officers. The records must be retained as long as their contents may become material in the administration of any Internal Revenue law.

Records supporting items on a tax return should be retained until the statute of limitations for that return expires. Ordinarily, the statute of limitations for an income tax return expires 3 years after the return is due to be filed or 2 years from the date the tax was paid, whichever occurs later. However, in many cases, the taxpayer should retain all records indefinitely. . . .

These statements establish the need for developing a good bookkeeping system, no matter how small or large your business may be. Since a free-lancer's tax returns already are suspect, inadequate records of receipts and expenditures can be a disaster should the return be audited.

The need for accuracy and completeness is almost self-explanatory. Every dollar received or spent to maintain the operation should be recorded to show the amount, the source of a payment received, the recipients of expenditures paid out, the reason for an expenditure, and the type of proof (receipt, check, credit card, etc.). It is necessary to be able to prove expenses listed as deductions, so some form of written proof should be available for even the most minor items like pencils or erasers.

The requirement for permanent records makes it necessary to follow certain procedures. First, the books should be permanently bound in such a manner that pages cannot be removed easily. Looseleaf notebooks or pads of paper do not constitute appropriate records. Most office-supply stores stock a variety of record-keeping books, the best of which use a two-page spread for each calendar week. One page is devoted to listing the expenses, with a provision for categorizing them according to the type of expense. The opposite page provides a list of categories where totals may be entered for the current week alone, the year up to the beginning of the week (carried from the previous week's entries), and the total to the end of the week. The columns then are totalled to provide both the expenses to date for each category and the overall business expense incurred. The same page also provides room to enter payments received and carries a running total of the receipts to date. Additions done across the page and down the columns provide an automatic double check of the calculations since the results obtained in either direction should lead to the same totals.

Keeping permanent records also implies that they must be recorded in ink. Pencil entries are not acceptable in an IRS audit. Erasures are not acceptable either; corrections should be made by crossing out the erroneous entry with a single line, not by obliterating the entry with a covering of ink or correction fluid. Corrections made by erasure or complete obliteration are highly suspect in any audit.

You may choose either single- or double-entry bookkeeping. The single-entry system is the simplest method and is the one most often used by free-lancers and other small businesses. However, it lacks the built-in checks and balances that are found in the double-entry system. Nevertheless, double-entry bookkeeping can be a real burden because of its complexity, and it usually shows up only in corporate business structures where there are needs for recording more complex information.

> **Single-entry bookkeeping** is a partially complete system of accounts in that it usually concentrates only on the profit and loss statement and not the balance sheet. While this system has its limitations, it may be used effectively by one starting out in a small business. A single-entry system can be a relatively simple one, which records the flow of income and expense. Through the use of a daily summary of cash receipts, a monthly summary of receipts, and a monthly disbursements journal, this system can be used to record income and expenses adequately for tax purposes. . . .

> **Double-entry bookkeeping** usually is the preferable method for business records. This system makes use of journals and ledgers; transactions are entered first in a journal, and then summary totals of the transactions (usually monthly) are posted to the appropriate ledger accounts. Ledger accounts are of five

types: income, expense, asset, liability, and net worth. Income and expense accounts are closed on the basis of the annual accounting period; asset, liability, and net worth accounts are maintained on a permanent basis. . . .

Few free-lancers have the time or inclination to deal with double-entry bookkeeping unless they hire a CPA. The single-entry system is simple enough for most individuals to handle themselves, and the weekly bookkeeping record already described is an easy method of maintaining adequate single-entry records.

If you employ others in your business, you also must withhold income, Social Security, and unemployment taxes, and you must keep records of those withholdings and payments to the IRS for a minimum of four years. The procedure can become quite involved, but it affects few free-lancers unless they develop a consulting-type business that grows to require additional full-time employees. Since most free-lancers would probably choose to subcontract rather than employ additional people, IRS regulations governing employers can be disregarded.

## DECLARING INCOME

The matter of declaring all items of income is the chief concern of the IRS in examining a free-lancer's tax returns. It's easy to forget or to deliberately omit listing $5 payments for quips and fillers sold to publishers, but the omission of even a single dollar of income is strictly viewed as an attempt at tax evasion. The IRS permits you to take steps that avoid the payment of unnecessary taxes, but they take a dim view of outright evasion.

If you are a regular contributor to a publisher or are dealing with a client as a consultant, your buyer ordinarily files a nonemployee compensation report to the IRS on Form 1099. You should receive a copy of any such filing, but some buyers have been known to forget to send your copy. If you deal with a large number of people, it's not always practical to run down every past buyer to check whether they sent you a copy. Form 1099 looks very much like an employee's annual W-2 form except that it lists fees, commissions, and other compensations without any withholdings for tax liabilities. If your declared gross income on Schedule C is less than the total of the payments indicated on the 1099 forms received by the IRS, an audit is almost unavoidable.

A certain conflict inevitably arises since a buyer may include his payments in late December of one taxable year, while you use a cash accounting method and don't list the income until received in January of the following year. I've even had a few buyers who dated checks in December to get their deductions in one year, but didn't mail them out until February or March to protect their cash flows. In either event, there may be a substantial difference between your recorded gross income and the IRS determination of payments made to you. If enough buyers don't file Form 1099, it may go unnoticed because the IRS total is less than your total, but you should be prepared to explain the situation and to document when and where you recorded any discrepancies.

The IRS uses very specific definitions of what constitutes a business, an income, and a profit. By IRS definition, a pursuit not showing a profit may not qualify as a business, thus losing eligibility for deductions of expenses incurred. Just a few of the applicable provisions are:

> A business is a pursuit carried on for livelihood or for profit. For a pursuit to be recognized as a business, a profit motive must be present and some type of economic activity must be involved. . . .

> An activity is considered a business if it is entered into and carried on in good faith for the purpose of making a profit. Thus, a profit making activity (a business) must be distinguished from an activity engaged in purely for personal satisfaction.

> Two characteristic elements of a business are regularity of activities and transactions, and the production of income. If, in a given year, no income or a small amount of income is coupled with expenditures that produce a loss, there may be a question as to whether a business was carried on in that year.

These provisions can be troublesome for a new business that may take several years to become established and show a profit.

They are a particular problem for a part-time free-lancer who cannot demonstrate a business intent other than as the difference between money received and money paid out. The full-time free-lancer at least has records of office equipment and similar items that help support his claim to a business activity. Similarly, the part-timer may have other sources of income that allow the IRS to view his pursuit as a hobby, while the full-timer can demonstrate that he has no regular employer and thus relies on his free-lance income for his livelihood.

The IRS further complicates the matter by defining when a profit must be shown:

> Absence of income in itself does not prevent you from deducting the ordinary and necessary expenses directly connected with or pertaining to your activity that constitutes a trade, business or profession. . . .

> An activity is presumed to be engaged in for profit if it produces a profit in any 2 out of 5 consecutive years unless the Internal Revenue Service establishes to the contrary. . . .

In 1975, I called an IRS information number for clarification of some details. During that call, I was informed that the IRS would not consider my pursuit a business until after I had shown a profit for one year, and that I would not be able to deduct any expenses until I had shown such a profit. That was a clear disagreement with the foregoing definition which allows a loss in any three of five consecutive years (including the first three years). That serves to illustrate the unreliability of information received from the IRS, but it also points out the problems you can expect in trying to identify exact requirements. Assuming that the tax guide is correct, you can show a business loss for the first three years, but you had better show a profit for the next two. I have known people in various businesses who have gotten away with showing a loss for many years in succession, but they are playing a dangerous game.

Of course, you can do what you want as long as you don't get caught. But if you do get caught, you could be in a situation in which the business is declared a hobby for personal satisfaction, and the costs of operating the business are eliminated as deductions. Done retroactively, this could result in large tax payments, penalties, and interest due and payable immediately. It could open up the possibility of tax-evasion charges. Furthermore, it is possible to wind up in a situation that has you receiving payments that must be declared as income, being ineligible to deduct the actual costs of earning that income, and paying taxes on what may be a net loss instead of a profit. A complicated IRS system of evaluating deductions in such a case allows the IRS considerable flexibility in deciding what you can and cannot deduct if you lose the business qualification.

> . . . You may not use losses from an activity not engaged in for profit to offset income from other sources. Generally, expenses of an activity not engaged in for profit may be deducted only to the extent of earnings from that activity.

> These deductions are allowed only in the following order, only to the following extent, and only if you elect to itemize your deductions on Schedule A (Form 1040).

> First, amounts allowable as deductions during the tax year, which would be allowable without regard to whether the activity giving rise to the deductions was engaged in for profit, are allowable to the full extent after taking into account any limitations or exceptions on the deductibility of such amounts. . . .

> Second, other expenses allowable as business expenses for an activity engaged in for profit, but only if such deductions do not result in an adjustment to the basis of property, are allowed only to the extent the gross income attributable to the activity exceeds the deductions allowed or allowable under the first category.

> Third, depreciation and other deductions that involve adjustments to the basis of property are allowed only to the extent that

the gross income attributable to such activity exceeds the deductions allowed or allowable under the first and second categories.

What this boils down to is a sequential application of deductions. Assume that you have lost your business qualification by not showing a profit after four years of operation and that you have $18,000 of income from some other source such as a spouse's full-time employment. Also assume that you have invested a considerable amount of money in office furnishings that include an expensive word processing system. Now, if you suddenly sell a manuscript for $2,000, you have to declare that amount as income. After applying your personal nonbusiness deductions to your total income, you have to derive a pro rata income from the manuscript as a proportion of your total income. The manuscript value would be 10% of a $20,000 total income, so 10% of your nonbusiness deductions would be applied to the $2,000.

Assuming the balance then is $1,500, you then can apply nonproperty deductions such as paper, postage, etc., against that amount but you may not be able to apply deductions attributed to other unsold manuscripts. Assuming you can apply $500 of deductions to the $1,500 manuscript balance, you then have $1,000 against which to apply your property deductions.

Now assume that your normal equipment depreciation would total $3,500 per year. Only $1,000 of that could be applied as a deduction, leaving you a cost of $2,500 that cannot be deducted from your overall income but that still counts as part of the costs of producing and selling that one manuscript. As if that's not bad enough, the costs you incur probably have to be prorated as the proportion of the manuscript actually sold to the total number of manuscripts produced whether sold or not. If that one manuscript amounts to only 5% of the total work you turned out in a year, only 5% of your expenses and depreciation might be allowed as deductions. This could leave you having to pay tax on at least part of the $2,000, even though your costs of producing all your manuscripts far exceeds the value of that one sale.

It's also important to remember that the IRS requires all income to be declared, regardless of the source or the nature of the receipts. If a publisher wants to pay you with live chickens, those chickens have a market value that must be declared as income. The IRS also has regulations concerning when certain types of income must be declared. The following excerpts from the tax guide are offered without further comment.

> Any income you receive, regardless of its source and whether it is in cash, property, or services, must be reported on your tax return, unless it is specifically excluded by law. In addition to the gross income derived from your trade or business, your tax return must also reflect gross income from any other source. This includes but is not limited to: Compensation for services, including fees, commissions, and similar items. . . .

> **Business income** arises from your business activity whenever there is a sale of your product or services in the ordinary course of business. . . .

> **Property or services.** Income received in the form of property or services must be included in income to the extent of its fair market value on the date received. . . .

> Advance payments for services to be performed by the end of the next succeeding tax year under an agreement (written or otherwise) can be deferred from income until earned through performance of services. However, you must be an accrual-method taxpaper to defer such advance payments and you may not defer them beyond the year following the year of receipt. . . . [author's note: this could be appropriate for book advances received contingent upon delivery of an acceptable manuscript.]

## BUSINESS DEDUCTIONS

Without getting involved in the special considerations afforded to corporations, the free-lance writer has quite a few deductions available. It's not practical to list and describe every possible deduction, and the deductions actually used vary from one business to another. However, it is useful to list some of the more important ones, with an observation or two pertaining to restrictions that may apply. Note that any items attributed to an office at home are subject to severe restrictions, and I'll describe those difficulties in a later section of this chapter. Before actually treating a particular expense as a legitimate deduction, you should examine the applicable instructions and information sheets that can be obtained from the IRS.

1. Accounting costs. Hiring or contracting a CPA to do your accounting is a legitimate and deductible expense. Paying to have your tax returns prepared also is deductible, but only the business forms are deductible as business expenses; costs for preparing the personal part of a tax return are not a legitimate business cost. Purchases of bookkeeping records, journals, and ledgers are deductible.

2. Advertising. Expenditures for media space, preparing an advertisement, and preparing and printing letterheads, client lists, and brochures are deductible.

3. Transportation. Costs of public transportation are deductible provided adequate records are kept and that the business nature of the trip can be proven. Costs that are reimbursed by a client or publisher may be listed as expenses only if they also are listed as income. Automobile expenses, including parking fees, also are deductible. Actual costs of operating an automobile are deductible as a ratio of business use to total use; this requires accurate cost records and a determination of the percentage of use that is business oriented. Alternatively, automobile costs may be treated as a fixed cost per business mile driven (the allowance per mile changes annually according to IRS guidelines).

4. Entertainment. The allowable deductions for entertaining a client, publisher, or other business contact have been

sharply curtailed by the IRS. Qualifying such expenses for deduction has been made quite difficult, and the current laws and regulations should be checked each time a return is filed.

5. Supplies. Normal operating supplies such as pens, paper, typewriter ribbons, and so on are deductible expenses. However, the IRS requires that the cost of any such items be reduced by the value of any items removed for personal use. If you are buying something like paper for both business and personal use, it is advisable to make separate purchases and obtain separate receipts.

6. Office expenses. Costs incurred for photocopying and similar office-type expenses are deductible if incurred for business reasons. Copying a manuscript prior to mailing or delivering it to a prospective buyer is a legitimate office expense. Other expenses may include file folders, index cards, address books, diaries, and similar items not associated with one particular project or assignment.

7. Taxes. Taxes paid are deductible, including sales taxes on items purchased for business use. Sales taxes collected from a buyer are treated as income when collected and a deductible expense when paid to the local taxing authority. The Self-employment Tax (Social Security) is *not* deductible under any circumstance.

8. Postage. The postage for mailing manuscripts, sending letters, and conducting mass-mailing campaigns is deductible. However, accurate records should be kept and receipts obtained whenever possible. Don't forget to include any prepaid return postage for manuscripts and other materials in your computation of costs under this category.

9. Reference materials. Most books and magazines obtained for reference use are deductible expenses. However, some

items such as dictionaries, encyclopedias, and specialized texts used over a period of several years should be treated as depreciable property and not as one-time expenses in the years of purchase. Simple practicality may dictate setting a dollar value below which the item is treated as a one-time expense and above which the item is treated as depreciable property.

10. Equipment rentals. Equipment rented or leased for business use can be treated as an actual expense when incurred. Equipment purchased outright and having a useful life of several years must be depreciated over its entire life.

11. Repairs. The cost of repairing a piece of business equipment to restore its usefulness is deductible when incurred. However, special considerations are required if the repair procedure adds to the actual value of the equipment and, thus, constitutes an improvement to a capital investment. The costs of service contracts for business equipment are deductible expenses when incurred.

12. Rent and utilities. For an office outside the home, the actual expenses for rental, electricity, water, sewer, natural gas, heating oil, telephone service, and insurance are fully deductible when paid. Special restrictions are imposed by the IRS on having an office at home, and the requirements must be satisfied before any of these deductions can be claimed. If you can qualify for deducting the cost of an office at home, you then must determine the percentage of the home used for business purposes on the basis of both physical area and amount of time involved. That percentage then applies to the *interest* on the home mortgage to become the rental cost; it never applies to the principal portion of the mortgage or to amounts held in escrow for taxes and insurance. The same percentage then is applied to all utilities, property taxes, and homeowner's

insurance policies to determine the amounts deductible for those items.

13. Interest. The interest costs incurred for business indebtedness such as commercial loans are fully deductible when incurred. Remember that mortgage interest on a home used partially for business must be qualified and then is deductible only to the proportion actually used for the business.

14. Miscellaneous expenses. A wide variety of other deductions may be taken for items such as professional memberships and dues, license fees, packaging materials, delivery expenses, subcontractor's payments, legal expenses, bad debts not collected, etc. As long as you retain your qualification as a business, the costs you incur to operate that business generally are deductible in one way or another.

The preceding list is certainly not all-inclusive, but it does provide a starting place to examine what may or may not qualify as a legitimate deduction to avoid paying excess tax without actually evading payment. The tax laws are subject to continual change, with some items being added and others being removed from the list of available deductions. As a result, you should order all pertinent information from the IRS every year before starting to work on your return. A complete stack of IRS information measures about three inches thick and requires a lot of intensive study. Even if you have a CPA doing your work, it's your signature on the bottom of the return and your responsibility for the accuracy of the return. Since the accountant's abilities are limited by the information you provide, you should still make it a point to know what you can and cannot claim on the return; if the accountant makes a mistake, he's not the one who's going to pay the penalties or go to jail.

## AN OFFICE AT HOME

Until the mid-1970s, one of the most attractive business deductions for a free-lancer was the office at home. By charging off a portion of the home expenses for business use, individuals were able to reduce their tax obligations significantly. The available deductions included a percentage of the mortgage interest, utilities, repairs and maintenance, trash collection, and so on. In the case of mortgage interest, bigger savings could be achieved by deducting the applicable percentage as a business expense on Schedule C rather than by taking it as a personal deduction on Schedule A.

The possibilities were so attractive that many people in many occupations began to claim offices at home. Insurance agents, sales representatives, corporate executives, and many others all claimed a percentage of their homes for studying paperwork, storing files, writing letters, and hundreds of other tasks associated with making a living in their primary occupation or with a second income from "moonlighting."

Then the IRS closed the loophole! Regulations were put into effect to eliminate the deductions for individuals working in a job and keeping an area at home to do work such as reading professional journals. At the same time, moonlighting to earn additional income also was eliminated from consideration for home-office deductions, essentially penalizing those who need to earn additional income just to keep pace with the cost of living. For regular employees earning their primary incomes from corporations, the change was annoying but not completely disastrous. For free-lancers, the change and subsequent enforcement of the regulations had a major impact, particularly on writers and others just trying to get established. They lost a major portion of their deductible expenses.

The IRS makes some very specific statements concerning the use of your home in your work, but their application of those statements may not always be uniform. Again, the fastest way of summarizing the restrictions is to quote directly from the IRS tax information, in this case from IRS Publication 17, *Your Federal Income Tax*. Additional information is available in IRS publication 587, *Business Use of Your Home*, which is recommended reading for all free-lancers.

If you use a portion of your home *regularly and exclusively* for certain business purposes, you may deduct a pro rata portion of the operating and depreciation expense on your home.

**Qualifying business use.** The allocable business expenses are deductible only if the portion of your home is used *regularly and exclusively:*

(1) As your principal place of business;

(2) As a place of business that is used by your patients, clients, or customers in meeting and dealing with you in the normal course of your trade or business, or

(3) As a separate structure used in your trade or business and not attached to the dwelling unit.

If the regular and exclusive business use specified here is in connection with your service as an employee, the use must be *for the convenience of your employer,* and not merely appropriate and helpful in your employment.

The business use of your home must be directly related to or used in connection with your trade or business. Activity which does not constitute a trade or business does not entitle you to any deduction for business use of your home. . . .

*The use of a portion of your home for both personal and business purposes* does not meet the exclusive test and any expenses attributable to business use are not deductible. . . . Thus, if you use the den of your home to write legal briefs, prepare tax returns, or perform similar activities as well as for personal purposes, no deduction will be allowed for expenses in connection with the use of the residence.

The dual requirement for regular and exclusive use as your principal place of business is the bugaboo for the free-lancer. To be the principal place of business, the office at home must be your primary source of income. As a writer, this means that you must make more than 50% of your gross income from free-lance writing—a condition nearly impossible for part-timers and beginning writers. If you make 50% or less of your income from your free-lance activities, the interpretation is that your other activities, salaried or not, are your principal income and, thus, your principal business. The result is an automatic loss of the business deductions for the office in your home. Note that losing those deductions doesn't mean losing the ones for supplies, equipment, postage, and other expenses directly incurred to prepare a manuscript. Instead, it means losing the pro rata deductions for mortgage interest, electricity, heating fuel, insurance, water, sewer, etc.

The test for exclusive use can be even more tricky. The word *exclusively* used in the IRS context means exactly that—no other activity can take place in the area designated for office use. The simple act of hanging an item of personal clothing in the office closet could lose you the qualification for the business deduction. Many tax-advice columns in newspapers have advised against the practice of simply designating some portion of the kitchen, living room, or family room as an office. Such an area is subject to other uses and does not qualify for a deduction. The usual view of what constitutes a qualifying office is that it must be a room of the house that can be closed off to other activities by a door, that it may not be used for any family purposes including the storage of personal possessions, and that it be used regularly in the business activity and not merely set aside and left unused.

There is one consideration, however, for which there is no clear-cut solution. What happens when the business outgrows the area set aside exclusively for the pursuit? For example, assume that an otherwise unused bedroom of a house is devoted to the business solely and exclusively and that all other qualifying conditions are met for that room. Then the business requires expansion for a combination of reasons such as installing a large drafting table, setting up a word-processing system, providing an area to meet with consulting clients, and so on. When the actual office itself cannot accommodate these items, can other parts of the house, not necessarily sealed off from other activities, be added to the allocated office space? Advice from different sources provides different opinions. Some say you still are limited to the original office space. Others say you can add a pro rata portion of the other areas to the original space allocation as long as the original space remains qualified. IRS advisors are themselves uncertain and deliberately vague on this point, and much may depend upon whether the business is conducted on a full- or part-time basis with the full-time business that shows a profit more easily entitled to add the extra space.

The allocation of expenses associated with an office in your home is accomplished most easily by comparing the number of square feet of floor space qualifying as an office to the total number of square feet in the entire house. Dividing the first by the second gives a ratio or percentage of the house used for business purposes. The same thing can be accomplished by dividing the number of rooms used for business by the total number of rooms in the house, but this method may not be a true indicator of actual office area when rooms are of different sizes. Once the ratio is determined, it is applied to all eligible expenses to determine the portion of those expenses that can be charged off as business deductions. Some of the expenses that can be treated in this manner are mortgage interest (not principal), electricity, natural gas or fuel oil, homeowner's insurance, home repairs affecting the business area, property taxes, telephone service, water, sewer, and trash collection. If you meet clients at your home, you may even be able to take a portion of expenses such as landscaping, provided such expenses enhance your business by making it more attractive to new clients.

If you can qualify, the deductions and tax savings for an office at home can be surprising. Assume that about 32% of a house is devoted to a consulting business, that a $32,000 mortage is financed at about 9% interest, and that utilities and expenses are about average. A reasonable estimate of the allowable pro rata deductions could be $1,600 for rent (mortgage interest), $230 for electric and gas utilities, $65 for homeowner's insurance, $240 for property taxes, $40 for telephone service, $95 for water and sewer, and $20 for trash collection. These total to $2,290, meaning that nearly $2,300 of your free-lance earnings would not be subject to income taxes. If your federal tax rate is about 20%, you can save about $450 in federal taxes alone.

It's interesting to note that the presence of the business itself may not influence your expenditures for the deductible items. Your home mortgage has to be paid whether the business is there or not. Homeowner's insurance, property taxes, local telephone service, water and sewer, and trash collection are costs you incur whether or not you have a business on the premises. Electricity and heating fuel may be increased by operating the business at home, but a substantial portion would be incurred anyway. However, the IRS does not require that the business increase the costs to make them deductible, so the pro rata amounts that can be charged off are just money in your pocket.

## EQUIPMENT DEPRECIATION

Depreciation is the means of recovering the cost of tangible property used for business or trade purposes. Items such as typewriters, desks, and cameras all have a useful life, and they decline in value from year to year. Their costs cannot be deducted as one-time expenses when purchased and must be recovered in smaller yearly amounts over the entire useful life.

Since depreciation can get to be a very complex subject, thorough treatment and explanation is well beyond the scope of this book. The IRS *Tax Guide for Small Business* devotes many pages of small type to the subject, describing what is and is not depreciable, the amounts allowed, the determination of a useful life and a salvage value at the end of that life, the additional allowances for first-year depreciation, and the methods of computation.

Depreciation of assets is an important tax deduction for all businesses including free-lance writing, and you should become thoroughly familiar with the applicable sections of the tax guide. The IRS descriptions are difficult to understand, but the examples they provide can help you make the necessary decisions regarding things such as which method of depreciation to use. The situation is further complicated because different pieces of equipment may be depreciated by different means, using equal yearly amounts for one item and accelerated methods for others.

Additionally, there are provisions for changing from an accelerated to a slower method of depreciation partway through the life of an item.

It's not my purpose here to define the requirements and procedures, but merely to alert you to their existence. Beginning freelancers, in particular, are apt to be unaware of depreciation or to ignore its importance to the way they handle their deductions. Depreciation not claimed when applicable cannot be recovered later and could result in paying some unnecessary taxes. In reading through the IRS tax guide, certain statements seem particularly important to the writer, so I'll excerpt them here without commenting on them individually. I leave it to you to obtain a copy of the tax guide and study the information therein, keeping in mind that the depreciation provisions are applicable to all of your tangible office and business equipment.

> . . . If income-producing property or property used in a trade or business has a limited useful life that can be determined or reasonably estimated, you may deduct its cost or other basis over its useful life. . . . The cost of property with a useful life of more than one year, such as buildings, furniture, machinery, . . . may not be deducted entirely in one year. . . .

> . . . The depreciation deduction is allowed only for property you use in a trade or business or hold for the production of income. . . .

> *If property is used for both business and personal purposes,* depreciation is deductible only to the extent that the property is used in your business. . . .

> *Professional libraries* are depreciable if their value will diminish. The cost of technical books, journals, and services that have a usefulness of one year or less is deducted as business expense. . . . [Author's note: a "business expense" is deducted all at once in the year incurred.]

Any reasonable method that is consistently applied may be used in computing depreciation. The three methods most generally used are: (1) Straight-line; (2) Declining-balance; and (3) Sum of the years-digits. . . .

*Straight-line method.* This method is the simplest for computing depreciation. Under this method, the cost or other basis of the property less its salvage value is deducted in equal annual amounts over the period of its estimated useful life. . . .

*Declining-balance method.* Under this method, the depreciation, which you take each year, is subtracted from the cost or other basis of the property before computing the next year's depreciation. The same depreciation rate applies to a smaller or declining balance each year. Thus, a larger depreciation deduction is taken for the first year and a gradually smaller deduction in succeeding years. . . .

*Sum of the years method.* Under this method, as a general rule, you apply a different fraction each year to the cost or other basis of each single asset account. . . . The denominator (bottom number) of the fraction, which remains constant, is the total of the digits representing the years of estimated useful life of the property. . . . The numerator (top number) of the fraction changes each year to represent the years of useful life remaining at the beginning of the year for which the computation is made. . . . [Author's note: this is the most complicated method but provides the best way of accelerating the depreciation and obtaining maximum deductions as soon as possible after the purchase.]

In selecting a method to apply to a particular item, it's useful to calculate the depreciations over the entire life with all three methods. Straight-line depreciation is a good choice when you want the same deduction each year, allowing you to predict an even level of deductions over a long term. The other methods are good when you want to obtain as large a deduction as possible and as soon as possible. Different methods are allowed for each item and for each group of items, but a method once selected must be applied consistently throughout the life of the item unless a change (usually only from accelerated to straight-line depreciation) is allowed.

Figure 8 compares the three methods of depreciation as they apply to the same piece of equipment. In this case, the item was purchased for $224.95 in August of 1980, had no salvage value, and was used 100% for business over seven years. Each tabulation lists the annual and actual depreciations (differing where a full year is not allowed), the additional 20% first-year depreciation allowed, and the number of tax dollars saved each year. Totals are presented for the allowable tax credit, dollar savings in taxes, and monthly tax costs incurred by delaying the purchase. Notice the difference in the annual depreciation amounts and the distribution of the deductions for the three methods.

Remember that items with a life of less than one year are not depreciable; you would not depreciate pencils, paper, typewriter ribbons, etc., but you would depreciate office furniture, typewriters, photographic equipment, tape recorders, and similar items.

## INVESTMENT CREDITS

An area frequently overlooked by free-lance writers is that of investment credits. Few free-lancers realize that purchases of typewriters, office furniture, word processors, cameras, and other depreciable business equipment may qualify for an actual credit on the federal income tax return. Some states also allow an investment credit.

Again, I must refer you to the IRS *Tax Guide for Small Business* for the details. However, I will point out that if you purchase new or used equipment or other property having a useful life of three years or longer and use it for your business, you may very well be entitled to the investment credit. This credit does not affect the normal depreciation deduction and is allowed separately and in addition to that deduction. Therefore, you can both deduct a portion of the purchase price and get a tax credit on the same item in the same year.

FIGURE 8. Comparative Depreciation Methods

## SUM-OF-YEARS METHOD FOR 7 YEARS INCLUDING ADD'L 20% 1ST YEAR DEPRECIATION

| Year | 1980 | 1981 | 1982 | 1983 | 1984 | 1985 | 1986 | 1987 |
|---|---|---|---|---|---|---|---|---|
| Full Yr Depr | 44.99 | 38.56 | 32.14 | 25.71 | 19.28 | 12.85 | 6.43 | |
| Reg Yr Depr | 18.75 | 42.31 | 35.88 | 29.46 | 23.03 | 16.60 | 10.18 | 3.75 |
| 1st Yr Depr | 44.99 | | | | | | | |
| Tax $ Saved | 22.95 | 15.23 | 12.92 | 10.60 | 8.29 | 5.98 | 3.66 | 1.35 |

| | | |
|---|---|---|
| Tax Credit | 22.50 | Total $ Saved 103.48 |
| First Year $ | 45.44 | Waiting Cost/Month 5.09 |

## DECLINING BALANCE METHOD @ 2X ST. LINE FOR 7 YEARS INCLUDING ADD'L 20% 1ST YEAR DEPRECIATION

| Year | 1980 | 1981 | 1982 | 1983 | 1984 | 1985 | 1986 | 1987 |
|---|---|---|---|---|---|---|---|---|
| Full Year Depr | 51.42 | 36.73 | 26.23 | 18.74 | 13.38 | 9.56 | 6.83 | |
| Reg Yr Depr | 21.42 | 45.30 | 32.35 | 23.11 | 16.51 | 11.79 | 8.42 | 3.98 |
| 1st Yr Depr | 44.99 | | | | | | | |
| Tax $ Saved | 23.91 | 16.31 | 11.65 | 8.32 | 5.94 | 4.24 | 3.03 | 1.43 |

| | | |
|---|---|---|
| Tax Credit | 22.50 | Total $ Saved 97.33 |
| First Year $ | 46.40 | Waiting Cost/Month 5.28 |

## STRAIGHT LINE METHOD FOR 7 YEARS INCLUDING ADD'L 20% 1ST YEAR DEPRECIATION

| Year | 1980 | 1981 | 1982 | 1983 | 1984 | 1985 | 1986 | 1987 |
|---|---|---|---|---|---|---|---|---|
| Full Yr Depr | 25.71 | 25.71 | 25.71 | 25.71 | 25.71 | 25.71 | 25.71 | |
| Reg Yr Depr | 10.71 | 25.71 | 25.71 | 25.71 | 25.71 | 25.71 | 25.71 | 15.00 |
| 1st Yr Depr | 44.99 | | | | | | | |
| Tax $ Saved | 20.05 | 9.26 | 9.26 | 9.26 | 9.26 | 9.26 | 9.26 | 5.40 |

| | | |
|---|---|---|
| Tax Credit | 22.50 | Total $ Saved 103.48 |
| First Year $ | 42.55 | Waiting Cost/Month 4.51 |

The actual amount of the federal investment credit ranges up to 10% of the purchase price, subject to certain dollar limitations and adjustments for the useful life of the property. Typically, the credit is figured as 10% of some fraction of the cost, with the fraction determined by the life of the item. A life of two years or less uses a zero fraction, so 10% of zero is zero. A life of three or four years applies the 10% credit to ⅓ of the cost. A life of five or six years applies 10% to ⅔ of the cost. A life of seven or more years applies 10% to the entire cost.

The importance of the investment credit is that it is treated as tax already paid to the government. Suppose you buy a $660 camera setup solely for use in your journalistic endeavors and that you expect the camera to have a useful life of seven years. You further assume that after seven years, the equipment could be sold for $100. For depreciation, your basis would be $560 ($660 less $100). Using straight-line depreciation without any additional first-year depreciation, you would be able to deduct $80 each year as a cost of doing business. In the year of purchase, you also would be eligible for the investment credit of 10% of the entire purchase price since the expected life is seven years. That credit would be $66 entered on Form 1040 and credited as tax paid in the same manner as employer's withholding taxes and estimated tax payments made earlier in the year are treated as credits. In a 20% tax bracket, each dollar of tax paid equals something like $5 earned, so the $66 credit shelters about $330 of your earnings from tax liability. Meanwhile, the $80 depreciation deduction saves you additional taxes of about $16 within the same tax bracket.

## ESTIMATING TAXES

The IRS requirement to estimate and pay your income tax in advance is an outright nuisance. You are required to file an estimate and make quarterly payments if your total income and self-employment tax liability exceeds $100. Incidentally, full-time employees also are obligated to estimate their taxes if the employer's withholding leaves the employee owing more than $100 at the end of the year.

The declaration of estimated tax for the coming year is required on the same day as filing the tax returns for the previous year. For example, if you file your 1981 tax returns on April 15, 1982, you must file your declaration of estimated income and tax for 1982 on the same date even though you haven't earned that money. Your estimated payments of taxes due for 1982 then would have to be made on or before April 15, June 15, and September 15, 1982, with a final payment due on January 17, 1983. You then would file your 1982 income tax return on April 15, 1983, as usual to recover any overpayments or to pay any balance due.

Failure to pay the estimated tax or paying too little estimated tax results in daily percentage penalties and the burden of trying to figure out how to complete Form 2210 for nonpayment penalties. If completing all of the regular schedules and the 1040 Form are difficult, the nonpayment penalty form is nearly impossible. The calculations involve quarterly allocations of income and deductions, calculations of excess tax carryovers or deficiencies, and the application of different quarterly interest rates on a daily basis from the date of delinquency to the date of payment. Filling out the form is a worse penalty than paying the interest.

The biggest problem is in trying to estimate how much you are going to earn before you earn it. Most writers find it very difficult to judge their earnings in advance during the first five years of their business operations. Even consultants have a fluctuating income that can vary widely from year to year. Even worse, you may start off the year with no income during the first two quarters and anticipating a loss for the year, and then have a burst of activity at the end of the year to invalidate your earlier estimate and necessitate an adjusted estimate.

There is no easy way around this problem other than to ignore estimating, pay the penalties when you file your taxes, and hope you can justify your actions to an IRS auditor if they decide to challenge you. The IRS doesn't particularly care what problems you have in making the estimate, they just want it done. Incidentally, there are no extensions on filing estimated tax declarations or the quarterly payments. They are either filed by the date specified or they are delinquent and subject to penalty.

## SELF-EMPLOYMENT TAX

Self-employment tax is the sole proprietorship's equivalent of Social Security except that the self-employed individual pays a rate about 2.1% higher than that withheld from an employee's salary. According to the IRS tax guide, "The self-employment tax is part of the system for providing social security coverage for persons who work for themselves."

If you have net earnings (a profit) from self-employment of $400 or more, you must file Schedule SE with your 1040 Form to compute the self-employment tax. About the only break you get here is that the tax is computed on net earnings from self-employment; i.e., after the business deductions have been subtracted. There have been rumors at various times about converting this to a tax on gross earnings before the deductions, but nothing has ever come of that.

Like Social Security withholding, the percentage of tax or the maximum dollar amount of taxable earnings (or both) increase every year. The 1978 rate was 8.1% of the first $17,700 of earnings. The 1979 rate was 8.1% of the first $22,900. By 1990, the rate is projected to be at least 9.75% of the first $66,900. Your ultimate retirement benefits are determined as a percentage of the maximum payments you make, so the farther away from the maximum you are, the lower your percentage of maximum benefits will be at retirement. Few free-lance writers can expect to continue increasing their annual earnings and self-employment taxes by nearly 30% a year to remain entitled to full retirement benefits, so they, like most other self-employed individuals, constantly lose ground in what they can expect to receive back at retirement.

The actual computation of self-employment tax is simple and straightforward. You take your net profit from Schedule C, enter it on Schedule SE, and pay the percentage on either the entire amount or the stated maximum amount, whichever is lower. If the maximum is at $22,900 and you had net earnings of $20,000, you apply the percentage to the $20,000. If you earned $30,000, you apply the percentage to only $22,900. Note that self-employment tax is on the profit from Schedule C, before taking standard or itemized personal deductions on Form 1040 or Schedule A.

## MANUSCRIPT LOSSES

There is an odd quirk to the tax laws. For income purposes, a writer's manuscripts are assigned a fair market value. Accrual-method accounting systems must show that value as income when the manuscript is produced. However, should a manuscript be lost, the market value cannot be taken as a deduction.

In Chapter 1, I mentioned the publisher who ceased operations and cost me some 660 puzzle manuscripts with a market value of $4,330. Even though the manuscripts were never returned and were unsalable to any other publisher, and even though I lost a substantial amount of my earnings, the IRS forbade me to take the value of those manuscripts as a deduction. In their eyes, my loss was limited to the cost of the paper and materials used to prepare the manuscripts, with no allowance for time or value. Since the costs already were included in the deduction of business expenses, the IRS assumed that no loss had taken place. Trying to treat the loss as a bad debt was disallowed on the basis that the manuscripts did not constitute actual merchandise for which any debt was owed.

This creates a real problem for a writer. He can spend vast amounts of his working time preparing materials only to have a publisher go out of business and leave him with nothing to show for his efforts. It also implies that there are going to be difficulties for a consultant trying to write off a nonpaying deadbeat as a bad debt, even when a substantial amount of the writer's own money is invested in the unpaid project.

Of course, the rationale is to keep writers from claiming losses for work they never intended to sell, since it would be possible to flood the market with manuscripts and then just write off the losses. Nevertheless, it's painful for a writer who assumes a good working relationship with a buyer only to find himself without a regular buyer and with no way of offsetting what may be direct and substantial losses.

## STAYING OUT OF TROUBLE

There is no guaranteed way to avoid trouble with the IRS. You may be audited purely at random or for a specific reason. All you can do is make the most honest effort possible to keep accurate records and follow instructions. An honest mistake is a lot less trouble than deliberate evasion of a regulation, but ignorance is no excuse in dealing with the IRS.

However, to avoid nonrandom audits, you should take care to avoid those things that may trigger the IRS computers into selecting your return. The most obvious is to avoid simple arithmetic errors. Carefully check your addition and subtraction, and that of any outside accountant; check every item and every calculation at least three times, preferably with an electronic calculator. Avoid rounding your numbers; your rounding technique may not be the same as that of the IRS computer, and rounding can cost you several dollars in excess tax (one accountant has told me that up to $15 in extra tax can be incurred just by rounding). Make it a point to carry all entries and calculations in dollars *and* cents.

The IRS computers score tax returns according to a formula that identifies high probability errors by looking for deductions unusually high for the overall income level; contributions are one area of particular concern. Don't make unusual claims unless you can document them thoroughly. If your return exceeds two or three of the computer's scoring indices, it will be selected for an audit. The IRS always watches for unreported income, and it is possible to be charged with tax evasion for not reporting all income, even if you overpay your taxes for some other reason.

If you are called for an audit, don't panic. Your notification may specify the area being audited, so unless otherwise directed, take only records pertaining to that area of interest. Don't volunteer information in areas other than that of specific concern; by doing so you open those areas to question. You don't need a lawyer to prepare your returns or for the audit, but you do need one if you wish to appeal the audit or if you are investigated for or are charged with a criminal tax violation.

Above all, remember that tax avoidance is legitimate, but tax evasion is illegal!

# 8

# Day-to-Day Operations

As a free-lancer, your daily operations are no less important than the procedures used to set up your business. It would be nice if all you had to worry about was writing, but that's rarely the case. Instead, you have to be a businessman first and a writer second, tending to all of the miscellaneous business chores before you can sit down at a typewriter and begin creating.

The portion of your time spent managing your business can easily exceed the portion available for actual writing. Consulting services, in particular, require a considerable overhead in time spent on negotiating contracts, conducting meetings, scheduling hours, invoicing assignments, collecting delinquent payments, coordinating vendors, and assigning subcontracts. All free-lancers, whether operating as consultants or not, have the every-day problems of bookkeeping, searching for new publishers or other buyers, and managing finances. You don't necessarily have spare time just because you don't have an assignment in progress. There's always something that should or could be done to fill those idle hours.

## PRACTICAL PROFESSIONALISM

If you think I've been harping on the subject of professionalism, you're absolutely right. And I'm not quite done with it yet. I've already presented the subject in terms of preparing and starting your business, establishing a business image, and conducting client-contact meetings. Now, it's necessary to examine the subject as it affects your daily operations.

If you're going to be a free-lancer or a consultant, you have to be 100% professional. Anything less is roughly equivalent to committing financial suicide. If your image or reputation are tarnished by unethical or unprofessional behavior, you lose clients, find prospects are unwilling to contract for your services, and experience a substantial loss of income. If word gets out that you don't live up to your promises, you might as well close down your free-lance business and go back to working for some corporation. Your publishers and clients have every right to expect a high standard of performance on your part, and if you burn them they'll not easily forget it.

### Meeting Deadlines

From an operational standpoint, the first and most critical requirement is that you deliver your work on time. Delivering early is even better. When you agree to provide a draft, manuscript, or camera-ready art by a certain date, there is no excuse for being late. If your client imposes late changes affecting the delivery date, it is up to you to advise him of the revised date. In some cases, the delivery date may be so critical that the buyer will do without those late changes simply to expedite the delivery of your materials. In other cases, the material may be critical, but the buyer may have to adjust typesetting, printing, or other schedules to accommodate a new delivery date.

In any event, the buyer is waiting for your delivery, and failure to meet a deadline can cause him enough problems to make him avoid using your work in the future. Publishers who issue assignments often schedule their production efforts prior to receiving a finished manuscript; a delay on your part causes innumerable other delays in production and may leave a publisher with an almost unfillable space. A consulting client waits on you to provide the materials he needs to launch a marketing campaign or to support the products he is ready to ship to his customers; delays cost him in losses of revenue from the actual or potential sales of his product that are postponed. Preparation of camera-ready art for brochures and similar pieces often requires advance press reservations for the printer; your delay may mean that the presses don't roll when scheduled and that your client may have to pay for the press time allocated to the job even though it wasn't used. At best, your delay causes other procedures down the line to be done on a rush basis, often with premium charges because of the rush.

## Refusing Assignments

The need to deliver committed assignments and deliver them on time implies refusing impossible or impractical assignments. You should never get in over your head by accepting work you know is beyond your capability. Similarly, you should never accept an assignment with a deadline that will be difficult to meet under ideal circumstances—the buyer may add more work to the assignment and make it impossible to meet the deadline. And, you should never take on more assignments than you feel you can handle comfortably.

It's difficult for a free-lancer to walk away from any assignment, but it's sometimes necessary to do so. Since the rule of feast or famine usually is in effect, it's possible to acquire too many projects too quickly and wind up in trouble on the delivery dates for all of them. Consultants have a particular problem in that their clients may tend to release information and assignments at the last possible moment, and if several long-term clients do so simultaneously, an overload situation can develop almost overnight.

Discussing delivery dates should be an integral part of negotiating every assignment. If you are already well loaded with work, the client should be advised of that fact, and delivery dates should be adjusted to accommodate your time availability. If the buyer cannot live with the dates you provide, it is better for both you and him if the assignment is given to someone else. Refusing an assignment is far better than disappointing a buyer when you are unable to deliver it on time.

## Terminating an Assignment

Refusing to take on a new assignment is an altogether different matter from bailing out of one already in progress. Refusing a new assignment usually does no harm to your reputation since most executives realize that everyone's work load and availability fluctuate with demand. However, terminating a project in work is extremely ill-advised. When you take a job, you make a personal and professional commitment that must be met. If doing so requires working 24 hours a day, sacrificing vacations and holidays, and disrupting family plans, you must do exactly that. Your reputation and integrity are at stake, and, as a result, your business itself is on the line.

I've been through a number of situations where I've contracted several apparently small projects for different clients, all to be done within the same general period of time. Then one or more assignments suddenly expanded due to client changes, immediately jeopardizing the dates on all of them. Under such situations, I had had no choice but to switch onto a 20-hour a day, 7-day a week schedule until the overload was relieved. That kind of schedule has extended for months on end as projects kept increasing in scope and complexity, yet I always consider the expanded work schedule far preferable to the alternative of aborting a project already committed. I get myself into those problems, so I can't justify charging the 100% rate premium for a rush job. Thus, I can charge only normal rates for late nights, Saturdays, Sundays, and holidays unless the client has requested the rush specifically.

About the only reason for quitting a project is an overall change in the scope of the assignment that takes it out of your realm of expertise. Sometimes what first appears to be a chore well within your capabilities suddenly takes on a completely new character as the client changes direction in mid-stream. Under that circumstance, it may be preferable to advise the client that you can't comply with the new directions and expect to do an acceptable job. If you then help him locate someone more suitable to that project, you can escape it without endangering your image or reputation. In fact, it's preferable to abort a project like this as soon as you discover you can't handle it adequately, rather than waste the client's time and money on efforts that are going to be less than satisfactory.

In my case, this usually happens when a project proposed as a straightforward technical assignment suddenly takes on the character of a powerful, consumer-oriented public relations task. Since I do not specialize in consumer-directed marketing and PR work, circumstances such as a technical brochure suddenly being retargeted for the general public as a PR piece force my withdrawal, although I do so quite reluctantly.

There has been one instance in which a client and I could not agree on the approach to be used in preparing some technical manuals. After I had put in a lot of time detailing precise procedures for operating the equipment, the client decided that he wanted to force his customers to sign up for expensive training sessions. To do that, he demanded that the information in the manual be minimized and that much of the pertinent information be eliminated so that the manual could not serve as a stand-alone operating guide. As a direct conflict with my philosophy on materials of that type, I resisted the idea and eventually terminated my efforts, feeling that my reputation would be better preserved by refusing to complete the job rather than turning out a piece of work that would violate my personal and professional principles.

The important point in any such termination, regardless of the reason, is to convince the client that his interests would be served better by the withdrawal. The trick is to convince him that someone else can do a better job on that one assignment, without jeopardizing the entire client-consultant relationship you may have built.

## Staying Accessible

All free-lancers and consultants have to be accessible to their publishers and clients at all times. Since the buyers' needs may develop or change suddenly, they must be able to contact you as quickly as possible.

One obvious provision is to install a telephone answering machine that enables callers to leave messages when you are away from your office. A client or publisher who tries to call several times over a span of days and gets no answer is apt to assume you've disappeared. It's quite likely that you may be running back and forth to meetings and vendors and just happened not to be at the office when the calls arrived. The answering machine allows you to receive the messages and respond appropriately, eliminating the danger of missing out on a good assignment just because you weren't home when the buyer called.

Vacations are a special problem. Being away from the office for one or more weeks increases the chances of missing an important assignment. I make it a point to send out notification letters to all existing clients and the editors of magazines to which I contribute regularly. The first notification is sent three months before the planned shutdown, advising the recipients of the date I expect to close, the date I intend to resume operation, and the cutoff date for receipt of new assignments. The cutoff date usually is a month before the actual closure to allow me to finish work in progress without becoming encumbered by new assignments. About a week before the cutoff date, I telephone each client and editor to remind them of the shutdown and to collect any last-minute jobs they may need done. At that time, I also give them a contact number for messages—someone who will know how to reach me for important matters and whom I will call each week to check for nonurgent messages. During my absence, that same contact will check my answering machine, collect the messages, and respond to any that seem important.

Since vacations typically are several years apart, this procedure does not inhibit normal work flows. It does, however, safeguard important contracts against loss resulting from a client's sudden inability to contact me. Of course, the vacation itself is subject to postponement or cancellation in the event of an urgent assignment or a sudden increase in the work load during the weeks just prior to the cutoff date. No matter how carefully the work load is projected and the vacation is scheduled, there remains an element of uncertainty that can upset even the best laid plans.

Remaining accessible also implies developing a good flow of information between yourself and your buyer. This is a two-way street. The buyer has to keep you posted on new developments and requirements as soon as the information becomes available. You, in turn, have to keep him advised of the progress and current status of any assignment currently in work.

Large assignments may span several weeks, with little occasion for direct communication. It's good practice to call the affected client at least once a week to let him know you're working on the project, check for any changes or new information that may have become available, and advise him of how you stand with respect to the delivery date. At any time you find that you are going to be late delivering the work or are likely to exceed any estimate of either time or charges, you should call the client immediately. Waiting until the last possible minute to advise him of a possible late delivery, or waiting until a billing date to indicate charges exceeding an estimate, are mistakes.

The sooner the client knows of a change in the job parameters, the easier it is for him to adjust his schedules and budgets, so it's just good business sense to let him know what's happening. Secrets and surprises between writers and buyers do not make for good working relationships.

The editorial free-lancer should maintain as much communication as possible with his publishers and editors. Many editors, however, do not appreciate being bothered by telephone calls, particularly if they are up against tight deadlines themselves. In such cases, a writer working on assignment or under contract should still provide occasional progress reports, but in the form of written communications that the buyer can examine at his pleasure.

If you are a regular contributor to a publication, it is your responsibility to advise your publisher of interruption to the flow of your work, doing so as soon as possible after you realize that a temporary halt will be necessary. Failure to do so may leave the publisher with insufficient material for an issue and no time to arrange for substitute materials. That can be instant death for a regular working arrangement because the publisher will not be able to rely on you any longer. It's good practice to maintain a file of spare material on hand to cover periods when your work would be interrupted. By having reserve materials, you can arrange to have someone drop packages into the mail while you are away, or you can do the same thing for yourself while you're busy on some other major project.

### Educating Your Buyers

It's important that you educate your publishers or consulting clients as to your particular capabilities. The buyer who knows what you can produce is more likely to contact you when he has a need for your work than one who doesn't know what you can do. You also can save your buyer a lot of wasted time because he doesn't have to check with you on projects which would obviously be beyond your capabilities.

For consultants, it's also necessary to educate clients in the procedures, limitations, and overall requirements affecting the documentation you are producing. It's not uncommon to have a client who knows nothing about printing request a format that either cannot be printed or would be priced prohibitively. Others have no concept of what information is required for a consulting writer to do his job properly. Still others expect the writer to perform more tasks than the ones he is capable of performing. All of these points and others require that you inform your buyer of the rationale behind a particular approach or a refusal to do something in the way demanded. You can't just refuse to do something like a four-color printed piece on general principles; you have to justify your reluctance with an explanation of comparative printing operations, costs, and appearance considerations.

For example, I had one client who requested a full-color, 12-page brochure on some computer services he was offering. His reason for wanting full color was that his plotting equipment generated multi-color graphs that he wanted to reproduce. However, the graphs used nine ink colors. The problem was that printing the graphs as line art would have required nine separate plates, nine separate inks, and nine separate press runs at a totally unrealistic price. On the other hand, printing the graphs as half-tones (dot screens) in a four-color process would have provided lines that were sequences of different dot colors, would not appear continuous, and probably would be misaligned—still at a cost above what was budgeted. It took several meetings, a lot of arguing, and joint effort with a high-quality printer to explain the problem to the client and convince him that he wouldn't be happy with the results even if he could afford to have the job done. Eventually, the job was printed as a two-color brochure, and the multi-color graphs were either reduced to straight black-line art or eliminated altogether. The client got an attractive sales piece at only a fraction of the cost that would have been required to do it his original way.

## Maintaining Supply Lines

If you function as a documentation consultant and offer services such as the preparation of camera-ready art, coordination of printers, and other tasks beyond normal writing, the logistics of an assignment can be another major concern. You probably have to commit to a firm deadline for delivery of the finished product in its printed form, usually meaning that you must have the camera-ready art done at least 10 days prior to the delivery to allow for the printer to make plates, pull proofs for approval, print the document, and do the binding and packaging.

Throughout the course of an assignment like this, you have a number of deadlines for the first draft, first review and revision, second draft, second review and revision, ordering type, shooting photographs, obtaining illustrations, etc. Each of the deadlines must be established in advance by working backward from the deadline for the finished product and building in the various

intervals required by outside vendors. If you do not allow sufficient time for your suppliers to perform their tasks, or if they
exceed their normal intervals for any reason, you can find the
whole assignment jeopardized rather suddenly.

For that reason, it's crucial to maintain adequate lines of
supply and communication, remaining current on vendor intervals and the availability of supplies at all times. When you first
negotiate an assignment, you should check with your proposed
vendors to make certain that they are completing jobs within the
normal intervals and that the materials such as the paper you
intend to design into the project are readily available. The point is
best illustrated by two examples of personal experiences.

At one point, I contracted with a company to prepare a brochure for their product line. It was a six-page, double-folded
brochure to be printed in two colors on a glossy cover-stock paper.
I had been doing a lot of similar assignments at the time and was
relying on one large supplier to handle all of the quality printing.
Since I had been using that printer regularly and they had been
turning out their work within eight or nine days, I felt safe
allowing two weeks for the printing interval. I didn't bother to
call the printer to check their anticipated work load for the time
interval around my scheduled printing dates. The entire job went
smoothly up to the point of releasing the camera-ready art. When
I delivered the art to the printer, I was informed that there would
be a two-week delay before they could even start the job.

What I had overlooked in my haste to get my part of the job
done was that my schedule had hit a month when all large
printers were fully loaded with annual reports. Twice a year, at
the end of the standard corporate fiscal years, every advertising
agency and public relations firm in the city releases a large
number of annual reports to be printed for their clients. These
are critical items, having to be printed and distributed by certain
dates to meet Securities and Exchange Commission (SEC) regulations. They usually are behind schedule, and are released to the
printers on a rush basis, completely blocking any other jobs
during the three or four weeks immediately preceding the SEC
deadline. The end result was that my client received his brochures more than two weeks late and had to attend a national

product show without his supporting literature. Of course, I was blamed for the client's inability to secure orders at that show and for what he saw as a major loss of business. I never got another assignment from that client because the printed product had not been delivered on time, even though I met my personal deadlines and the final printing situation had been beyond my direct control.

In another case, I was preparing a series of three instruction manuals for the hardware and software support of a business computer system. In designing the covers for the manuals, I had found a cover paper that had a high-gloss finish and was available in a shade of tan exactly matching the paint color of the computer itself. The three manuals extended over a period of two months, each being printed as the final artwork was readied. The first manual was delivered without incident, and I was quite pleased with the way the cover color and design worked with the equipment itself. When I took the second manual to the printer two weeks later, the cover stock was unavailable. Furthermore, the paper distributor advised us that the stock was a special production run at the mill and would not be resupplied for six to nine months. To expedite the job, I had to choose an alternate color— still a tan, but not a match with the first manual. On the third manual a few weeks later, the whole thing repeated again, except there was a three-week delay to get the glossy stock in any color. The end result—late delivery of the final manual, three different cover colors, and an irritated client.

These two examples illustrate problems with printing and paper supplies, but similar considerations also effect typographers, photographers, artists, graphic designers, and other vendors normally used by a documentation consultant. Even office supplies can be a problem. I've suffered delays of two or more weeks waiting to receive a carton of suitable paper for preparing typewritten printing masters on oversize paper for ultimate reduction to the final page size. I've had jobs requiring special type elements for mathematical or engineering symbols and found the elements available only by special order from the manufacturer with a delay of several weeks.

The whole point is that basic supplies and vendor intervals are critical to your performance. Even with the most careful planning, you can run headlong into serious or even devastating delays beyond your control. Therefore, you constantly have to seek ways to minimize such problems by checking each possibility in advance. It's also advisable to schedule some slack to accommodate unpredictable problems such as lengthy review intervals by the client. The more slack you can build into a schedule, the better off you will be. It's always acceptable to deliver a job ahead of schedule, but it's never good to deliver it late.

## INVOICING A CLIENT

Editorial free-lancers almost never have the opportunity to invoice a publisher for their work. The publisher's rates and method of payment are preestablished, so the writer usually has to wait until the work is used. On the other hand, consulting writers have to invoice their clients for everything they do, and such invoicing amounts to more than just writing the amount due on a scrap of paper.

### Invoice Requirements

Certain information is required on every invoice you prepare. Obviously, the invoice must state your name and mailing address as well as the name and address of the client. The easiest way to accomplish this is to prepare the invoice on your letterhead, typing the client's name and address just as you would on a letterhead. Other required information includes:

1. A statement of how the check is to be made out, usually in the form of a line reading, "Make all checks payable to," followed by either your business name or personal name depending on how you want the payment.

2. An invoice number unique to the particular bill. Invoice numbers can be sequential single numbers, or can be multi-part numbers keyed to the client. A particular client might be assigned a base number like 1550. Individual

projects then can be assigned an added number, and different invoices against the same project can be assigned another number sequence. Therefore, an invoice number might read something like 1550-005-08, where 1550 designates the client, 005 designates the project, and 08 indicates the eighth invoice against that project.

3. The client's purchase order number or other authorization. Many companies refuse to pay invoices if they are not related to a purchase order. When you are working under the authorization of such a purchase order, clearly indicate the client's number on the invoice. If the job also has a project number, it also should be shown to enable the client's accounting department to allocate the charges to the correct project.

4. The date of the invoice. No invoice should ever be undated; there is no way to prove or disprove payment delinquency on an undated invoice.

5. The statement of terms. Usually this is a simple entry reading "Terms: Net 10 days" or "Terms: Net 30 days." This tells the accounting department how long they have to pay the bill before you begin to get agitated. When you impose nonpayment penalties, it also clarifies the point at which you consider imposing those penalties.

6. A statement of discount if you offer a price reduction for early payment. This can be a separate item reading something like, "Deduct 1.5% if paid within 10 days." Alternatively, it can be a part of the statement of terms as, "Terms: Net 30 days; 1.5% discount when paid within 10 days."

7. A description of the project, the name of the authorizing individual, and the date of authorization. This might be a line reading something like, "Total revision of the Model 100 User's Manual assigned by John Smith on October 20, 1980."

8. An itemized list of the work done, including the dates, number of hours, and a description of the tasks performed. A line might read something like, "8.5 hours Oct. 10 Review inputs and prepare text for Chapter 1."

9. A statement of each expense billed, reading something like, "$10.00 Oct. 11 Special press-on lettering sheets."

10. A concluding summary of charges showing the total number of hours billed, the number of nontaxable hours and the charge, the number of taxable hours and the charge, the taxes, the expenses, and the grand total. This might look something like:

```
22.50 TOTAL NONTAXABLE HOURS = $ 675.00
10.00 TOTAL TAXABLE HOURS     = $ 300.00
32.50 TOTAL HOURS             = $ 975.00
      EXPENSES                = $   0.00
      SUBTOTAL                = $ 975.00
      3.5% SALES TAX          = $  10.50
      TOTAL DUE AND PAYABLE   = $ 985.50
```

## Detailing an Invoice

Make it a practice to detail your invoices as thoroughly as possible. Charges entered as "miscellaneous" are highly suspect and may be challenged by your client. Even listings of items like, "Writing copy for manual," are suspect. It's far better to use a day-by-day itemization, listing the date, number of hours, and exact accomplishments. First, this tells the client what you did with the hours you're billing. Second, it is a valuable aid in estimating future assignments since it indicates the scope of the job and the distribution of charges. Third, it helps justify large charges for seemingly small tasks; doing a single illustration may take a full day or more, and itemizing allows that particular area to be isolated and justified if it should be challenged. Expenses are subject to the same consideration. Each should be listed and defined rather than being lumped under the heading of "miscellaneous expenses."

### Reducing Your Charges

There are occasions when it's necessary or advisable to reduce your charges to a level slightly below what you might be entitled to get according to the terms of the contract. Some examples might involve reductions because you feel you weren't working effectively on a particular day, you had to back up and redo something because you misunderstood the information you received, or you've decided that the job is sufficiently large to warrant waiving some minor expense items like car mileage.

Such reductions in the overall charge may cost you little but can gain you some prestige with a client if he recognizes that you are trying to minimize his costs. Sometimes a small reduction can be used to misdirect his attention from some other item that is actually overcharged, leaving the client thinking that you are doing him a big favor by knocking out something like mileage when you are more than making up for that reduction through some other charge. It's good practice to list all items on the invoice as they would be charged, but then to enter a "no charge" indication for an eliminated item. If the item does not appear on the invoice, the client soon forgets you did him the favor, but if it's a part of the invoice sheet, it's hard to overlook.

Discounting for early payment is a common business practice usually applied by offering a small reduction of about 1.5% for early payment within 10 days of invoicing. However, many businesses offering the discount pad up their charges to make up the difference, often multiplied several times. I've seen little advantage in offering early-payment discounts. The clients who are slow are going to stay slow because the discount doesn't offset the other cash-flow gains they get by delaying. Clients who are going to pay quickly, do so whether or not they get a discount. Instead, I prefer to bill all time and expenses as incurred, and then impose penalties against the clients who delay payment for intervals longer than I'm willing to accept as reasonable.

### When and How to Invoice

The question of when to invoice a job requires an individual assessment of the job itself. Some small jobs are best invoiced only when the job is done. Some larger assignments are better handled when invoiced for each segment, such as a draft of the text, a second draft, a package of finished artwork, etc. The largest assignments spanning many months are best handled on a bi-weekly or monthly basis so that payments do not fall too far behind the work being done. I always reserve the right to make such billing decisions after I'm well into the job and have a good feeling for its duration and scope.

The large majority of consulting assignments divide neatly into specific segments such as individual drafts, each separated from the others by a period for client review and revision. By invoicing for each segment and setting a payment interval of 10 days, I usually know if I'm going to get paid before the project is returned for continued work. If it looks like there's going to be a problem getting paid, I can suspend further effort until a check is received. Where that approach doesn't work, I impose a dollar limit on the client's total debt. If the total billings exceed that amount, I halt work and advise the client that I will resume only after I have received his check for the balance already due.

The object is to avoid having too much at risk in accounts receivable. If the money at risk can be minimized, the dangers from deadbeats who don't pay also can be minimized.

Despite all precautions, some clients still try to get away with unreasonable delays in paying their bills. They may pay eventually, but they're in no hurry to do so. Repeat clients who pull that stunt more than once become subject to special treatment. I simply demand that the full estimate for any future work be paid in advance of starting the work. I then hold that money in an escrow account until the job is completed, returning any excess over the amount of the actual charges, or billing any amounts that exceed the prepayment. This technique does, however, tend to alienate clients, and it is reserved only for those who are chronically late in paying their bills.

The question of how to invoice is easier to answer. An invoice should be prepared in triplicate, and you should retain one copy for your files. The original copy accompanies the package of materials sent or hand-carried to the client, and the other copy goes directly to the client's accounting department. The copy for the accounting department should bear a notation stating who received the original and on what date it was presented.

In most corporations, the person who authorized the assignment is the one who must authorize payment of the invoice. However, the copy accompanying the materials may get sidetracked and sit on someone's desk for weeks before being countersigned. By arranging for a copy to go directly to accounting, they are alerted to the existence of the invoice, can schedule the payment, and can track down the original if it's not countersigned by the payment date. For clients not out to delay payments deliberately, I've found that this approach has expedited handling and has eliminated accidental delays resulting from misplacement of the original invoice.

## Invoicing Consistency

It's a good idea to check invoices for consistency. First, this allows you to develop a better sense of estimated time and charges for new assignments. Second, it assures that billing to a particular client for a particular type of work is relatively uniform. When a client undertakes a major audit of accounts, large discrepancies in amounts paid for similar work become evident and are subject to challenge. If one assignment was charged significantly higher than the others without any evident reason, a question arises as to whether or not you might have padded that invoice. If you did it once, you could do it again. An invoice unaccountably smaller than the others generates questions like, "If you could do it that cheaply once, why not all the time?"

When you are acting as a consultant, there is always a temptation to pad your bill, particularly if the client has approved an estimate that turns out to be a lot higher than the actual charges for the job. Besides, advertising agencies, vendors, and other suppliers all seem to be padding their bills! Applying a "fudge factor" to increase your charges is always a dangerous practice. After all, you're selling yourself on your reputation, and, if a client detects a major discrepancy, that could end your relationship quite quickly.

Believe it or not, I've known clients who have compared my invoices between each other. The probability is low, but it can and does happen when one client has referred another, and the one having been referred decides to check back. For that reason, I also make it a habit to do a consistency check between different clients to make sure that the billing practices are as uniform as possible. Although different clients may be signed at different hourly rates so the total charges vary, the number of hours for similar jobs should remain comparable. If, during that check, I detect a major discrepancy between the charges for the current assignment and those for prior assignments, and if I can't attribute that discrepancy to some particular difference between the jobs, I then adjust my hour count to minimize the difference.

When a downward adjustment is made in this manner, I always advise the client of what I have done, showing the actual hours incurred on the invoice and stating clearly that certain hours have been subtracted from the total. Over a period of time, this impresses my clients and makes them feel confident in my billing procedures. As a result, they accept the charges without question and rarely consider diverting assignments to other free-lancers who may offer a lower estimate but whose final billing may not be predictable.

## KEEPING REGULAR HOURS

If you're an editorial free-lancer, you probably don't have to worry about what hours of the day you work. Since your direct contact with publishers and editors is minimal, you can work late at night or early in the morning without being concerned with availability for phone calls or meetings.

If you are a consultant, however, the situation changes radically. The need for direct communication with your clients forces you to keep roughly the same business hours as those prevailing in your community. If clients start work at 8:00 A.M. and quit at 5:00 P.M., you must be open for business and accessible to them during those hours. You may not actually be working during those hours, but you do have to be available for telephone conversations and meetings.

At the same time, there are some executives with no respect for normal hours. At various times, I've had clients who liked to call late at night, as early as 5:30 in the morning, or on weekends to discuss a project or to set up a meeting. For nearly a year, I worked with an in-house advertising agency where the president liked to call me late on Sunday afternoons or evenings to set up meetings for 7:00 on Monday mornings. Projects of extreme urgency sometimes require working or meeting with clients on Saturdays, Sundays, and holidays. I've even had one client who moved part of his staff right into my own home and office for 12 hours a day just to minimize the delay of transmitting information back and forth.

The point is that a consultant has to be open for business during normal hours, plus any other hours that the clients may demand. As the work load builds, it also becomes necessary to allocate hours before and after normal business hours for effective working time not subject to disruptive meetings and phone calls. Eventually, it reaches the point where a consultant may be on call 24 hours a day every day, with effective working hours scheduled to make the best possible use of any time available.

## USING SUBCONTRACTORS

Outside talents may be required to complete a particular project. These may include photographers, designers, illustrators, pasteup artists, and affiliated individuals handling different tasks associated with a particular project. Both editorial writers and consultants may have to depend upon such other individuals at various times, usually on a subcontract basis. A consultant also may have to use other writers as subcontractors to alleviate an overload situation or to handle part of an assignment requiring someone particularly adept at a different style of writing.

Notice that I've referred to these other individuals as subcontractors, not as employees. Few free-lance writers can afford to hire someone as an employee, even on a part-time basis. From an accounting viewpoint alone, hiring help is impractical because it carries the burden of withholding taxes, paying unemployment, and filing a number of additional papers with federal and state governments. Subcontracting is nothing more than assigning someone else to work on the project, with that individual contracted to you just as you are contracted to your client. You pay them a rate based on the contracts, and forget about fringe benefits, taxes, and insurance.

The usual problem is to find reliable people to work on a subcontract basis. Since you are responsible for the final quality of the work, you must be satisfied that the other individuals can live up to your standards. If they don't, you either have to have their work redone by someone else or have to do it over yourself. You also have to pay them less than you receive, further complicating the process of finding someone reliable. In normal subcontracting arrangements, you might charge your client $25 an hour for your own time plus that of the subcontractors. To make a reasonable profit, however, you might be able to pay the subcontractors only $15 an hour, allowing for your time to examine, edit, and revise their work. The discrepancy between your rate charged and what you can pay is significant enough to make it difficult to find suitable talents.

In addition, there is a definite danger in subcontracting. If your client defaults on paying your bill, you still are liable for paying the subcontractors out of your own pocket. Even under the best of circumstances, you can wind up with a severe cash-flow problem when your client delays his payment for 45 days while you have to pay your help within 30 days.

As a rule, I prefer not to subcontract any tasks. When I need additional talents such as illustrators and photographers, I have them contract separately with my client. I make the recommendations as to who can provide suitable work, introduce the people to the client, and let them work out their own terms. That keeps me from being financially responsible, and it puts the burden of assessing the suitability of the other individual on the client. If the client defaults on payment, I'm not obligated. If the client is unhappy with the work, they made the final choice, so it's out of my hands. Of course, I still try to recommend the best people possible, simply because it makes my part of the job a lot easier.

When it comes to additional writers, I again avoid using sub-contractors. Since every writer has his own style, it's impossible to expect another writer to prepare text that would be compatible with mine when used side by side in the same document. There-fore, subcontractors would be useful only if they were assigned complete jobs of their own for which there would be no necessity of merging two different styles. However, that doesn't help my problems in handling overloads on projects already in progress. So instead of using subcontractors, I've adopted a direct referral procedure. Jobs that I can handle personally I take on without hesitation. Those I cannot handle, I don't take on at all. In the latter case, I make every effort to match a potential writer with the prospective client, giving the writer's name to the client and calling the writer to inform him of the client's interest. From that point, they can handle it between themselves.

When I first tried this approach, I expected that I would never hear from the prospective client again. A month later they called to see if I was free to tackle their next project. That pattern has repeated many times since then; by helping a company find help when I'm not available, they think of me first when their next need arises. Of course there's no guarantee that you won't lose a portion of these prospects to the referred writers, but my expe-rience has been that the portion lost permanently is not large enough to endanger my overall business.

## SETTING A DAILY ROUTINE

Obviously, there is no one correct way to conduct your daily operations. Only experience will enable you to set the procedures you will use, and a lot of reflection and adjustment will be neces-sary to accommodate your unique needs. After a year or so, the day-to-day methods and approaches should become routine, work-ing well for the majority of your business dealings, but adjust-ments still may be needed from time to time for special cases or when you stumble over some practice that makes the operation smoother. The important thing is to run your operation in the most businesslike and professional manner possible.

# 9

# Simple Self-Preservation

Self-preservation! It's defined as a natural or instinctive tendency to act so as to preserve one's own existence. It is, after all, the prime prerequisite of survival in any endeavor, and it has to be a free-lance writer's foremost concern. Your ultimate survival doesn't depend upon how well you can write. Instead, it depends upon your ability to preserve your existence in the business world. That need for self-preservation demands that you plan ahead for every contingency and that you be ready to respond quickly and automatically to anything that threatens your survival.

Throughout your day-to-day operations, you can expect to encounter many difficult and potentially hazardous situations. Although you can't necessarily avoid them, there are some things that you can do to minimize their impact. In this chapter, you'll find a selection of problem areas and some specific recommendations for their treatment. There are, of course, a great many areas not addressed, but the guidelines herein should help direct your thinking toward the subject of self-preservation and give you the

211

basic background necessary to anticipate the problems you are likely to find in your own business dealings.

## GET A CONTRACT

The most obvious means of self-preservation is to have a written contract for everything you do. Naturally, an editorial writer working on small, speculative assignments such as fillers, gags, articles, and so on cannot expect to obtain a contract for each item. In fact, most magazines won't even contract regular contributors working on-spec, and reserve their contracts only for those receiving specific assignments.

If you do most of your work in those areas, you have no real means of protecting yourself against a publisher who is less than completely honest. You are at the publisher's mercy! If he ceases publication without paying for or returning your manuscripts, you probably have to absorb the loss. You can suffer similar losses when a publisher copies your materials, takes your ideas and assigns them to staff writers or other free-lancers, publishes your work and refuses to pay, or makes it a habit to issue multiple assignments and then pay only the small kill fee when the work is unused. Your only recourse in cases such as these is through the civil courts, but you have no written documentation with which to prove the validity of your claim.

Most publishers are honest! Their continued existence often depends upon how they treat their contributors because without contributors they might not have a publication to produce. But there are those few who aren't as honest, and the contributing free-lancer simply has to accept the risks and take the losses when he runs into one of them.

For book authors and consulting writers, the situation is completely different. All work in these areas should be under written contract. There are no exceptions! Book publishers always require a written contract, so the procedures are automatic when dealing with these buyers. However, consulting writers have the option of using or not using a contract that they themselves create. It's often tempting to take on small assignments without a written contract, particularly when the project may take only a day or two to complete. However, it's been my experience that the small assignments run the highest risk of nonpayment, so I require a formal agreement for projects requiring as little as two hours of work.

It may seem ridiculous to ask for a formal contract on an assignment worth only $60 to $100, but those assignments tend to have the lowest profit levels and the highest costs for record keeping and associated tasks. It takes time to pick up the job, deliver it, prepare invoices, update accounts receivable records, tabulate expenses, and so on. As a free-lancer, time translates directly into dollars, so a job that may take two hours to complete also may require an hour or two for running back and forth to the client, another half hour for invoicing, another quarter hour for updating accounting records, etc. If additional time has to be added for collecting a delayed payment, the margin of profit can disappear altogether.

Meanwhile, the client finds the idea of postponing small payments attractive. If he can stall off enough small debts, he has more money for his major expenses and investments. He tends to assume that a small bill probably won't be subject to collection actions by the consultant simply because it wouldn't be worth the time and effort. On the other hand, the consultant may be waiting for that client's check to provide the money to pay a vendor or supplier, and any delay forces him into having to make his payments out of other funds. If there is no written agreement as to the terms for payment, a consultant has little ammunition with which to fight for the money he is owed. Verbal agreements and a handshake aren't worth a thing when it comes time to collect money; the only protection a free-lancer has is what may or may not be in writing.

Large consulting assignments generally are paid more promptly than small ones, but nonpayment of a bill that may amount to several thousand dollars becomes a very serious matter. Where the small nonpayment was annoying and may have meant temporarily diverting other funds to cover expenses, a large nonpayment can pose severe problems. If, for example, an entire month is devoted to one project, excluding all others, and payment is not received promptly, there may be no cash to juggle around. If too much is tied up in receivables, a consultant can find himself in a position where his suppliers, vendors, and other creditors are launching collection actions against him while he has no money with which to pay the bills. In very short order, a few large and unpaid assignments can lead a consultant directly into bankruptcy court, even when he has been working steadily and has what appears to be a good income on paper.

In addition to outright nonpayment, a free-lance writer working without a contract can find himself with no way to recover expenses incurred on the client's behalf. Unless stated otherwise in writing, the client expects all costs to be included in any estimate of charges. He then may make changes that require new typography, a second photo session, or other out-of-pocket expenses by the consultant. If a consultant can't add those onto his bill, the charges may have to be absorbed.

As I've indicated earlier in this book, I've had little trouble getting clients to agree to a formal contract. The few prospects who wouldn't sign were of dubious reputation anyway, so not doing any work for them was probably to my advantage. My philosophy has become one of "no contract, no work." I both expect and demand a written agreement to terms and conditions before I will do anything at all for someone with whom I'm not completely familiar. For at least the first year, I require that agreement, and I relax my requirements only after the client has proven reliable.

## GET WRITTEN AUTHORIZATIONS

If you work under a general contract or written agreement that specifies terms and conditions for all assignments over a period of time, be sure to have individual jobs authorized in writing. A consulting contract such as the one I presented in Chapter 3 does not require any particular assignments to be issued, and it provides no proof that charges for a project are legitimate. After working with a client for a year or so, you may be able to accept a verbal order to start a project before the paperwork clears, but you shouldn't turn over any completed work until you have the papers in hand. For new clients, it's highly inadvisable to even start the project until all paperwork has been completed.

In most cases, you can work from a company's purchase order, as long as you don't depend upon that purchase order as a contract. Since purchase orders are not as legally binding as companies claim, they really can't be used for anything more than to support a verbal request to undertake a particular project. In most cases, I prefer a letter of intent from the client, signed by an officer of the corporation, to initiate an individual project. It need not contain any terms or conditions since those are covered in my general agreement. However, the letter does have to specify the job, the extent of my responsibilities in completing the assignment, and an undeniable statement that the tasks are authorized and that the project has been approved through official channels.

In most editorial work other than book publishing, the authorization is not so specific. Drawing upon the example of my work in the word-puzzle field, my authorization is nothing more than the letter from the editor stating that the style and format of a puzzle can be used by the magazine and that he would like to have a quantity of manuscripts for his files. In such cases, the editor does not commit himself to using the work in any specific quantity but does express sufficient interest for me to assume the risk of preparing manuscripts on speculation. Once a particular type of puzzle begins to appear in print on a regular basis, there is an implied authorization to continue contributions.

However, I rarely see a specific request for a particular type of manuscript in a given quantity. Only one publisher I've dealt with has ever said anything like, "I will use five of this type each month." For the most part, it's necessary to prepare and submit large quantities of material in each acceptable format to be held in the publisher's files until they are needed. Maybe they'll be used! Maybe they won't be used! I view this as an "assignment-on-speculation" in which contributing enough manuscripts hopefully will generate enough publications and payments to offset the losses suffered on the unused materials.

## ENFORCE COLLECTIONS

The tightest contract in the world is of no value if it is not enforced. When you have a contract, each and every term and condition specified therein must be followed to the letter. If the contract is from a book publisher, you can expect them to enforce it, right down to the punctuation marks. You had better provide the manuscript on time. You had better return the advance if they notify you that your manuscript is not acceptable. You had better own the rights to the work when you sign them over to the publisher. If you fail at any point, you are in default and the publisher will launch legal actions without hesitation.

As a consultant, you must treat your own contract the same way. Every statement in that agreement must be followed to the letter. If you say you are going to impose penalties and launch collection activities after a certain interval, do it. You can make allowances for good clients, such as a few extra days when they indicate a cash flow problem of their own, but make them only when there is sufficient reason. If the client simply ignores your requests for payment, take action immediately.

Collecting the money you're owed can be one of the most trying experiences of your career. Anytime you have to commence collection proceedings against a publisher or client, you are jeopardizing that relationship and must accept the fact that there probably will be no more work to be done for that buyer. It's amazing how awkward a feeling can develop when it's necessary to go after a payment, but it's important to remember that the money is owed and that you have every right to receive it. Most deadbeats have a knack for finding ways to make you feel guilty for asking for the payment that's rightfully yours. If you find yourself feeling such guilt, ignore it. Nobody's going to feel bad about trying to collect from you, and you shouldn't feel bad for doing it to someone else.

When working under contract to a book or magazine publisher, the dates and conditions of payment are stipulated in the contract. Should a date go by without receiving the statement of account and any payment due, allow about a week for slow mail deliveries. Then send a polite but formal letter to the editor or publisher with whom you have been dealing, and inform him that you haven't received the statement or payment. Ask for his assistance in determining whether or not the missing payment actually was sent out, and request that he advise you of the date on which it was mailed. Under ordinary circumstances, this should be as far as you need to go.

If you don't get a response within 14 days, send a second letter. This one should be polite but firm, making pointed references to "Dun and Bradstreet." You can apologize for taking his time, but indicate that you are getting quite concerned over the missing payment and the failure to get a response to your first letter. If, after another 10 days, you still have not resolved the situation, use the telephone. Some people advise a third, strongly worded letter instead of a phone call. However, I feel that if no response is received after two letters, none is forthcoming and the buyer is subject to whatever disturbances I care to make. On the phone, remain as polite as possible, but be extremely firm. You want your payment or you want to know why you've not received it. If the publisher claims to have sent a check on the original due date, you can assume it's been lost. Ask for the original check to be voided and a new one issued.

Collecting nonpayments requires both diplomacy and persistence, yet bad-tempered communications have to be avoided. Angry or threatening letters do little good and may actually make your contact resistant to providing any assistance in obtaining the money he owes you. In many cases, the delay may be due to the accounting department, not the editor with whom you've been dealing. Sending a polite but firm letter allows the editor to forward the information to his superiors, but threats and accusations may be sufficiently embarrasing to keep him from forwarding your communications.

If your communications with the editor don't get you the payment to which you're entitled, you can try addressing your correspondence to the publisher or president of the firm. If that doesn't work, it may help to contact the business manager. In some publishing houses, it is the business manager who is most likely to be concerned with the firm's reputation—the publisher and the editor have a great many other things on their minds and have little time to become deeply involved in the day-to-day financial affairs.

If all else fails, and you find yourself with neither the payment due nor a reasonable explanation for the delay, you have to take some kind of action. Your choices are to use either a large, reputable collection agency such as Dun and Bradstreet or an attorney. In either case, it's going to cost you a substantial portion of the money you're owed and is going to destroy any possibility of future dealings with the particular buyer. Therefore, such collection activities have to be a final resort, but they are necessary in extreme cases.

The procedure for noncontracted magazine contributions is much the same. However, you have no contract and no guaranteed date of payment. Instead, publishers typically pay "on publication," so they send checks only after the magazine has appeared on the newsstands. You have only two ways of knowing when your work has been used. The first is getting a check; the other is seeing the work in print. Obviously, if you've gotten the check, you have no problem. However, if you see the material in print and haven't been paid within 30 days of the magazine's appearance, you should contact the publisher. The procedure from that point is the same as that for a book author—a couple of letters, a phone call or two, and an attorney or collection agency, in that order.

In written communications, it's advisable to include a bill for the unpaid material, basing the charges on the publisher's highest rate of payment plus about 25%. For example, a publisher specifying a payment range of $0.06 to $0.08 per word should be billed at the rate of $0.10 a word. Typically, this results in a payment somewhat less than that indicated on the bill, but moves the amount offered as a settlement by the publisher toward the high end of his range rather than the low end.

The same procedure is applicable to editorial material sent for a publisher's consideration. You can expect a book or magazine publisher to respond to your manuscript within 30 to 45 days, either accepting or rejecting it. If you haven't heard anything after 45 days, write to the publisher and ask them to track down the manuscript. There is a possibility that mail gets lost, so I use

Registered Mail with a return receipt whenever possible. If you have a receipt and get no response from the publisher after two letters, try the telephone. If you can prove they received the manuscript and they neither return it nor acknowledge it, you will need legal assistance to recover it.

For the consultant, the situation is a little different. With a contract in hand, you have proof that the client is obligated to pay for the materials. Under a 30-day payment interval, I find about 75% of my clients pay within three weeks. For those that don't, I send a notification on day 26 stating that the final date for payment is approaching and that a retroactive penalty will be invoked if payment is not received. On day 31, I place a phone call to my contact, asking why payment has not been received and advising him that the penalty clause may have to be invoked. If payment has not been received within four days, I calculate the retroactive penalty and send a statement of the original bill and the penalty to the client's accounting manager, along with a notification of the date I plan to file for collection. If I haven't been paid and haven't received a satisfactory explanation by day 45, I turn the debt over for collection.

On occasion, I've been a little more casual in my attitude toward collecting money, but when I've relaxed my procedure for any but proven clients, it's led to some extreme difficulties. The worst instance occurred in mid-1979 when a small firm attempted to escape paying for a promotional brochure. I had designed, written, edited, photographed, and prepared camera-ready art for a formal promotional piece under my standard contract terms. The typographer and printer had contracted separately to the client and had been issued individual purchase orders. My part of the job was billed at about $2,500, with the typographer charging about $3,000 and the printer charging about $5000.

I delivered the camera-ready art and an invoice for my work during the last week of July. A 30-day payment interval was allowed, making the payment due in the last week of August. The printing was done in mid-August, so the client had taken possession of the brochures before the final due date of my payment. A week before the payment was due, I sent the usual notice, but received neither payment nor any other response. After the due date, I visited the client's office and was assured that the check would be ready the following Friday. On Friday I was told it would be Monday. From there on, the client made daily promises of payment, right up to the morning I was scheduled to board a plane for a month-long vacation.

On the morning of my departure, I again visited the client's office and was informed that the check was ready but nobody was available to sign it. I spent the rest of the morning doing some last-minute financial juggling to cover my bills while I would be gone, and I sent a letter to the client informing him that he was to send the check to my appointed agent within seven days or I would have to take legal action when I returned.

When I returned in mid-October, no payment had been received. I checked with the typographer and printer and found they had not been paid either. To give the client one more chance, I visited his office again, but the receptionist had been given orders to turn me away, telling me I had no right to expect to walk in and talk to anyone. Furthermore, I was informed that if I wanted my money I would have to sue for it. Since the materials had been printed and were being used, there was no question of the brochure being satisfactory, simply a statement that they did not intend to pay the bill.

Back at my office, I tried to call the company president, but couldn't get past his secretary. I did inform her, however, that I knew the typographer and printer had not been paid, that I would be contacting my attorney, and that I would be launching both a civil suit for my money and a criminal investigation for theft and fraud. I also informed her that I would be pursuing a court order to seize the printed brochures since my contract stipulated that the image printed on them was my property and they were using it without authorization. Within three hours, I received a call from the client assuring me that the typographer and printer had been paid (an outright lie) and that they would like to arrange to pay off their debt to me.

To keep the matter out of an expensive legal process and to avoid losing most or all of the money in the collection activity, I had to settle for payments over three months, although I did get a daily percentage penalty. Finally, in February of the next year, I received the last of my money, but my cash flow was totally disrupted for several months and I had some problems in meeting my debts and bills. The typographer and printer never did receive any payment at all.

Throughout the attempts to collect the money owed, the client's whole attitude changed dramatically—the company president actually had the nerve to act insulted by reasonable demands for payment, and the more he delayed, the more insulted he pretended to be. After that experience, I reinstated absolute payment intervals, with no exceptions for anyone other than long-term clients who provided satisfactory explanations for short delays. Delays of more than 15 days past the due date would not be tolerated from anyone. I also shortened my payment interval from 30 to 10 days for all existing and newly acquired clients. Furthermore, I lowered the amount of maximum indebtedness I would allow a client to incur without halting work on the project, reducing that amount to about $1,500. Finally, I reinstated a process of conducting a complete financial investigation of all new clients, requiring that any client whose estimated bill would exceed $500 be able to prove that he is worthy of credit.

## GIVE AN ESTIMATE

If you are acting as a consultant, you may be required to estimate or quote an assignment. Since most assignments you can expect to receive will be of widely differing complexities, providing a client with a firm quotation is nearly impossible. Besides, committing yourself to an inflexible price for an entire project is both impractical and unwise.

When you have to provide an estimate, your best practice is to examine past billings for projects of a similar nature, add from 50% to 100% to those billings, and use that amount as a general estimate. You also should give an estimate of probable costs that will be passed through to the client, again doubling what you think might really be required. You probably will find it better to overestimate a job and then bill a lower amount rather than underestimate the job and have to bill higher amounts.

Even after deliberately overestimating a job, you should not indicate that the amounts stated are absolutely binding. You need flexibility to incorporate changes, account for unforeseen difficulties, and recover unanticipated expenses. Therefore, your estimate should indicate clearly that it is based on approximations only and that you reserve the right to adjust your charges as necessary. In my written estimates, I place two paragraphs right at the beginning to clarify these points. The typical form is:

> Prices herein are estimates for the completion of two drafts of the manual. These estimates are approximations only, based on the anticipated time required in relationship to similar documents of parallel length and complexity done for other clients in the past. Generally, these estimates tend to be somewhat higher than the costs actually charged, and every possible effort is made to provide materials at or below the costs estimated herein. Actual billing is for time spent, on a basis of $30 per hour. When the time required is less than that estimated, the charges are correspondingly lower, but when the time required is greater than estimated, the right is reserved to charge for that time and prior notice of additional charges will be provided.

> No allowance is included for client-generated changes to the project, functions of the equipment, internal or external operations, or project guidelines. Any such changes are additions to the task, are charged at the full hourly rate for incorporation into the project, and are assumed to have been approved at the time the changes are issued. No allowance is made for cancellation or termination of the project once underway; such action by the client obligates the client to pay for all work performed up to the point of notification to discontinue efforts. No allowance is made for non-use of the materials; should the delivered materials not be used by the client for any reason, the client shall be obligated for payment of all charges associated therewith.

In response to your estimate, you should receive a confirming purchase order or letter of intent from the client prior to starting any work. In checking the purchase order or confirming letter, make certain that any hours or charges are clearly indicated as estimates. If the purchase order does not indicate that it contains estimates only, your acceptance of that document could obligate you to hold to the stated prices as fixed charges, even though you intended them to be estimates only.

The purchase order or letter also might contain a statement reading something like, "Not to exceed $5,000 without prior written approval." That's usually added by the purchasing department in an effort to fix the price more exactly, but it should cause you few problems. Although you have to obtain separate authorization to overrun the charges, it's rarely difficult to do so. Furthermore, you still have the option of halting work on the project if the client refuses to approve the additional charges.

## AVOID COMPETITIVE BIDDING

Consultants may be asked to submit competitive bids. Since estimating a writing project in advance is difficult in itself, competitive bidding is nearly impossible. Most clients will view your bid as a binding flat-rate price, removing the flexibility of charging for changes or unforeseen problems. Furthermore, you have to adjust your rates and terms to try to undercut the competition, and you can wind up losing a great deal of money on a project.

It's my stated practice not to engage in competitive bidding at any time. I will prepare an estimate based on my standard rates and the anticipated number of hours determined from past experience. I will make every attempt to keep my charges reasonable. But I will not try to provide the lowest price obtainable for a project, knowing quite well that my rates are not the lowest around. Since I have very specific skills and often have directly related experience in the field, I expect to be paid accordingly.

When I negotiate with a prospective client, I make it quite clear that the work probably can be done less expensively by someone else, but that the lower-cost consultant may not be able to do the work as well or within the delivery interval required. I present my estimates on a take-it or leave-it basis, and I'll never revise my estimate because someone else has quoted the same project at a lower rate. Underbidding and then overcharging is a common business practice, but it's one with which I don't care to be involved. Since I state that I will give the best price possible while charging my standard hourly rate, I don't feel it's necessary or advisable to further cut the prices by trying to shave the hourly rate itself.

Small companies are the ones most likely to be looking for competitive bids. Their budgets are limited, so they think that taking a low bidder is going to save money. Oddly enough, that's rarely the case since low bidders tend to do inferior jobs and employ undesirable cost-cutting methods. The prospective clients who insist on using a low-bid selection process may find that the documentation they receive is less than totally suitable and may have to be revised extensively before it can be used. I've lost a few such assignments over the past five years, but most of those companies eventually came back to me to rectify the problems caused by the consultant they selected. When I am approached by such a company after having originally lost the assignment, I increase my hourly rate above what was quoted originally. For example, if I lose an assignment I estimated against a base rate of $30.00 an hour, I would charge $40.00 an hour if approached again by the same company to rework the project in order to make it usable.

Most larger companies don't use competitive bidding for consulting work. They usually are aware that documentation tasks are difficult to estimate, and they are more interested in having the job done well the first time than in getting the lowest possible price and possibly having to rework the assignment. In fact, most of the larger companies have more respect for a high-priced consultant than for a low-priced one. If they have more confidence in higher-priced consultants, they are more likely to choose such writers over those who quote low rates and thereby imply limited abilities and experience.

## AVOID SPECULATIVE WORK

Working on-spec is a characteristic of most editorial freelancers, and there's no way to avoid it in that market. The large majority of writers dealing with filler materials, articles, stories, and books have to do their work without any guarantee of sale, usually trying to find a buyer after the piece has been at least partially completed. In markets such as puzzle magazines, many manuscripts are submitted and may or may not be used over a period of several years. The editorial writer working on speculation has to assume the inherent risks and be willing to take his losses when work isn't published or when a major buyer suddenly quits operation with a large number of manuscripts already on hand. Even magazine assignments are little more than speculative work done by special request since many such assignments are never printed and pay only a kill fee.

When I'm asked to name the one major drawback to editorial writing, I always identify it as the speculative nature of the market. Since we all work to make money, spending a lot of time on projects for which there is no guaranteed return is a risky business. For that reason alone, I've always recommended that aspiring writers examine the consulting possibilities before committing themselves to the editorial field. Although marketing and technical writing don't offer the prestige of being a published author, they do offer a regular income and the ability to expend most efforts on a profitable basis instead of on speculative and potentially nonprofitable pursuits. A writer who can make his living as a consultant can use those profits to offset the lost time and expenses involved in creating speculative manuscripts for the editorial market. When a writer does not have to rely on editorial sales to earn a livable income, he can work on-spec with less risk of being wiped out when publishers reject his contributions.

A consulting writer need never work on-spec and should avoid doing so at all times. There are some prospective clients who will ask a consultant to do a trial job as a test of his abilities. If you have a portfolio, there is no need to accept that kind of assignment—your samples prove or disprove your abilities, and unpaid trial work or speculative work are totally unnecessary.

Accepting a consulting job on-spec also has its dangers; some companies try to use such assignments to get their work done at no cost. The worst situation of this type I've run into involved a trade school. In scanning the classified ads of a Sunday paper, I spotted one seeking free-lance technical writers for an assignment in electronics. I responded to the ad and set up a meeting with the head of the department. At the meeting, I showed my samples, talked about my rates, and received a definition of the task. The project involved preparing 18 lesson books to be used by classes in the school and for a mail-order course in a particular type of electronic repair work. The individual in charge asked me to submit a formal estimate and gave me an outline and the reference materials to be used. Up to this point, negotiations had gone normally.

I worked up the estimate for the 18 small books and submitted it about three days later. Then, I got a call informing me that I would have to prepare one of the books as a sample before my estimate could be approved or a contract signed. I became suspicious, but I went out to meet with the prospect again. While I was waiting in the reception area, someone else came into the building to drop off a package for the individual in charge of this project, and I saw the receptionist add it to a pile of other packages, each of which obviously included the same reference materials I had been given. Already being suspicious, I waited till the receptionist had left her desk, and then took a quick look through the stack, finding a series of sample books for the same project I was negotiating.

Had each of the sample manuscripts been on the same section of the course, I might not have paid too much attention, but each was a different segment, and none were on the same part I was told to prepare as a sample. At that point, I had a fairly good idea of what was being done, and I left immediately without waiting to talk to the prospect. I later confirmed that the entire project was done by 18 different writers, each of whom prepared a sample segment on speculation and was then turned down for having done unsatisfactory work. The organization itself got the complete set of lessons written at no cost since they didn't have to pay for the samples they "rejected" and never contracted with anyone to undertake the program. The writers were cheated out of their work, though I doubt that many of them ever realized what a slippery scheme had been worked.

As a result of that experience, I swore never to take on an unpaid task and to never give my time to anyone without being paid. Jobs that don't pay are jobs I don't need, and I have more than enough work to keep me busy without tempting fate by taking on free work in the consulting portion of my business. I assume the risks of speculative work for my editorial work, but I cannot and will not assume those risks in the consulting phase that generates the majority of my income.

## KEEP JOB RECORDS

Accurately accounting for your time is important on any consulting assignment, so you have to keep accurate records of what was done and when it was done. Every project should have a log sheet similar to that shown in Figure 9 on which you note the date, the time of day you start, the time you quit, and exactly what was accomplished during the interval. When you prepare an invoice, you can go right down the list, determining the number of hours from the starting and quitting times, and obtaining an itemized day-by-day invoice of every task associated with the job. You also can use the log sheet as a valuable estimating tool for other projects because it clearly indicates the distribution of your time among the individual tasks you had to perform. Over a period of years, you can develop averages for different types of assignments, allowing you to look at a new project and calculate a fairly good estimate of the range of hours required for writing, illustrating, proofreading, preparing camera-ready pages, etc.

When you deliver a project, you should get a receipt for it. A signed statement that you have delivered certain materials on a certain date normally is sufficient. The important point is to avoid the situation in which a client receives a package, misplaces it, and then accuses you of not delivering it in the first place. When you send your materials through the mail, it's advisable to use only Registered Mail and to get a return receipt card. Mail does get lost, so you need to prove when you sent the package *and* when it was received. Although it does cost a little more, I prefer Registered Mail to insured or certified shipments simply because the registration guarantees a special handling that minimizes the possibility of loss.

In most cases, you will be delivering or sending original typed pages to your client or publisher. However, you should keep a

FIGURE 9. Typical Log Sheet for Consulting Projects

## CONSULTING PROJECT LOG SHEET

Project Name:
Client:                          P.O. #:                          P.O. Date:
Auth. Indiv.:                                        Title:
Street Address:
City:                                    State:          Zip:
Telephone:                                                Hourly Rate:
Quoted Charge:                                            Date of Quote:

| Date | Time In | Time Out | Work Done | Hours |
|------|---------|----------|-----------|-------|
|      |         |          |           |       |
|      |         |          |           |       |
|      |         |          |           |       |
|      |         |          |           |       |
|      |         |          |           |       |
|      |         |          |           |       |
|      |         |          |           |       |
|      |         |          |           |       |
|      |         |          |           |       |
|      |         |          |           |       |
|      |         |          |           |       |

Delivered to:

| Invoice | Date | Amount Billed | Amount Paid | Date Paid |
|---------|------|---------------|-------------|-----------|
|         |      |               |             |           |
|         |      |               |             |           |
|         |      |               |             |           |

copy for yourself in case of loss. Before I acquired a word-processing system, I had every project photocopied before delivery. However, I soon found my files overflowing with materials and had to start conducting regular purges in which I discarded preliminary copies of documents and kept only the latest version. But that proved unsatisfactory when a client came back a year after a project had been completed and was looking for justification for a particular paragraph in a manual. I remembered being instructed to include that paragraph but couldn't document the fact because I had only the final copy. With a word-processing system, I now keep each revision level of a project magnetically stored for about two years after the close of the project, making each level accessible almost immediately while not requiring the bulk storage capability necessary for printed copies.

Editorial writers should keep track of every manuscript and every submission by means of log sheets similar to the one shown in Figure 10. Each manuscript should have such a log sheet, and each submission should be recorded in terms of the date it was sent out and the date it was received back. Additional information on the log sheet should include the title of the work (as written and as published), the source of the idea, the buyer, the purchase price, and the date of publication. By keeping such log sheets, you develop a total index of your work and can identify any one item's status immediately.

I've also picked up the habit of tape recording business meetings and telephone conversations. I sometimes have some serious doubts about things I am directed to include in a project, and I feel a bit safer if I have the directions and information from my buyer clearly recorded on tape. Since I never know in advance what's going to be covered in a meeting or a phone conversation, I record nearly every conversation and keep those recordings indefinitely.

Some caution is advisable in taping telephone conversations since the legality of such actions may be questionable in specific locales. Usually, the front matter of the telephone book "white pages" states some specific restrictions on taping calls for business uses, often requiring that a beep tone be generated every 15 seconds. Since most small recorders are not equipped to provide

FIGURE 10. Typical Log Sheet for Editorial Submissions

## EDITORIAL SUBMISSION LOG SHEET

Working Title:
Subject:
Source of Idea:
Other Files Referenced:

File No.:
Length:

Bought by:
Published Title:

Price:

Date Paid:
Pub. Date:

Comments:

| Publisher | Date Out | Date In | Comments |
|-----------|----------|---------|----------|
|           |          |         |          |
|           |          |         |          |
|           |          |         |          |
|           |          |         |          |
|           |          |         |          |
|           |          |         |          |
|           |          |         |          |
|           |          |         |          |

that tone, it always is necessary to advise the other party that you are recording the conversation. Calls should never be recorded without the other party's knowledge and consent since that would constitute an invasion of privacy and leave you open to either criminal or civil actions. In addition, any time the other party wishes to go "off the record," it is necessary to cease recording.

## MANAGE FINANCES CAREFULLY

Earlier in this book, I emphasized the importance of having an adequate cash reserve to float through difficult periods. Even after the business is established and doing fairly well, you should keep enough cash available to cover at least six months of living and business expenses in the absence of any income. Free-lance writing is anything but a secure way to make a living, and it's possible to go from a high income of several thousand dollars a month to absolutely no income. The transition literally can happen in a single day; all it takes is receiving a few letters or phone calls that terminate projects in progress.

When that happens, the cash reserve is the only cushion you have until you can realign your efforts, find new buyers, and restore your cash flow. At best, the process of turning around a major business decline will take three months and will average even longer under circumstances that are less than ideal. First, you have to find the new business and get the authorizations to do the work. Then you have to do the work before you can consider its value a part of your accounts receivable. Finally, you have to wait out the payment intervals before you get a check. That whole process can be quite lengthy, and your bills and expenses continue to mount up while you're trying to generate some income. If you don't have enough cash to pay your bills, you are in serious trouble.

It's advisable to make use of tax shelters such as retirement plans, but the bulk of your cash assets have to be readily accessible. Even short-term investments have to be considered carefully and in terms of cash availability when it's needed. Stocks, bonds, and investment funds offer a way to increase your earnings on money to come closer to keeping up with inflation, but they can be difficult to dispose of when you need immediate cash. Certificates of deposit have the disadvantage of severe interest penalties for early withdrawal, and retirement accounts add high tax rates for premature use.

Since you can't predict your cash flow in advance, you may find, as I have, that six months' cash supply has to be kept in a relatively low interest passbook account. Only the excess earnings over the amount needed in that account can be invested in higher paying but less liquid accounts or securities.

In 1980, a new type of savings account became readily available and is of special interest to free-lance writers. Known as a group savings plan or "synergy" account, this type of savings is offered by organizations such as the National Writers Club (1450 Havana #620, Aurora, Colorado 80012). The advantage is that a deposit of as little as $100 can earn 10% interest or higher without being tied up in long-term certificates. These types of accounts are established and administered by the offering organization and are deposited with a commercial bank or savings and loan institution so that the depositor has an individual account in his or her own name. To administer the account, the sponsoring organization charges a nominal fee, usually less than $20 a year. At the same time the account is drawing a high rate of interest, the funds are easily accessible and are fully insured in the same manner as regular passbook accounts.

Under this type of plan, the organization such as the National Writers Club charges $17.50 per year to establish and maintain the account (you must also be either an associate or professional member of the organization). The account they set up in your name is essentially a 30-day self-renewing certificate with a minimum balance of $100. It matures one month from the date of the last deposit, at which time a 7-day grace period is allowed for making withdrawals without forfeiting interest. Every deposit (but not withdrawal) changes the maturity date of the account, so some care is needed in determining when to add funds to the account, but the penalties for withdrawing money at the wrong time are not so severe as to prevent immediate access to the account.

Assuming a 10% annual interest rate on such a synergy account as compared with a 5.25% passbook rate, the difference in the interest earned by $850 left on deposit for one year would pay for both an $18 account maintenance fee and a $35 membership fee for the organization. Since your money is not tied up for long periods, you retain the element of liquidity you need, yet still achieve an attractive rate of return on your investment when compared with a passbook account.

You also have to learn to be conservative. Large projects may pay very well and in large amounts earned over short intervals. As a result, you may be tempted to increase your expenditures while the money is available. It's fine to do so, but only after you've repaid your own cash reserve for any withdrawals you've made, set 25% aside for income taxes, and paid any outstanding bills. Remember that the windfall you are getting from one project may stop suddenly, but your liabilities won't. It's quite likely that the high-paying months are going to be followed by a longer interval of low income, and you have to protect yourself accordingly.

## OBSERVE TAX REGULATIONS

Never take your income tax return for granted. The way you filed last year may not be applicable this year. First, the government has a habit of making changes to the tax laws every few years. Most of those changes usually don't have a significant impact on your small business, but something like the attempt to disqualify an office at home can have a serious bearing on the way you do things. There are frequent changes to the lists of expenses you may or may not be able to deduct, the allowable mileage rate you can write off for your automobile, the allowable investment credits for equipment, etc.

Second, your income may change substantially from year to year. In turn, this may necessitate examining the benefits of single versus joint filing, income averaging, forming a corporation, and so on.

When you use an outside accountant to handle your taxes, remember that his work is only as good as the information you give him. Also remember that you are the one who's held responsible. It's a foolish decision to rely totally on an accountant who may or may not be up to date on new regulations and who probably doesn't know all the details of your business anyway. Since you are the only one who can make certain decisions, it's up to you to keep current on new tax laws and changes to old laws that affect the way you do business and file your tax returns.

Each year, order the applicable IRS publications concerning small businesses. Read those publications from cover to cover and compare them with those of the previous year. When you find a difference, make certain that it has no effect on your business or that you have incorporated the new procedure into your way of doing things.

## STAY DIVERSIFIED

The adage about putting all your eggs into one basket has a special significance for a free-lance writer. Quite simply, you can't afford to rely on one buyer or even one type of writing to make a living. You may prefer to write historical fiction or poetry, but you may not be able to make a living at it. Instead, you might have to hack away at other more profitable pursuits in order to afford the luxury of doing the writing you enjoy.

As a general rule, the more things you can do, the more sales you can achieve. That leads to a better income and a better chance of survival as a free-lancer.

If you can mix pursuits, you have a broader market base and a greater potential for sales. When one market tapers off for a while, you can emphasize a different one while you wait for the first to be revitalized. If the markets are highly diversified themselves, there is little chance that all of them will decline at the same time. For instance, a marketing copywriter who also does some anecdote-style fillers for magazines, a little pornography, an occasional how-to article for a trade journal, and some simple instruction manuals would likely find one or more of the other fields picking up speed whenever companies in his locale were cutting back their advertising budgets.

It's even worse to rely on a single buyer. I made that mistake over a period of a year when a large contract required essentially full-time attention. During that period, I worked that project almost continuously, turning away new clients for fear they would endanger my progress on the one job. I did handle work on older accounts, squeezing them in whenever I could, but I took no new clients at all and let some of my second-line business concerns slide into inactivity. During that year, I made a great deal of money, and the payments were absolutely dependable. I received a check on or about the tenth of each month, the checks were several thousand dollars apiece, and each month paid roughly the same amount as the preceding one. For a free-lancer, the situation seemed almost too good to be true—a high level of income on a constant basis.

Then one Monday morning I got the telephone call terminating the project. The assignment died then and there; it was reassigned to a staff writer recently hired by the client, and there was no chance of it being reactivated. My income died at the same time. Through neglect, my broad business base had almost disappeared. I had no immediate way to generate enough new business to offset that loss and to accommodate the level of expenses I had been incurring. It took an entire year before I was able to reestablish myself in the local market and achieve what I considered a comfortable income level. I never did achieve an income as high as the one I lost, but I was able to live and operate off bank accounts long enough to survive that sudden decline.

As usual, I had to learn by making a mistake. I'll no longer commit myself to those kinds of projects. Assignments of long duration are deliberately broken into small segments and separated by other endeavors. While I may not make as much money in as short a time, I achieve a level of diversity that prevents any one client or any one failing endeavor from doing too much financial harm. When one particular pursuit declines, I can make up the difference within a month or two just by shifting my emphasis to an immediately available alternative.

# 10

# Try It Yourself

In the preface to this book, I drew an analogy between a free-lance writer and a sailor navigating through treacherous waters. In the body of the book, I've attempted to chart those waters, spotting some of the reefs and shoals and establishing a few buoys and other navigational aids that should help you reach your destination. By introducing some of the economic, financial, and tax considerations, I've also tried to identify shifting currents and tides that can sweep you far away from your objective.

What I haven't been able to do is chart a specific and safe channel that will lead to survival and success under any possible set of circumstances. Such a task would be impossible, and each of you must find your own way. Neither I nor any other writer can tell you exactly what you should do, and any advice you receive should be applied in terms of what not to do rather than what to do. In this book, I've identified many of the major problems I had to discover the hard way, and, by sharing my experiences, I sincerely hope that I helped you avoid the same pitfalls.

If I've saved you a single, costly error, then I've achieved my purpose.

Remember that all of the good advice in the world is no substitute for actual experience, and you learn to survive as a free-lancer only by getting out there and trying it for yourself. I suspect that many of you who have read this are just toying with the idea of starting a free-lance career, and many of you will never go beyond just thinking about it. If that's the case, you'll never know whether you could have made it or not. For those of you who try free-lancing and survive past the first few years, there is the intense feeling of satisfaction that comes from beating the odds and knowing that you have taken control of your own fate. For those who try but fail, at least you will have had the experience and will have eliminated the lingering doubt about whether or not you could have done it.

I have no doubt that this book has discouraged many of you. You may have decided that even trying would be a futile effort because you're too shy to be an aggressive salesman, because you can't develop a good financial cushion, because you don't have the experience to function as a businessman, or for any of a variety of other reasons. These and others all are important considerations, but no one reason should be sufficient to stop you completely, only to slow you down a little so you can base your decisions on thorough evaluations rather than sudden impulses. Being a free-lance writer may not be the easiest way of life, and I can't delude you into thinking that it's not going to require a lot of effort, a number of risks, and a bit of good fortune. But it's not beyond the reach of any writer who's willing to work at it and make the sacrifices it demands during the first few years. The difficulties can be minimized by developing the business slowly, preferably on a part-time basis at first to test the water, developing a firm business base and then expanding into a full-time enterprise when finances and experience permit it.

If you've got the itch, scratch it! Give it a shot! Get your talent into gear and send something—anything—off to a publisher! Do some checking—see if there's a local need for your talents on a consulting basis! But don't just sit there calling yourself a writer when you aren't really trying! If you have some manuscripts sitting in a drawer, dig them out and send them off to a publisher! Take that first step and others will follow almost automatically!

I've a friend who pretends to be a writer. She's written many pieces, some seemingly good and others not so good. But she's never sent them out to a publisher, never gotten a rejection slip, and never found out whether she has anything of value to the literary world. She's afraid of the rejections she might receive, afraid that an editor won't like her work, and afraid that her ego is going to be a bit bruised if she doesn't get a buyer on the first try. As a result, her work sits in file folders and she'll probably never know whether or not the pieces could have been published.

In closing this book, I'll summarize the major points I've tried to convey. You can think of them as the free-lancer's commandments if you wish, but remember that they must be tempered and modified by your own needs and experiences.

1. Do your preliminary planning. Identify your goals, investigate the available markets, evaluate your talents, and develop your financial capabilities.

2. Establish your business structure and plan your accounting, tax, investment, and other financial approaches before you begin your operation.

3. Operate as a professional, not as a hobbyist. Maintain your personal integrity at the highest possible level, and guard your reputation at all costs. Keep your deadlines, even if you have to work 24 hours a day.

4. Take pride in your work and command respect for your efforts. Inferior work reflects poorly on your integrity and professional standing.

5. Utilize your talents to the fullest. Be as diverse as you can, offering as many different services and approaches as possible. Remember that diversity of talents and pursuits offers expanded areas in which to sell yourself and your work.

6. Provide as much assistance as you can to both your buyers and other free-lancers. The more favors you do, the more are likely to be returned when you need them. Don't be afraid to share information, knowledge, and potential sales leads with others.

7. Accept the blame for your own mistakes. If you make a mess of a project, don't point the finger at someone else when it was your own fault. Dodging responsibility again reflects poorly on your professional standing.

8. Be prepared to work impossible hours on occasion, including weekends and holidays. Be prepared to disrupt your own plans and those of your family and friends. If you aren't willing to pay this price, don't attempt to free-lance.

9. Don't waste a lot of time idling. In the words of Mary Heaton Vorse, "The art of writing is the art of applying the seat of the pants to the seat of the chair." If you're not writing, there are plenty of other tasks that have to be done, so you can't afford to waste your time. Make writing a habit—an integral part of each day.

10. Be persistent! Don't give up writing every time you receive a rejection slip. Success as a free-lancer requires perseverance, so rejected work should be submitted again and again.

11. Recognize the simple fact that you're out to make a profit. Some people would have you think that profit is a dirty word and that it's not an honorable motivation. In fact, profit is the only real motivation you have—pretending noble goals in writing an earth-shattering exposé is nothing but window dressing designed to conceal the desire to cash in on a bit of sensationalism. There's nothing wrong with making a profit, so you should set out to do so from the very first moment.

Figure 11 is provided as a final aid in helping you organize

FIGURE 11. Free-lance Writer's Checklist

(W. O. Metcalf. *Starting and Managing a Small Business of Your Own*, 3rd ed., Small Business Administration, pp. 87–94.)

---

# FREE-LANCER'S CHECKLIST

### Are You the Type?
____ Have you rated your personal qualifications using a scale similar to that presented in Figure 1?
____ Have you had some objective evaluators rate you on such scales?
____ Have you carefully considered your weak points and taken steps to improve them or to find an associate whose strong points will compensate for them?

### What Business Should You Choose?
____ Have you written a summary of your background and experience to help you in making this decision?
____ Have you considered your hobbies and what you would like to do?
____ Does anyone want the services you can perform?
____ Have you studied surveys and/or sought advice and counsel to find out what fields of business may be expected to expand?
____ Have you considered working for someone else to gain experience?

### What Are Your Chances for Success?
____ Are general business conditions good?
____ Are business conditions good in the city and neighborhood where you plan to locate?
____ Are current conditions good in the line of business you plan to start?
____ Are publishing houses increasing or decreasing their purchases?
____ Can you develop enough diversified endeavors to accommodate a sudden decline in one area of business?

### What Will Be Your Return on Investment?
____ Do you know the typical return on investment in the line of business you plan to start?
____ Have you determined how much you will have to invest in your business?
____ Are you satisfied that the rate of return on the money you invest in the business will be greater than the rate you would probably receive if you invested the money elsewhere?

### How Much Money Will You Need?
____ Have you filled out worksheets similar to those shown in Figures 2 and 3 of this book?
____ In filling out the worksheets, have you taken care not to overestimate your income?
____ Have you obtained quoted price sheets for equipment and supplies you will need?
____ Have you estimated expenses only after checking rents, utilities, and other pertinent costs in the area where you plan to locate?
____ Have you allowed for inflation and rising costs in your estimates of expenses?
____ Have you added an additional amount of money to your estimates to allow for unexpected contingencies?

# FREE-LANCER'S CHECKLIST (continued)

**Where Can You Get the Money?**

\_\_\_\_ Have you counted up how much money of your own you can put into the business?

\_\_\_\_ Do you know how much credit you can get from your suppliers—the people you will buy from?

\_\_\_\_ Do you know where you can borrow the rest of the money you need to start your business?

\_\_\_\_ Have you selected a progressive bank with the credit services you may need?

\_\_\_\_ Have you talked to a banker about your plans?

\_\_\_\_ Does the banker have an interested, helpful attitude?

\_\_\_\_ Have you cleared as many personal debts as possible?

\_\_\_\_ Have you set aside a sufficient amount of money to cover your day-to-day living expenses while establishing the business?

\_\_\_\_ Have you considered a part- or full-time job to supplement the business income until the business is fully established?

**Should You Share Ownership with Others?**

\_\_\_\_ If you need a partner with money or know-how that you don't have, do you know someone who will fit—someone you can get along with?

\_\_\_\_ Do you know the good and bad points about going it alone, having a partner, and incorporating your business?

\_\_\_\_ Have you studied the tax regulations pertinent to the different types of business structures?

\_\_\_\_ Have you talked to a lawyer about it?

**Where Should You Locate? (primarily for consultants)**

\_\_\_\_ Have you studied the make-up of the business community in the city or town where you plan to locate?

\_\_\_\_ Do you know who will want to buy what you plan to sell?

\_\_\_\_ Do potential buyers exist in the area where you want to locate?

\_\_\_\_ Have you checked the number, type, and size of competitors in the area?

\_\_\_\_ Does the area need another business like the one you plan to start?

\_\_\_\_ Do you consider costs of the location reasonable in terms of taxes, average rents, utilities, and costs of supplies?

\_\_\_\_ Is there sufficient opportunity for growth and expansion?

\_\_\_\_ Have you had a lawyer check any lease and zoning restrictions (particularly for an office at home)?

**How Will You Price Your Products and/or Services?**

\_\_\_\_ Have you decided on your method of billing and price ranges?

\_\_\_\_ Do you know how to figure what you should charge to cover costs?

\_\_\_\_ Do you know what your competitors charge for similar services?

\_\_\_\_ Have you set your prices so that you neither overcharge nor undercharge for a given assignment?

## FREE-LANCER'S CHECKLIST (continued)

**What Marketing Methods Will You Use? (primarily for consultants)**
___ Have you studied the marketing methods of your competitors?
___ Have you studied why clients buy your type of product or service?
___ Have you thought about why you like to buy from some salesmen while others turn you off?
___ Have you investigated the available media and approaches for advertising and public relations?
___ Have you weighed the merits of direct mail, telephone solicitation, and personal sales calls?
___ Have you or can you overcome shyness and feel comfortable talking to editors, publishers, and corporate executives?
___ Have you decided what your marketing methods will be?
___ Have you outlined your sales-promotion policy?
___ Have you set up your resume, client list, and sample portfolios?

**What Other Management Problems Will You Face?**
___ Do you plan to sell your work for credit?
___ If you do, have you set aside the extra capital necessary to carry accounts receivable?
___ Have you determined how to handle collections for unpaid manuscripts or assignments?
___ If you act as a consultant, have you drawn up a general contract and had its terms checked by an attorney or legal advisor?
___ Have you established a policy for rejected and returned manuscripts, correcting your own errors in consulting assignments, etc.?
___ Have you planned how you will deliver editorial manuscripts and/or consulting assignments?
___ Have you determined just what services you are willing to offer (editing, writing, designing, photography, layout, etc.)?
___ Have you considered other policies which must be made in your particular business plan and endeavor?
___ Have you made a plan to guide yourself in making the best use of your time and effort?

**What Records Will You Keep?**
___ Have you planned a system of records that will keep track of your income and expenses, what you owe other people, and what others owe you?
___ Have you worked out a way to keep track of your inventory of manuscripts, including a log of recipients, dates submitted, and dates returned or accepted?
___ Have you worked out a way to keep track of your time and invoices on consulting jobs?
___ Have you developed a plan for handling tax reports and payments?
___ Do you know what financial statements you may have to prepare from time to time?
___ Do you know an accountant who will assist with your records and financial statements?

# FREE-LANCER'S CHECKLIST (continued)

**What Laws Will Affect You?**

\_\_\_\_ Have you checked with the proper authorities to find out what, if any, licenses are necessary to do business?

\_\_\_\_ Have you received advice from your lawyer regarding your responsibilities under federal, state, and local laws and ordinances?

\_\_\_\_ Have you examined the legal aspects of copyrights and trademark registrations, as well as possible infringements thereof?

\_\_\_\_ If using an office at home, have you complied with the IRS restrictions that qualify the office for tax deductions?

\_\_\_\_ Have you become familiar with the tax laws governing business operations (including records, income, expenses, depreciation, investment credits, self-employment tax, estimating taxes, etc.)?

**How Will You Handle Taxes and Insurance?**

\_\_\_\_ Have you chosen an appropriate accounting system?

\_\_\_\_ Have you planned an adequate record system for the efficient preparation of income tax forms?

\_\_\_\_ Have you planned a worksheet (with dates and requirements) for meeting your tax obligations?

\_\_\_\_ Have you investigated appropriate tax shelters such as retirement accounts and tax-deferred investments to shelter your income?

\_\_\_\_ Have you talked to an insurance agent about the kinds of insurance you will need and how much it will cost (be sure to check the impact of an office at home on your homeowner's policy)?

**Will You Set Realistic Goals for Yourself?**

\_\_\_\_ Have you set goals and sub-goals for yourself and your business?

\_\_\_\_ Have you specified dates when each goal is to be achieved?

\_\_\_\_ Are the goals realistic; will they challenge you while not calling for unreasonable accomplishments?

\_\_\_\_ Are your goals specific enough so that you can measure performance?

\_\_\_\_ Have you allowed for obstacles?

\_\_\_\_ Have you prepared a business plan that can be amended as dictated by circumstances?

\_\_\_\_ Do you have the motivation to undertake a business enterprise and make the sacrifices it demands?

your efforts and get underway. This is a checklist of the most important items you have to examine as you prepare to start your free-lance business, and you may feel free to add other items as you see fit. As you examine and account for each item on the list, check it off. By the time you actually get started, you should have most or all of the items checked and will have developed a good understanding of exactly what you face.

With these things in mind, go ahead and get started! I wish you every possible success and the best of luck!

# 11

# References and Associations

## REFERENCES

*American Book Trade Directory*, New York. R. R. Bowker Company, published periodically.

*American Publishers Directory*, New York, K. G. Sour Publishing, published periodically.

*Bowker Annual of Library and Book Trade Information*, New York, R. R. Bowker Company, published annually.

Burack, A. S. *The Writer's Handbook*, revised ed., Boston, The Writer, Inc.

*Business Use of Your Home*, Department of the Treasury, Internal Revenue Service, Publication 587, published annually.

Casewit, Curtis. *Freelance Writing: Advice from the Pros*, New York, Collier Books.

Clarke, Tim. *International Academic and Specialists Publishers Directory*, New York, R. R. Bowker Company.

Gearing, P., and E. Brunson. *Breaking into Print: How to Get Your Book Published*, Englewood Cliffs, NJ, Prentice Hall.

Greenhood, D. *The Writer On His Own*, University of New Mexico Press.

Gunther, Max. *Writing and Selling a Non-Fiction Book*, Boston, The Writer, Inc.

Gunther, Max. *Writing the Modern Magazine Article*, Boston, The Writer, Inc.

*International Literary Market Place*, New York, R. R. Bowker Company, published every two years.

Jacobs, Hayes B. *Writing and Selling Non-Fiction*, Cincinnati, Writer's Digest Books.

Komroff, Manuel. *How to Write a Novel*, New York, Simon & Schuster.

*Literary Market Place/Directory of American Book Publishing*, New York, R. R. Bowker Company, published annually.

Mathieu, Aron. *The Creative Writer*, revised ed., Cincinnati, Writer's Digest Books.

Metcalf, Wendell O. *Starting and Managing a Small Business of Your Own*, Vol. 1, *The Starting and Managing Series*, 3rd ed., Washington, Small Business Administration.

Palmer, W. R. *Freelance Business-Writing Business*, Monmouth Junction, NJ, Heathcote Publishers.

Rockwell, F. A. *How to Write Nonfiction That Sells*, Chicago, Contemporary Books.

Rockwell, F. A. *How to Write Plots That Sell*, Chicago, Contemporary Books.

Schwarz, Ted. *How to Be a Freelance Photographer*, Chicago, Contemporary Books.

Schwarz, Ted. *How to Start a Professional Photography Business*, Chicago, Contemporary Books.

*Tax Guide for Small Business*, Department of the Treasury, Internal Revenue Service, Publication 334, published annually.

Van Zandt, Joseph H. *How to Start Your Own Newspaper*, Chicago, Contemporary Books.

Wilbur, L. Perry. *How to Write Books That Sell: Cashing in on the Booming Book Business*, Chicago, Contemporary Books.

Wilbur, L. Perry. *How to Write Songs That Sell*, Chicago, Contemporary Books.

Williams, W. P., and J. H. Van Zandt. *How to Start Your Own Magazine*, Chicago, Contemporary Books.

Williams, W. P., and J. H. Van Zandt. *How to Syndicate Your Own Newspaper Column*, Chicago, Contemporary Books.

Williams, W. P., and J. H. Van Zandt. *How to Write Magazine Articles That Sell*, Chicago, Contemporary Books.

*Writer's Market*, Cincinnati, Writer's Digest Books, published annually.

*Your Federal Income Tax*, Department of the Treasury, Internal Revenue Service, Publication 17, published annually.

## ASSOCIATIONS

American Advertising Federation, 1225 Connecticut Avenue NW, Washington, DC 20036.

American Medical Writers Association, 5272 River Road #370, Bethesda, MD 20016.

American Society of Journalists and Authors, Inc., 1501 Broadway #1907, New York, NY 10036.

Associated Business Writers of America, 1450 South Havana #620, Aurora, CO 80012.

Authors Guild, Inc., 234 West 44th Street, New York, NY 10036.

Aviation/Space Writers Association, Cliffwood Road, Chester NJ 07930.

Garden Writers Association of America, Inc., 680 3rd Avenue, Troy, NY 12182.

International Association of Business Communicators, 870 Market Street #928, San Francisco, CA 94102.

International Women's Writing Guild, Box 810, Gracie Station, NY 10028.

Mystery Writers of America, Inc., 105 East 19th Street, New York, NY 10003.

National Association of Science Writers, Inc., Box 294, Greenlawn, NY 11740.

National Writers Club, Inc., 1450 South Havana #620, Aurora, CO 80012.

Outdoor Writers Association of America, Inc., 4141 West Bradley Road, Milwaukee, WI 53209.

P.E.N., American Center, 47 Fifth Avenue, New York, NY 10003.

Poetry Society of America, 15 Gramercy Park, New York, NY 10003.

Poets & Writers, Inc., 201 West 54th Street, New York, NY 10019.

Science Fiction Writers of America, c/o Peter D. Pautz, Executive Secretary, 68 Countryside Apartments, Hackettstown, NJ 07840.

Society for Technical Communication, 815 15th Street N.W., Suite 506, Washington, DC 20005.

Society of American Travel Writers, 1120 Connecticut Avenue #940, Washington, DC 20036.

Society of Children's Book Writers, Box 296, Los Angeles, CA 90066.

The Word Guild, 119 Mount Auburn Street, Cambridge, MA 02138.

Women in Communications, Inc., Box 9561, Austin, TX 78766.

# Index